Federal Organization and
Administrative Management

To:

J. V. E.

Federal Organization and Administrative Management

by

HERBERT EMMERICH

The University of Alabama Press

University, Alabama

On behalf of my husband and myself, I wish to express my deep appreciation to Laurin L. Henry, friend and colleague, for his discussions with the author on substantive matters of the book and for seeing the book through to its readiness for final publication after the untimely death of the author on September 7, 1970.

JANET V. EMMERICH

Some parts of the material in this book appeared in 1950, in Dr. Emmerich's *Essays on Federal Reorganization,* copyright © 1950 by The University of Alabama Press.

CONTENTS

Federal Organization and

Administrative Management

INTRODUCTION

THE PROBLEMS OF FEDERAL ORGANIZATION AND ADMINISTRATIVE MANAGE-
ment, given the astronomic increase in the size and complexity of
American domestic and foreign obligations, have achieved new dimensions of importance. They have fascinated me during the thirty-five
year period in which I have been both a participant in and a watcher
of efforts to solve them. In a kaleidoscopic era of crisis and accelerating change, reorganization becomes increasingly a continuing process
of adaptation of structures and methods to new needs, new programs,
new insights, and new capabilities. In the American system the constant pressure for specialization and autonomy requires a strong
countervailing force for integration and coordination. The presidency
seems to be the institution in a position most likely to provide the
overall view and the countervailing influence.

Federal organization accordingly is treated here primarily from the
standpoint of executive organization and in respect to the ability of
the chief executive to modify it. Administrative management is intended to convey the unique executive function of providing the
relationship between desirable ends and effective means, to correlate
policy making with execution, to supply *a link between program
formulation and implementation.* It is not enough to insist that policy
and administration are interrelated. One of the high functions of
administrative management is to achieve their proper integration.
And the power to take initiative on reorganization of structure is an
essential tool of administrative management.

An examination of this subject cannot avoid the question of the

3

machinery the President has for decisions concerning both ends and means, and their close links. Nor can it refrain from references to the political environment in which the executive branch must work, particularly in the American scene, in which the legislative branch intervenes so freely in administration. An examination of the historic landmarks in governmental reform reveals that substantial progress has been made and that Congress has given the President and his department heads many new forms of authority and staff to discharge their managerial tasks. Among these the executive budget, the executive office, and the power to initiate reorganization plans subject to the legislative veto rank high in the annals of administrative history. The historic continuum receives special emphasis because of the importance of the long-term view in organizational matters. New departures need to build upon the experience of the past, modified in the light of new needs and new administrative and technical potential. Administrative changes of yesterday and today will determine the manageability of the establishment in the future. The President is the temporary guardian of the presidency and must be careful of his stewardship of the estate he bequeaths to his successors.

In the main, I continue to adhere to the still useful doctrines of the Brownlow Committee and of the first Hoover Commission. However, I have endeavored to identify their shortcomings and to indicate points at which they no longer seem to be adequate to present-day needs. Where possible I have documented my sources, but at some points I have not hesitated to refer to unrecorded incidents and observations. Nor have I attempted to repress or disguise my own opinions and biases. Suggestions for constitutional change have been avoided, and I am aware of the many profound problems of political organization and practice that are not treated.

That the overall structure and processes of the government need drastic simplification is overwhelmingly indicated by the evidence. In restructuring, a new emphasis is needed on the view from the bottom up as well as the view from the top down and across the board. I identify these three viewpoints as reorganization by triangulation. With the increasing use of indirect administration through grants-in-aid to cities and states, and through contracts with private bodies, the federal government must take care to conserve its chosen instruments. A more precise prescription for the functions of the Executive Office, including the White House staff, is undertaken. Questions are asked on the effect of automated systems and communications on regionalization. A caution is raised that some of these powerful new drugs may have unpredicted side-effects. The need to respond to the insistent demands for more consultation and citizen participation in decisions is acknowledged with the caveat that new forms of minority vetoes and roadblocks cannot be permitted indefinitely to postpone decision and action which are imperative in the democratic world-power service-state. Neither violence at home nor abroad is conducive to the development of men and their resources in a complex interrelated technical society.

My own unstructured and varied career has given me the opportunity to know and appreciate many fine specialists, but has served to incline my sympathies to the generalists. I have been involved in industrial management, the building of new towns, cooperative credit institutions, industrial mobilization, national and international associations of public officials and of scholars, and in government administration at local, state, federal, and international levels. My knowledge of the government was updated by contacts with mid-career men and women who attended my graduate seminars at the University of Virginia, and by my work with graduate students at the University of California in Berkeley and with federal executives at the Federal Executive Institute in Charlottesville, Virginia. My long association with faculty members at the University of Chicago and Harvard University helped my assimilation as a professor so late in life. To my earlier association with two great teacher-administrators, Louis Brownlow and William I. Myers, I attribute the fact that I learned to regard the practice of administration as essentially a teaching and learning experience.

In a sense this was my first book and will probably be my last one. It started out to be a revision of my *Essays in Federal Reorganization*, written in 1950 and based on lectures to the fellows of the Southern Regional Training Program at the University of Alabama. It ended up by being a new production, although a few older readers may identify occasional borrowings from the earlier material. I was born too soon to master the contemporary vocabularies and numerologies of social science, so I have been compelled to use traditional English. In spite of this shortcoming, my readers may find that the book contains some hitherto unpublished material and an occasional new idea.

My acknowledgments must be selective as I owe too much to too many to give all the credit that is due. The work has been made possible by the senior research grant made by the Social Science Research Council. The University of Virginia has assisted the project in a number of ways. Early in the project, I had the benefit of the research services of two gifted young scholars, Dr. Alex Lacy, Jr., now Dean, School of Urban Studies, Georgia State University, and Dr. Dennis S. Ippolito, now Assistant Professor of Political Science at Emory University. They helped me to track down sources and to assemble and formulate much material and many ideas. The Bureau of the Budget in the Executive Office of the President was most helpful. Miss Ruth Fine, its able librarian, made its outstanding collection of documents available to me. Mr. Fred Levi of the Bureau staff gave me invaluable assistance on the compilation of the reorganization acts in Appendix III. Dr. Harold Seidman, while he was Assistant Director for Management and Organization of the Bureau and since he started his own researches in the National Academy of Public Administration, has generously shared his immense store of knowledge and ideas with me. Mrs. Gladys Hess rendered expert typing and editorial services. I am deeply grateful to my wife for her unfailing encouragement and her perceptive comments on each chapter. I thank all those who have helped me and accept full responsibility for any errors and omissions in these pages.

CHARLOTTESVILLE, VA.   HERBERT E. EMMERICH
MARCH, 1970

I wish to record my appreciation for the help of several people in the final work on this book after the untimely death of the author. Mrs. Carolyn B. Sears provided secretarial assistance; Mr. Larry L. Owsley checked proof and footnotes; and Miss Virginia Thatcher prepared the index. We have sought to be faithful to Herbert's intentions.

CHARLOTTESVILLE, VA.   LAURIN L. HENRY
FEBRUARY, 1971

Chapter I

EXECUTIVE REORGANIZATION:
A CONTINUING PROCESS

1. Administrative Change and the Presidency

THE ADMINISTRATIVE REORGANIZATION MOVEMENT HAS SOMETIMES BEEN viewed as a periodic surge of revivalism in governmental reform. There is a widely held notion that reorganization occurs only as a result of waves of outside agitation for reform and major deliberate efforts to rationalize administrative organization and methods. This notion is predicated on a concept of a static federal executive structure. It springs, I believe, as so many administrative concepts do, from an engineering-legal approach which conceives an organizational structure as it does a bridge or a constitution. It fails to perceive the constantly changing nature of human organizations. In studying these organizations a biological or sociological orientation would give us greater insight into the realities of their growth and change than we can obtain from regarding them as rigid, inanimate edifices.

Federal reorganization is essentially a continuing process. It is going on all the time as a result of both internal and external pressures. Structural change is incessant, and the increase of the rate of change in governmental structure in the last quarter century has been the greatest in American history. It reflects the rate of change, the dislocations and tensions in society as a whole, in technology and in the vast escalation of our international responsibilities. Acute and complex problems, internal and external, face our country; government is asked to under-

7

take new programs for their solution, and is constantly adjusting the structure of its vast establishment to respond to these demands.

The occasional major reform efforts have the value of shock treatments for the rationalization of an organism which is subject to chronic imbalance. From the first organized investigation of administrative procedures by the Fifth Congress in 1798, to the surveys of the two Hoover Commissions over 150 years later, federal administration has undergone periodic reexamination and reform.

These, however, are but periodical purges whose effects can be traumatic as well as therapeutic. They are not always as high-mindedly motivated as the language of the act creating them would suggest. They are ponderous undertakings, requiring much uncosted time and money, as well as the distraction and anxiety of hundreds of people in dozens of agencies. They are slow in their effect, and the process of legislative implementation often brings forth amendments which the recommendations did not contemplate. Congress has recognized these factors and has devised means for the executive to expedite the process of adaptation of structure to program and, in fact, to strengthen generally his ability to discharge his duties of administrative management.

Executive responsibility for administrative management of a vast series of activities calls for the means to formulate sound national policies, to interpret and espouse them, and, when approved, to see that their administration is appropriately assigned and vigorously implemented. In our rapidly changing world-power service state, the chief executive, more than ever before, needs the means constantly to adapt organizations, structures, and systems to new national policies and priorities and to new operational needs and techniques. The ability to initiate promptly needed organizational changes is an essential tool of administrative management.

Reorganization needs to be appreciated, therefore, as far more than a species of "streamlining"—a reshuffling and consolidation of bureaus into a more logical pattern of related functions. It is more than the neat realignment of agencies into uni-functional groupings. Reorganization, I submit, takes place whenever there is a change in the size, distribution, and nature of the executive functions, or their staffing and financing, and particularly when these changes measurably affect the ability of the heads of the executive branch—the President and his department heads—to supervise and direct the manner in which the functions are exercised. This is another way of saying that it needs to be taking place all the time. It is going on even when the process is not labeled "reorganization." In this sense, the executive establishment has undergone profound and continuous reorganization since its establishment in 1789. In fact the Constitution itself was our first great document of administrative reform; and, although it was of course much more than that, one of the strong urges for its adoption was to substitute order, effectiveness, and responsibility for the impotence resulting from the almost complete lack of executive provisions in the Articles of Confederation.

Consider the difference in dimension of the problem of administrative management in 1789 and 1969. The contrast is in large part, of course, the sheer difference in size between an establishment of three departments and several offices, manned by fewer than 800 employees performing a limited number of simple well-defined functions, and the activities of over two and one-half million civilian public servants in twelve departments and scores of agencies, engaged in a myriad of complex functions of world-wide scope and pervasive impact. Another two and one-half million citizens are in the armed services. It is noteworthy, in contrast to the large mobilization of staff consultants for the inventory of the executive branch by the two Hoover Commissions, that President Washington, on his accession to office, personally undertook a comprehensive survey of the entire administrative business of the new government.[1]

Particularly spectacular has been the development in executive functions since the turn of this century. President F. D. Roosevelt told Louis Brownlow that he personally acted on more matters every day than President McKinley saw in a month.[2] Twenty-five years later, President Nixon can go nowhere unencumbered by the elaborate apparatus for rapid communication and instant decision.

But even more burdensome than this increase in breadth of the President's span of supervision is the transformation in depth of the problems claiming his attention. The first President, James Hart tells us, concerned over the decrease in profits of the Post Office, requested the records of that office in order that he might personally examine the receipts and expenditures "in detail."[3] The thirty-seventh President, steering the country through recurrent crises, is confronted with complex and grave national and international issues that defy the limits of time and energy of a single human being. The American President of the twentieth century has been aptly likened by A. Merriman Smith to a "fortress under constant siege."[4] The demands upon the President are now so great that he must be rigorously selective in the matters on which he intervenes at all. He cannot even yield to the temptation to linger over many of these.

With these incomparably more burdensome responsibilities, the President cannot with confidence depend exclusively on the hierarchical loyalty of his principal subordinates, the heads of the executive departments. Leonard D. White has pictured for us in *The Federalists* the acceptance, early in Washington's Administration, of the doctrine of complete and wholehearted subordination of department heads to the President.[5] The secretaries were viewed not as independent officers but as assistants to the President; their relationship was one of intimate and loyal identification. But even in this period this relationshp began to be impaired by the rising conflict between Jefferson and Hamilton, and it never became a durable tradition. The Presidents have for a long time found their purposes frequently subverted by their department heads. Burton J. Hendrick has illustrated and at the same time explained this development in his vivid description of Lincoln's Cabinet.[6] General Charles G. Dawes, the first director of the Budget, characterized the department heads as the operating vice-presidents of the government and the "natural enemies of the President." Today the problem is less one of sectionalism and of political rivalry with the President than of segmentation and preoccupation with a specialized part of the government program. This in turn makes the American Cabinet less useful than some writers would like it to be as a deliberative body. Dean Acheson, who was vice-chairman of the first Hoover Commission, has said that the American Cabinet is not a collective body but a "plural noun." But in recent years the increasing use of cabinet councils on substantive problems has become a promising device. The President's task, as Brownlow suggests, is one in which he "exploits his position by whatever means he can devise to evoke the prime loyalty of divers parts of the great governmental machine, each part being also animated by a loyalty to its particular purpose."[7]

The presidency is the focal point of any study of the interrelated aspects of executive organization and administrative management. In its development over the years it has evolved into a unique institution and remains one of the characteristic American contributions to responsible government. The presidency as an institution has been fully treated elsewhere and it is not my purpose to attempt another analysis. Its significance to administrative management, however, is central. The presidency has the vantage point to focus on the general interest as contrasted with the centrifugal forces in the Congress and the departments for the specialized interests of subject matter and of region. As the presidency becomes institutionalized, it becomes increasingly important to preserve its overall perspective and to keep it clear of entangling alliances with all but the most critical sectoral programs. The presidency needs a certain detachment from the many operations it must coordinate and supervise.

The increasing burdens on the presidency and the primary responsibilities of that office point up the need for more precise analyses of the aims of organization efforts. The broadened view of organization here suggested envisions goals that necessarily transcend the objectives of efficiency and economy, important as they are. The drives, in some unexplained way, to provide great savings out of administrative expenses without cuts in substantive programs have been exaggerated as the primary aims of reorganization. The real tests of effective reorganization are: (1) Is administration made constantly more responsive to the general interest of the country and better able to meet its ever changing responsibilities and needs? (2) Is the ability of the President to make far-seeing recommendations for the general welfare of the country strengthened? (3) Is his ability enhanced to see that the "laws are faithfully executed" and that programs sanctioned by Congress are vigorously and fairly pursued?

Five specific types of agency structures and programs have, over the years, given rise to particularly acute problems and have tended, whatever virtues they may have, to impair the unity of the executive branch: the independent regulatory agencies, government corporations, intergovernmental programs, contractual programs, and programs requiring special coordination.

2. The Independent Regulatory Commissions

The first of these which has been a countervailing tendency to administrative unity has been the growth of the independent regulatory commissions. The development of administrative adjudication has caused a basic modification in the nature of the executive function, and the establishment of the independent regulatory commissions has posed novel problems of presidential coordination. It may be noted here that the wholesale proliferation of the "headless fourth branch" which challenged effective presidential control over increasingly numerous areas of federal regulation has apparently been arrested. In the five years before 1939, five new independent regulatory commissions were established; in the three decades since, the only major commission to be created is the Atomic Energy Commission, which is only partly regulatory and is not independent of the executive. A few minor commissions, however, have been created (Appendix II).

An important factor in the uncertain relationship of the independent regulatory commissions to the executive branch has been the attitude of the Supreme Court toward the appointing and removal powers of the President. Its several statements on the President's removal powers, for example, have resulted in fluctuations in the relationship of the President to the independent agencies. The sweeping language of Chief Justice Taft in the Myers case, equating the removal with the appointing power, seemed to reaffirm presidential executive powers.[8] But Myers was a postmaster and not a member of an independent commission. It is noteworthy, as Edward S. Corwin points out, that Taft in this opinion relied as much on the necessities of executive control as on constitutional interpretation.[9] "The imperative reasons," the decision read, "requiring an unrestricted power to remove the most important of his subordinates in their most important duties must, therefore, control the interpretation of the Constitution as to all appointed by him." In this case Mr. Taft spoke more like an ex-President than a chief justice.

It is to be noted that since the Court, in the subsequent Humphrey case, redefined the relationship of the President to the Federal Trade Commission,[10] the independence of the regulatory commissions was again greatly strengthened. As the first Hoover Commission Task Force on Regulatory Commissions observed, the members of the later commissions appear to be as sacredly independent of presidential control as were the members of the earlier ones.[11]

Justice Sutherland's extreme statement in the Humphrey case, moreover, that the Federal Trade Commission "occupies no place in the executive department," leaves the independent commissions in the realm of no man's land.

In regard to members of quasi-judicial commissions, the Humphrey doctrine was strengthened by a decision in the case of Wiener, a member of the War Claims Commission removed in December 1953. The Supreme Court reversed a decision of the Court of Claims which had upheld the removal. The effect of the Wiener decision appears to be that, in the case of a quasi-judicial agency, the President's power of removal may be exercised only for cause even if the legislation has no such proviso.[12]

In the Lovett case, an obvious usurpation of the President's removal powers by the Congress by means of a rider to an appropriation bill was delicately disposed of by the Court on the grounds of a bill of attainder.[13] The effect of the Court's articulation of the President's removal power in the Myers decision has continued to be an influential force in determining the President's powers over officers in the executive branch outside the area of the regulatory commissions. The Supreme Court declined to review a decision of the federal Court of Appeals which upheld the President's removal of Arthur E. Morgan, chairman of the Tennessee Valley Authority. It held that the T.V.A. Act did not limit the President's powers to remove board members and that the T.V.A. was not a quasi-judicial agency.[14] Even though his right to hire, in the case of presidential appointments, is subject to Senate confirmation, his right to fire without such approval, except in the case of the independent regulatory commissions, appears to be affirmed as the law of the land.

Most of the regulatory commissions now have their chairmen designated by the President and the chairman is given authority to act as chief administrative officer of the commission. These changes were endorsed by the first Hoover Commission, but extended research would be needed to determine whether they have had any durable effect on relating commission policies more closely to the policies of the executive branch.

3. *Other Centrifugal Forces*

The second of the special problems arose out of the free use of the government corporation, and of highly autonomous boards in the field of money and credit. The enthusiastic and indiscriminate use of the corporate device in the depression and recovery period began in 1936 to cause some concern. Many of those formed could not be self-supporting and had to depend on appropriations. The government in some cases was establishing state-chartered corporations without congressional approval. Little or no distinction was made as to the controls suitable to privately owned federal corporations, those having mixed ownership, and those wholly owned by the government. In 1937 the

President's Committee on Administrative Management adopted my report calling for greater restraint and suitable supervision of the government corporation. Congress had been concerned with the problem and in 1945 passed the Government Corporation Control Act. In the case of the wholly owned government corporations this act and other attritions of the corporate device brought it constantly nearer to the bureau form of organization and tended to end rather than merely to regulate its usefulness.[15] The Atomic Energy Commission and the National Aeronautics and Space Administration have demonstrated the capacity to innovate both technically and administratively without using the corporate form.

The first Hoover Commission report on *Federal Business Enterprises* proposed still further restrictions on corporate autonomy, although it recommended the extension of the use of the corporate device. The second Hoover Commission was particularly partial to the federal "mutualized corporation" in which private and public ownership participate. At times the independent corporation posed as much of a threat to the program of the government in this century as the Second Bank of the United States seemed to President Jackson. The Reconstruction Finance Corporation, begun in President Hoover's time and expanded in the four terms of President F. D. Roosevelt, achieved a dangerous degree of political and economic power under the shrewd and in many respects competent administration of Jesse H. Jones.

The latest enthusiasm for incorporating the United States Post Office, in the light of these limitations, may arouse expectations which cannot be fulfilled. Is it likely that Congress will grant to such a corporation the necessary powers, such as the determination of services, the fixing of postal rates, the negotiation of pay scales, the location of new post offices, and the use of any surpluses for purposes of development and betterments? Without such delegations, the organization would be little more than an incorporated bureau.

The boards regulating federally chartered lending institutions are practically extra-governmental bodies. Their administrative expenses are paid by levies on member institutions and are not subject to budgetary and appropriations controls. The President has little or no way of exerting influence on their policies except in the early days of a new appointment. Little or no coordination is possible in the making of fiscal and monetary policy in view of the great autonomy of the Board of Governors of the Federal Reserve System. The Farm Credit Administration, the Federal Home Loan Bank Board, and the Federal

Deposit Insurance Corporation are also virtually autonomous bodies. In raising these questions I am not arguing for complete subordination of the day-to-day operations of these bodies to the government of the day. A wide area of autonomy would appear to be justified for credit agencies that often have to make unpopular decisions. But a greater amount of formal liaison on policy matters between the Treasury, the Bureau of the Budget, the Council of Economic Advisors, and the monetary, banking, and credit agencies would seem to make much sense in concerted action in regard to the business cycle, and in counteracting undue inflationary and deflationary movements.

The third area of unsolved problems arises from the important adjustments in federal administrative organization which may be traced to the enormous increase in the size and number of the grant-in-aid programs. National programs in the most urgent and complex problems of protecting the person and the environment are being assigned to state and local governments and have raised administrative questions of crisis proportions. Many of these problems arise because of the tendency to enact each highly specialized program without relating it to existing ones. These problems will be treated later in a discussion of cooperative federalism. Perhaps the most significant feature of the system of categorical and conditional grants is the great extension of federal influence on the administration and budgets of state and local governments, whose personnel and financial resources have been stretched almost to the breaking point by their proliferation. And now that grants have been extended to foreign countries it might be said that today the federal budget influences not only every state and city budget in the United States but practically every national budget in the world.

The growth of the use of the contractual device has introduced a fourth group of problems to which the large statutory commissions on reorganization gave only superficial attention. Contracting our governmental programs has become a large segment of the national budget. It gives rise to new and intricate problems of public policy, but has some aspects in common with the fractionalized grant-in-aid relationships with public bodies. The fields in which the contract device has been used often with great effectiveness have been notably those of scientific research, technological development and invention, education and training, and production and procurement. Much of it has been weapon oriented. The variety of contractors is very great and embraces not only private corporations, but universities, research institutes, specially chartered and government-related corporations such as Rand, and more recently community organizations in the poverty program. The dependence of the government on organized science, particularly in the contracts and grants made for basic research, presents unusually profound problems to administration and the democratic process. But there are many other vexing questions in the contracting out of governmental functions to so large a variety of chosen instruments.

The fifth great problem of administrative management is that of coordination of inter-related programs, and this is at once the most serious, baffling, and difficult to solve of all of them. It is of particular gravity in the field of defense, national security and international relations in which the United States has been called upon to play a dominant role in a dangerous and divided world. The actual coordination of the three military services has now been made possible by the creation of the Department of Defense, under the Secretary of Defense and the Chairman of the Joint Chiefs of Staff, but a number of activities are not under the direct control either of the Secretary of State or the Secretary of Defense. Through the device of the National Security Council over which the President presides, and the office of the President's special assistant for National Security Affairs, a serious effort has been made to span the gap between State and Defense at the highest level. This machinery continues to present certain difficulties and a number of authorities still believe that the influence of the military arm on foreign affairs is excessive. In the complex way-of-life and environmental protection programs at home, no matter how perfect the functional distribution is among departments and agencies, there are many points of conflict and difference requiring coordination of policies and operations. In this case, too, a number of novel methods are being tried, but a solution has by no means been achieved.

4. The Pressures for Autonomy

The continuing process of reorganization and rationalization of the federal executive branch operates in a milieu of irrational and illogical pressures in the opposite direction. These counter-tendencies of particularism and separatism operate, in the first instance, to force departures from unified structure and, subsequently, to impede attempts at reform. Certain of these forces inhere in the democratic process: they spring from the pluralistic and equalitarian character of American life. Whatever their causes and whatever value judgments we apply to them, the forces of autonomy operate constantly to impair the President's ability to supervise and direct the administration of the executive function.

There is a persistent, universal drive in the executive establishment for freedom from managerial controls and policy direction. The devices par excellence for the accomplishment of this freedom have been the independent commissions and the government corporations. Nor, as we have seen, have the financial and lending, and the scientific agencies fared too badly in this regard. Paul H. Appleby's eightfold classification of government agencies on the basis of their degree of responsiveness to general controls underscores the independence of these forms.[16] Poised precisely at one of the most crucial points of contact between government and governed, these agencies for economic regulation and the conduct of economic enterprise have a degree of autonomy, complete apartheid from any considerations of national development, and a tendency to become the guardians of the vested interests they were created to regulate.

The desire for autonomy characterizes the operating administrations and bureaus. As one observer has remarked, every agency wishes to be outside departmental structure or in the executive office of the President. No bureau, administration, or operating agency would choose to be in a department, and each can find some special reason to justify its claim. This desire for independence is an apparently innate characteristic of administrative behavior. It is one of the dilemmas in defining the characteristics of the good administrator that the best bureau chief is frequently the most contumacious one. Some measure of independence may well be justified in the nascent stage of an agency to give it needed flexibility, but such independence should be curtailed before it becomes institutionalized into a bulwark against coordination and responsibility to the chief executive. Who in the executive branch wastes much time issuing orders to the Director of the Federal Bureau of Investigation, the Comptroller of the Currency, or the Administrator of Veterans' Affairs?

Parenthetically I should confess at this point a sympathy for the point of view of the chief of program of a bureau or administration. I have been one myself, and I have known many others—men and women of outstanding ability. They are the custodians of their own single-purpose programs; they have generally a high awareness of the aspirations of these programs, the struggles it took to achieve them, and above all a keen sense of responsibility for the integrity and continuity of their organizations. Hard experience has made them skeptical of the ability and the intentions of the transitory political officers to whom they should report. The wise incoming political executive will do well to take pains from the outset to win the indispensable cooperation of the able career men who today operate most of the government programs. They have a wealth of know-how and experience in getting things done and are usually eager to find out what it is that their new political masters want to do. Department heads need to create an atmosphere in which the operating chief feels he can operate, and thus prevent him from withdrawing into an attitude of protective hostility. An able and progressive career chief will make an extraordinary effort to orient a new political head and to be receptive to new policies. The department head needs temporary assistants for new ideas and political responsiveness, career men for continuity and expertness, and what Don K. Price has called "administrative middle men" to bring these two groups together.

Within the departmental system the administrations and bureaus are the embodiment of the spirit of organizational autarchy and self-sufficiency. The introversion of the federal bureaus and their resistance to coordination are familiar instances of the pressures toward autonomy in the executive branch. This resistance is explained in part by the sociology of bureau life—by the natural resistance to control by outsiders who are not of the same professional or vocational group. Compartmentalization is fostered by the patchwork process by which new programs are initiated with insufficient regard to their relationships to on-going activities. This process in turn has roots in the fractionalization of political forces which give rise to the new programs as though nothing had ever been done in the field before.

A large part of the separatist tendencies of the bureaus and administrations may be traced to professional particularism. The intensely specialized approach of the professionals in the public service is one of the strongest of the centrifugal forces that beset administration. The reconciliation of a professionally specialized public service with the general interest is an unsolved problem of American administration. Whatever its other shortcomings the British civil service appears to be more skillful than ours in the use of interdepartmental committees at career levels. Ministers expect the members of Her Majesty's civil service to come up with sensible and agreed solutions, even if an agency must yield a point. In the American scene it is considered a species of disloyalty if a departmental representative makes important concessions to a rival agency. Loyalties in the United States government accrue to the highly specialized program components, not to the government as a whole.

The drive for professional autonomy is reflected in the increasing trend to appoint assistant secretaries of departments to represent particular fields. Such a provision was included in the 1947 Taft-Fulbright bill for a department of health, education, and security, admittedly to placate the American Medical Association. Separate divisions for the three fields were to be administered by assistant secretaries representing the respective professional areas.[17] This structural scheme of "three verticals and four heads" failed to appease the medical group and was not enacted into law, at that time.

A similar scheme was envisioned in the majority proposal of the first Hoover Commission for a department of social security and education, subdivided into a social security service and an educational service, and staffed with two assistant secretaries. Although the report does not specifically suggest that these officers represent the professional fields of the two subdivisions, such expectation is implicit in the proposal. A minority dissented from this proposal. Recommending a more comprehensive department of health, education, and security without prescribing subordinate personnel and structure, Commissioners Acheson, Aiken, and Rowe pointed out that "assistant secretaries appointed to represent their respective professions are not likely to be very helpful to the secretary in the all-important task of giving a common direction to the several professional points of view within the new department."[18] The secretary, the dissent urged, "should *not* be hampered by statutory provisions which, directly or by inference, assign the supervision of various agencies of the department to specific assistant secretaries."[19] It proposed that the assistant secretaries be "generalists, not specialists." This sage advice has been all but forgotten and department after department is appointing assistant secretaries with specialized and substantive rather than department-wide assignments. In the department of H.E.W., posts of Assistant Secretary (Education) and Assistant Secretary (Health and Scientific Affairs) were eventually established. A wise and experienced old hand like James E. Allen, Jr., insisted that President Nixon appoint him to be Commissioner of Education as well as Assistant Secretary (Education) in the Department of Health, Education, and Welfare, knowing full well that there is no way on earth of separating out the duties of these two posts.

A most illuminating commentary on the autonomous proclivities of the American diplomatic corps is afforded by a classic public administration case study of the legislative history of the Foreign Service Act of 1946.[20] The leadership of this elite corps prevailed on Congress to amend the basic law for the governance of the Foreign Service. In spite of the weaknesses of the bill which the Bureau of the Budget had pointed out to President Truman and which were perceived in high quarters in the Department of State, it was reluctantly approved after Secretary James Byrnes cabled the President that a veto would be unwise, largely because of other pending issues. Here in action was a cohesive "guild" having "strong centripetal force, a thick protective coating," which succeeded in having itself constituted an isolated group within the Department of State and the government as a whole. As a direct result of the first Hoover Commission's report on *Foreign Affairs*, Congress brought the Foreign Service back into the government again and under the jurisdiction of the Secretary of State.

More generally, the principle of giving the department head statutory authority over functions, funds, and organization was one of the great contributions of the first Hoover Commission's report on the *General Management of the Executive Branch*.

The permanence of administrators and bureau chiefs, for example, insulates a wide latitude of policy control from the direction of politically accountable officials. Unless they can be reassigned, there is the possibility that they may be immune to control by department heads. I want to make it perfectly clear that I favor the present trend to place more of the bureau chief positions under the merit system. It is one of the hopeful means of adding rungs to the ladder which the career service may aspire to climb. I should like, however, to see more generalists selected for these positions. The civil service rules should be changed so that an incoming secretary can assign a career chief to other professional duties without loss of status, prestige, or pay. If it is a career post, the secretary should have the right to assign another career officer to it. In any event, incumbents should have no vested interest in these top positions.

An unsound device for hedging the power of politically responsible officers has been the use of statutory committees representing special interests and wielding some measure of control over administrative action. This practice needs to be appreciated as a serious threat to the principle of executive responsibility.

A flagrant attempt to withdraw a segment of the executive establishment almost completely from the control of the President occurred in the drafting of the vetoed national science foundation bill in 1947. The program of research promotion was to be governed by a part-time board of 24 members "eminent in the fields of the fundamental sciences . . . so selected as to provide representation for the views of scientific leaders in all areas of the nation."[21] The director of the foundation was to be selected by this group. Empowered to act for the group was an executive council of nine elected members. This attempt to usurp the President's appointing power was stopped by his veto. With his veto, President Truman administered a stinging rebuke to the Congress for trying to set up an appointive device by which administration of the research program would have been "insulated from the President by two layers of part-time boards."[22]

Almost as serious an impairment of responsible administration has frequently resulted from the establishment of statutory committees that are nominally advisory but which come to interfere actively in administration. It has been difficult to restrict these committees to advice, particularly where they are constituted to represent interest groups. Interest in the committee, even on the part of its own members, appears to demand that its ultimate recommendations be accepted by the administrator. Substantial failure of the administrator to concur and cooperate with the advisory committee is apt to cause defection of the groups represented.

The statutory advisory committee, then, tends to introduce an element of particularism into the administrative climate. The Congress in recent years has increased the centrifugal pressures on the executive branch by establishing more and more of these committees. The plethora of advisory bodies for the scientific functions of the government is particularly conspicuous. The first Hoover Commission, in the opinion of a number of dissenting members, pointed out that giving such bodies a statutory status "connotes something more than mere advice."[23] This is not to say that the government cannot profit greatly by wide use of consultants and advisers drawn from civilian life. The real problem is to keep these advisers in their advisory role. They should be neither irresponsible centers of power nor rubber stamps. The use of ad hoc committees on special problems, appointed by the responsible head of a program to serve in an advisory capacity for limited periods or at his pleasure, would seem to provide a solution to this problem.

A major invasion of the power of the President to control the executive establishment occurred, paradoxically, in the Budget and Accounting Act of 1921 which advanced executive management so greatly in respect to budgeting. This act gave to the comptroller general, an officer of the Congress, not only the proper power of independent audit, but also the right to interfere in administration through the power to settle accounts and to determine the government's accounting systems. The interference by the first comptroller general, J. R. McCarl (1921-1936), in the details of management was a particularly unfortunate chapter in the history of federal administration.

A highly centralized and arbitrary system of pre-auditing government disbursements was adopted. Many of his decisions were overruled by the courts. No agreement could be reached with the Treasury, the Bureau of the Budget, and the departments on a system of accounts that would meet their several managerial needs. The comptroller general's functions of control infringed upon the executive power and impaired the independence of his audit. In many cases his rulings were based on his interpretation of policy and law which undercut and vetoed the decisions of the responsible political officers of the executive branch.[24]

From the point of view of administrative management, the impairment of fiscal control resulting from the loss of authority over accounting procedures, expenditures control, and administrative audit functions was serious. The anomalous control of these functions by an independent comptroller general, as both the President's Committee[25] and the first Hoover Commission[26] pointed out, made impossible continuing executive control commensurate with executive responsibility for administration.

Nor did this system effectively hold the Executive accountable to the Congress. General Accounting Office procedures failed to provide the Congress with even a practical means of retrospective review of expenditures.[27] The confusion of federal accounting and audit powers dispersed authority and responsibility and left the government without either a proper accounting system or a current, truly independent audit.

An astonishing series of improvements has been effected since the reign of Mr. McCarl, the first comptroller general, starting with the enlightened administration of Lindsay Warren and continuing today under the wise and progressive leadership of Elmer B. Staats. The policies, procedures, and personnel of the General Accounting Office have been modernized. Great strides have been made in joint efforts with Treasury, Budget, and the agencies for the adoption of new systems of accounts. The passage of the Budget and Accounting Procedures Act of 1950 (31 U.S.C. 65) has further rationalized the operations of the office. Many authorities, however, still believe that there is a fundamental incompatibility of lodging the functions of control of expenditures and of audit in the same agency.

Political controversies on substantive issues periodically exert effect on the structure of government and the redistribution of legislative, executive, and judicial powers. This effect is far removed from considerations of economy and efficiency. Violent debates on structure and power become but a cover for profound differences on national policies. They may be accentuated, in an election year, by a motive to seize credit or to avoid blame for specific programs. The Tenure of Office Act (1867) was passed not because of an abstract principle of personnel administration but to curb President Andrew Johnson's reconstruction policies. The autonomy granted the General Counsel of the National Labor Relations Board by the Taft-Hartley Act (1947) was a result of a general attempt to achieve a stricter control of trade unions. The debate in 1969 over the power of the President in foreign affairs was the product of resentment against our long and costly involvement in Vietnam.

Although many Presidents confer from time to time with congressional leaders of their own party to good effect, it is a shortcoming of our governmental institutions that no responsible way has been found for the executive branch to obtain the advice of Congress. The President and his cabinet consult with representatives of the Congress at the risk of implying that they seek their prior consent. They will feel bound by their statements made in such a consultation but what senator or representative can assure them that their respective Houses will be bound as well by theirs? Nor can the problem be solved by appearances on the floor of Congress by a cabinet officer, a proposal long advocated by the late Senator Estes Kefauver (Tennessee). Elected representatives do not consider appointed officials as peers. They have no position of parliamentary leadership or privilege in either House, nor could they count on support of members of their own party. They would be cross-examined on some particular point by the members and the confrontation would be less in the nature of a constructive debate on policies than of a disorderly grand jury inquisition into specific cases and minor matters. The informal give and take in the appearance of department heads before congressional committees is the most useful device we have been able to contrive and it does offer many constructive avenues of communication and interchange.

It would be absurd, of course, to depend upon structural reorganization alone to solve the problems created for government by the centrifugal forces which continually tend to impede effective coordination and the fixing of responsibility. These forces have deep roots in the American scene and profoundly affect all our institutions, private as well as public. In an age of high technology and educational specialization the problem is worldwide, but for some reason we in the United States seem to have pushed the division of labor and minute specialization to absurd extremes. Our federal system and the separation of powers magnify the problem in the governmental area.

The specialized forces in our society have great positive values and in a sense are part and parcel of the institutions and arrangements we most cherish. Expert competence, decentralization, variety of patterns, and participation of citizens in public affairs are among the major values in the American democracy. Much of our progress has resulted from the pressures of dynamic and expert specialist groups. Former Senator William Benton (Connecticut) used to refer to the power of the "one man lobby" and the name of Mr. Ralph Nader comes to mind. But in the heat of their crusades and in their preoccupation with their special purposes, these groups often have improvised programs with little concern either for their workability or for their relationship to the rest of the government. The question is how to preserve their peculiar values while relating their programs to the rest of the body politic. The need is to find an antidote for the strong forces of particularism in order that they do not cancel each other out and so that national priorities can be responsibly determined. Otherwise the American people run the risk of allowing the strength of a pluralistic society to reduce its main organ of united endeavor, its government, to a schizoid state of helplessness.

There is no single easy formula to preserve our rich tradition of special competence, professional esprit de corps, wide participation in public affairs, and generous opportunities for local and regional differentiation, and at the same time to discover the means for making the general purpose supreme over the particular and parochial purposes. In large organizations, particularly in big government, a rational structural organization, varied and decentralized in pattern, can however be one important means to this end.

Chapter II

LANDMARKS OF ADMINISTRATIVE MANAGEMENT 1789–1933

1. *Management—A Twentieth Century Concept*

THE CONCEPT OF MANAGEMENT IN BUSINESS AS WELL AS IN GOVERNMENT is essentially a twentieth century product. A brief glimpse at other times and places affords a comparative perspective. Ancient empires, such as Egypt and Rome, had elaborate quasi-military systems of administration. In imperial China, whose system of civil service examinations started in the seventh century, A.D., the command of thousands of words (characters) was a main qualification for entrance and promotion. Powerful mandarins undertook literary and philosophic formulations on the art of administration. In medieval Europe monarchs who could neither read nor write Latin, nor their own vernacular, retained clerks and scribes who could. The writings of Machiavelli, the Florentine who wrote *The Prince* in the early sixteenth century, and of Henry Taylor, the Englishman who wrote *The Statesman* in the early eighteenth century, may seem quaint and cynical to us today, but their works contain still useful administrative insights. The Prussian kings of the seventeenth and eighteenth centuries founded university chairs of "cameralism" for the training of public officials, emphasizing public finance and indoctrination in the political economy of a specific school. One of the earliest manifestations of democracy in Europe was the separation of the privy purse of the king from the public exchequer with parliamentary control of the latter.

The French administrative system, starting with Napoleon the First, was designed to fill the vacuum resulting from the fall of the ancient regime and the weaknesses of the committees of the French Revolution by replacing them with a logical central structure of power and law. Since 1945, major reforms have taken place in French administration. Of particular note is the system of recruiting and training young people for the highest corps of the French civil service. After severe competitive entrance tests, those chosen undergo one of the most rigorous periods of training in the world, embracing graduate seminars, individual research, and periods of field work in prefectures and even in industry. Administrative regions are being formed of three or four prefectures. A keen interest in tangible results in matters social, economic, and technical has overtaken older preoccupation with abstractions and a kind of disembodied concept of administrative law.

In Britain the early colonial governments of the empire were often administered by a corporation chartered by the Crown with administrative, military, and commercial powers, such as the ones in India and in some of the American colonies. The Trevelyan-Northcote reforms of the 1850's actually followed those adopted in India under the influence of Lord Macaulay. They replaced an obsolete system of patronage appointments, in an age when an office was still regarded as a property. Competitive examinations were required for entrance to an elite administrative class almost entirely recruited from Oxford and Cambridge universities. The examinations were originally in the basic humanities and sciences. Many other options are now offered. The British have not favored vocational pre-entry training for the administrative class whose members learned by doing and had the opportunity, by outstanding performance, to rise to powerful posts such as the permanent under secretary of a ministry. Until recently, their high civil servants could look forward to knighthoods. Administrators in Britain took an exceptional interest in developing their younger colleagues, and the system produced magnificent figures such as Sir Henry Bunbury, Sir Warren Fisher, Lord Bridges, and Viscount Waverly (Sir John Anderson). More recently, brilliant women have risen to high posts as in the cases of Lady Evelyn Sharp and Lady Barbara Castle.

With the rise of technology, increasing criticism of the recruitment of "generalists," the versatile "amateur in everything," began to be heard in Britain. There was a movement to separate management of the civil service from its historic location in the Treasury. Modernization and democratization of the system has occurred over a period of a hundred years, culminating in 1968 in the reforms of the Fulton Report. At the local level, the most significant step in the 1960's has been the enlargement of the area previously governed by the London County Council to a government of metropolitan London and the adoption of the two-tier system. Other large British cities will probably emulate the London model as a result of the recent recommendations of the Royal Commission on Local Government, headed by Lord Radcliffe-Maude. Some of its proposals were influenced by American examples, such as increasing the managerial duties of the town clerk and the establishment of regional councils. Other managerial changes of note in the British government in our time are the provision of staff aides and a cabinet secretariat in the Prime Minister's office and the use of the public corporation in the case of the nationalized industries. A corporate form of structure is gradually being applied to the post office, which in the United Kingdom runs the telephone and telegraph systems as well as handling the mails.

In the American world of business, the advent of scientific management is largely a twentieth century development. Business management techniques and theory were by-products of the growth of large scale undertakings. The nineteenth century entrepreneur started as a merchant or mechanic; and if his venture prospered, he fostered its growth out of earnings. His sons and nephews were his understudies and marrying the boss' daughter was a frequent road to advancement. The more impersonal hierarchies came with the large corporation. Frederick W. Taylor and his disciples first applied their engineering principles of scientific management in the relatively large-scale metallurgical industries. Even the discipline of accounting remained rudimentary until the passage of the Federal Income Tax Law of 1913. Except for the sons of the wealthy and a scattering of lawyers and engineers, few businessmen were college graduates. The enormous growth of university preparation for business administration at both college and graduate levels occurred in this century. All kinds of subdisciplines have arisen. Starting with courses in economics, accounting and corporate finance, business law, marketing, management engineering, personnel and industrial relations, the curricula now embrace studies in industrial psychology and group dynamics, statistics, case studies, automatic data processing, systems analysis, and operations research. A great mass of published research accompanied these developments.

Compared to government, there prevails an almost complete delegation to chief executive officers of American business by their boards of directors and stockholders in the matter of structural change of the enterprise and in the selection and promotion of executive personnel. In large industrial aggregates and conglomerates, this power is regarded by top management as an essential element of its profit and control structure, shared at the most with a small executive committee. Except at the highest level, the board approval of corporate officers is usually pro forma. The developments of management theory and practice in business and government are exhaustively described in the definitive treatise of Professor Bertram M. Gross.[1]

American representative government is opposed to emulating the business pattern, and the emergence of administrative management in government has taken a different direction. The business practice is frequently arbitrary and ruthless and our system of representative government will not tolerate an abdication of legislative oversight and regulation of the methods, procedures, and structures of government as well as of its policies and expenditures. As will be shown later, such intervention also may become arbitrary and irresponsible. Since 1939, Congress has been willing to delegate to the President certain initiatives in respect to executive reorganization, reserving to itself a power of legislative veto, and, as will appear, has given the chief executive new tools of administrative management.

It is interesting to note that under parliamentary systems the legislature exerts relatively little influence on organization and management. The prime minister and his cabinet have wide areas of latitude in changes in the structure of the government as they have in other matters. The creation of new ministries, although subject to parliamentary approval, and the shifting of ministerial functions are in practice left to the Prime Minister and the Cabinet either to recognize a new administrative need or to make places for powerful political figures in the Cabinet.

2. Management and the Chief Executive Since 1789

The practice of management of the executive branch by the President actually started with Washington, but the development of a general theory of presidential administrative management did not emerge until this century and was to a great extent a function of the expanding duties and size of the executive establishment. There were cycles of fluctuation in the exercise of the managerial function by presidents depending partly on their own personalities and partly on the extent to which Congress exerted executive powers. The state of the administrative art, science, and system is graphically described in each of the four epic volumes on the administrative history of the United States by Leonard D. White.[2] President Washington, he tells us, had a sense of system and order derived from his experience with plantation management. His military career had given him a skill in staff relationships and the habit of making decisions. He sought advice, even in the wording of a letter, but in referring matters to his department heads set short time limits for their oral or written replies. Once the main lines of policy had been agreed to, he gave his department heads considerable leeway on the details of execution. He was constantly aware that, as the first president, his every act was setting a precedent.

Washington's original small tight-knit government with only three secretaries and two other officers (State, Treasury, War, Justice, Post Office) and eight hundred employees operated as if it were his own executive office. In spite of growing differences among members of his cabinet, particularly between Jefferson and Hamilton, his subordinates daily submitted matters to him for approval, responded promptly to his requests for information and advice, and accepted his decisions. They were called "secretaries" rather than "ministers" not only because the young republic disliked the royal connotations of the latter term but to indicate their subordination to the President. Washington's control of the executive branch was strengthened in the first month of his administration by the passage, on a very narrow margin, of the act to create the Department of State. It provided, after much heated debate on the point, that the President could remove a department head without the approval of the Senate. The constitution required senatorial confirmation for appointments but had been silent on the precise method of removal, except in cases of impeachment.[2-A]

The President's power to remove department heads was infringed in the case of the Tenure of Office Act, passed to restrain President Andrew Johnson in 1867, which was modified at the end of his term and repealed in 1887. The limitation on the President's power to remove members of regulatory commissions of the government has been restricted by the courts.

A violent trend towards congressional supremacy took place as a result of the reaction to the assumption of immense powers during the

Civil War by President Lincoln. He stretched the executive powers of the constitution to the limit on the assumption that it could not be preserved if the union were dissolved. The Tenure of Office Act was only one of many acts which characterized the bitter fight over reconstruction policies between the "radical" dominated Congress and President Andrew Johnson. He was finally impeached in the House and was saved from conviction and removal in the Senate by only one vote. The presidency sank to its nadir during the subsequent weak administration of General Ulysses S. Grant.

White's administrative history, alas, had to omit the complex period of the Civil War, but he resumes his narrative with the postwar Republican era. Concerning this period, he observed "for twenty years members of Congress acted as amateur organization and methods analysts, but they failed to rise to higher levels." The long succession of congressional inquiries which he describes included a Joint Select Committee on Retrenchment (1869-71) whose chairman was Senator James W. Patterson (N.H.); a Senate Committee (1875-76) of which the former Secretary of the Treasury, George S. Boutwell (Mass.) was chairman; the Cockrell Committee (1887-89) and the Dockery-Cockrell Joint Commission (1893-1895). Representative Alexander Dockery and Senator Francis M. Cockrell were both from Missouri and evidently "wanted to be shown" why the bureaus were so slow and cost so much. Two of the experts employed by the Joint Commission, Charles W. Haskins and Elijah W. Sells, later founded the well-known accounting firm of Haskins and Sells. An interesting disquisition might be written on business and professional enterprises that began by associations in government work.

While some useful results were obtained from these efforts, such as improving internal systems of agencies, expediting work, and slightly reducing the number of clerks, White asserts that the fundamental causes of mismanagement were disregarded. The weaknesses of the patronage system and the lack of overall management were not treated. The initiative in this period came entirely from Congress and not from the President. Even at the turn of the century, he tells us administrative management was not considered an important concern of the presidency:

> When William McKinley took the oath of office for the second time on March 4, 1901, he and the Republican Party were committed to well-understood national policies. They were committed to no pattern of administrative organization, because they neither had one nor were

expected by the country to have one beyond honesty and economy.
The following thirty years however were decades of unparalleled progress
in developing both the theory and practice of the art of administration.[2-D]

The progress to which White refers resulted from demands for better
services as new tasks were assumed by the federal government. These
in turn were the products of such factors as the passing of the frontier,
the settlement of the continent, the exploitation of natural resources,
the abolition of slavery, the development of agriculture, the growth of
industry, the improvements in transportation and communication, the
advance of science, technology, and education, the waves of immigration, the building of cities, the recurring booms and depressions, the
rise of large corporations and trade unions, and the emergence of the
United States in 1898 as a world power.

At the local level, which in 1888 Lord Bryce had deplored as the
worst failure of the American experiment, great progress has been
made. The changes, for the most part, have come about by steps to
reform specific abuses rather than as a response to a general theory
of management. They included civil service reform, reduction in the
number of elected officials by adoption of the short ballot, replacement
of administrative boards by single administrators, and stronger powers
for governors, mayors, and department heads. The business analogy
had its greatest influence in the American invention of the council-
manager form of government with a professional city manager and a
non-partisan city council, one of whom was chosen by the council to
act as mayor. It was invented circa 1912 by Richard S. Childs, a New
York businessman who was associated with the short-ballot movement
launched by Woodrow Wilson, and who at age 87 is still active in
state and local reforms. There were marked improvements in municipal
budgeting, finance, and purchasing, some of which antedated the reforms at state and federal levels. At the state level, simplification of the
executive structure was effected by Governors Byrd in Virginia, Mc-
Lain in North Carolina, Gardiner in Maine, Lowden in Illinois, and
Smith in New York. Many states granted the governors the item veto
over appropriation. Many have still to perfect their overall structures
and methods and their relations to local governments. County governments have improved, but antiques still abound among the three
thousand counties. Interesting movements are in the direction of state
decentralization to regional bodies, and in the creation of larger metropolitan areas for local government. There remains a big task ahead of
reducing the number of local authorities aggregating some eighty thou-

sand and of revising old state constitutions to meet contemporary needs.

3. *Management By-products of Civil Service Reform*

Civil service reform has not only transmuted government service into a respectable career, but has had other significant managerial by-products. The American merit system actually began in the military services where it contrived to avoid most of the abuses of patronage in spite of the requirements of congressional nominations to the military academies and senatorial confirmation of the appointment and promotion of officers. Although political appointments of military officers were made in several of our wars, particularly in the Civil War, and soldier heroes have frequently become active in politics, we have been remarkably free of military juntas. In the civilian bureaus, during the height of the patronage system, there were always capable and industrious chief clerks and auditors around who saw that some work was done and became too useful to be fired when the government changed. Even in the early days of "the scientific estate" it kept a watchful eye to see that capable professionals were appointed to head the scientific bureaus.

It is often forgotten that the Pendleton Act of 1883 (5 U.S.C. 1101), which was certainly a landmark of administrative reform, did not cover the entire establishment into the civil service in one fell swoop.[3] American personnel advisers working in developing countries often overlook the gradualism of our own civil service history in their eagerness to wipe out patronage overnight. Congress granted the President the authority in 1883 to "cover in" groups of public officials from time to time, giving the incumbents an opportunity to qualify by non-competitive procedures. Every President has extended the career service and it has taken over eighty years to bring its coverage to the present point of embracing over 98 per cent of all civil positions.

The immediate by-product of civil service reforms was the enormous release of the energies of administrative officials from the hours of haggling with politicians in the making of hundreds of patronage appointments, promotions, and dismissals so that they had more time to give to their executive duties. I remember that when Farm Credit Administration was covered into the civil service in 1935, our mail and telephone calls from the Hill went down about 50 per cent.

Members of Congress have frequently expressed their satisfaction, as well, at having been relieved of so much of this time-consuming and often politically embarrassing brokerage. The Classification Act of 1923, as amended, not only introduced an element of fairness in advancing the principle (not yet perfectly implemented) of equal pay for equal work, but served further to conserve executive and legislative energies from long disputes over rates of pay for individual minor posts.

Another major by-product of personnel reform was that the managerial control of the department heads and bureau chiefs was measurably enhanced. Merit appointees were inclined to take an interest in their work, to observe improved standards of discipline, ethics, and decorum, and to aspire by good performance to higher posts on the career ladder. Loyalty to their programs, as well as to their chiefs, began to develop when they were no longer beholden to a political boss for their appointments or in Henry Adams' phrase "in Senator's service." Those who castigate a merit bureaucracy, and there is a never ending stream of writing on this topic, fail to contrast it with the indiscipline, indolence, venality, incompetence, and arbitrary rudeness of a patronage-ridden one. Civil service reform, although bringing in its wake a new series of problems, has nevertheless made public service a self-respecting and honorable vocation compared to the nineteenth century when most government jobs were considered to be a form of outdoor relief.

There is still a large number of federal political or "excepted" posts, estimated variously at three thousand to five thousand, many of which are of a policy-forming character, including the judiciary. Presidents and department heads utilize appointments of this character to formulate and defend new policies, to insure the responsiveness of the agencies to such policies, to procure congressional support in regard to legislation, and to secure popular support in elections. In times of prosperity and with the growth of awareness of conflicts of interest, it has become increasingly difficult to recruit first-rate talent for these positions.

4. Upgrading of the Career Services

The improvement in the quality of the federal career services during the twentieth century has been spectacular. An entirely new type of public servant has been attracted to government service as compared to the average run of "government clerks" that came in as late as the 1920's. The initial emphasis of civil service recruitment was negative— to eliminate favoritism in appointments. It has gradually become positive: increasingly it reaches out for able people who are not only competing for a job at the entrance level, but have before them the prospect of promotion and a stimulating life career. Civil service, as recommended in the Brownlow report, has been extended "upward, outward, and downward."

A number of factors have contributed to this improvement. High posts have been opened to career personnel, such as departmental administrative assistant secretaries, bureau chiefs, chiefs of missions (ambassadors) in the foreign service, and major scientific and technical positions. Salaries in the top grades which stopped at $10,000 in the 1940's now have reached the $30,0000 level. Pensions and fringe benefits have been measurably increased. Intensive efforts have been made since the passage of the U. S. Government Employees' Training Act of 1958 to develop educated and motivated people by means of internships, midcareer and executive training programs, and after-hours or leave-with-pay opportunities for continuing professional training and education. A most constructive series of short training exercises is underway for federal executives at the training centers in Berkeley, California, at Kings Point, New York, and at the Federal Executive Institute in Charlottesville, Virginia. A 1969 study of 28,000 federal executives in the highest civil service grades (G.S. 15 through G.S. 18) indicated that two-thirds of them had in excess of twenty years of service, that 86 per cent of them had college degrees, and that over one-half of these held advanced degrees.[4] Although the proposal of the second Hoover Commission for a mobile, top level "senior administrative service" was not adopted, the United States Civil Service Commission has in recent years initiated an interesting job assignment system at top executive levels, designed to encourage mobility and the best use of its human resources.

Opportunities for training at the university level for people interested in public affairs careers have grown rapidly. Well over 150 American colleges and universities now offer undergraduate and graduate programs in public administration, public affairs, international relations and allied fields. Whereas most of the graduates have tended to accept staff positions, some of the schools have emphasized training for more generalized posts such as that of the city manager and of the foreign

service officer. Professional associations of public officials have multi-
plied and a great number of research and survey organizations have
arisen. These institutions present further opportunities for public
service on the part of trained young people in addition to those found
in government itself. Many university graduates are attracted today to
state and local services, and to community organizations.

The standards of competence and integrity of the American civil
service today are high and compare favorably with those of other
vocations. For the most part, the American people have career services for which they no longer need to apologize.

5. Some Problems of a Career Bureaucracy

Not all the by-products of a competent career bureaucracy are
benign, although the dysfunctional aspects tend to be exaggerated in
the press and in some of the research on the problem. Naturally, new
problems have arisen as a result of the assignment of so many major
tasks to a career bureaucracy enjoying a high degree of security.
However, the tenure rights of American civil servants are considerably
less absolute than those found in European civil services, and among
college professors at home. Bureaus and positions may be merged or
abolished by reorganizations, and individuals may be disciplined,
reassigned, and discharged for cause and frequently are. Early retirement and "selection out" systems are used to eliminate persons deemed
by an impartial board to have reached the limit of their capacities.
Lateral mobility to and from the world of business, science, and other
professions is frequent and gives us an "open civil service," in contrast
to the closed ones of older countries. This sometimes creates difficult
"conflict of interest" problems which, in my view, are more susceptible
of solution than those of a civil service too detached from the rest of
society. The Foreign Service, however, has tended to operate on the
closed career principle.[5]

Some of the negative aspects of a competent career bureaucracy are
found in large organizations of any kind. One of them, built-in juris-
dictionalism, is caused by the way we organize our government programs. They are narrowly defined and the positions to man them call
for highly specialized job descriptions. The result is that we tend to
recruit people with an overspecialized technical background rather
than those having the promise of ascending in a promotional line,

even in their own fields of competence. While the British may have placed excessive emphasis on generalists, we have placed too little on broad educational background and administrative aptitude at entrance levels.

Large organizations tend to become impersonal and rigid, and the factor of human relations is often neglected by management. It is difficult to maintain high standards of productivity, work interest, and morale in big groups of office workers performing highly routinized, subdivided, and repetitive tasks.

The rank and file tends to become overconscious of the clock and the coffee break. It is often preoccupied with its rights and privileges to the detriment of its obligations for productivity and service. There is the undoubted problem of resistance to change in regard to programs, methods, or structures which many civil servants fear may downgrade the status of their work units. The grade of their precise job classifications may thus be threatened. Because of their highly specialized missions, American agencies are peculiarly vulnerable to jurisdictional rivalries which delay the decision-making process or water it down. With the growth of trade unionism in the government it is essential to establish the point at which officials become identified with the management side of the table and to avoid undue emphasis on seniority in promotions. The experience with veteran's preference should make us cautious to what extent standards of competence should be lowered in respect to promotions and separations as we endeavor to give a fairer opportunity to minority groups.

In times of transition, new administrations and new political executives are greatly concerned about the responsiveness of the higher civil servants to a new regime. Many of them come into office with no knowledge of the government and with preconceived stereotypes about the permanent officials. They tend to regard any questioning of the soundness of a new program or method as resistance. Much has still to be learned concerning the interface relationships between new policy officials and career civil servants during a time of transition. In my view, the problem is rarely insoluble. The top career man or woman, if changes are to be made, will usually be more responsive to them than is generally believed. Their experience and skills are essential to the policy executive and should be enlisted from the outset, for they can make or break their programs. An indication of trust and confidence on both sides will usually establish a modus vivendi. If this is impossible to achieve after a sustained effort, the career man had better

begin to look around town for another berth. This view is supported
by recent conversations with a number of mid-career and top-level
officials. In all organizations, private as well as public, the enlistment
of cooperation of human beings in the effecting of changes in programs,
methods, and structures is a continuing ingredient and test of enlightened management. There has been a dearth of research and experimentation in regard to these interface relationships in the governmental
setting.

6. Theodore Roosevelt and the Executive View

President Theodore Roosevelt, unlike McKinley, had firm views on
presidential management. He was the undoubted originator of the
concepts of reorganization as a continuing need of administrative
management and as an executive responsibility. He thought that government should do things and that the President was the man to see
that they got done. To get something done, anything done, and hopefully the right thing, is the perpetual struggle of the government executive. A kinetic and articulate personality, "T. R." was the living embodiment of Hamilton's "energetic executive."

He was the first President to perceive and to assert the executive
view of reorganization which is concerned with efficiency of operations
as well as with their economy. He had been helped to formulate this
view by the reports of the Keep Commission, headed by Charles Hallam Keep, assistant secretary of the Treasury, which he had appointed
in 1905. This attitude coincided with Roosevelt's executive experience
and observation at three levels of government: as U. S. Civil Service
Commissioner from 1889 to 1896, as head of the New York City Police
Board, as assistant secretary of the Navy, and as Governor of the State
of New York, before he became Vice President and then President of
the United States. Both Roosevelt and the Keep Commission had been
influenced by the precedent set by the Act creating the Department of Commerce and Labor, approved February 14, 1903 (32 Stat.
827), which authorized the President:

> . . . by order in writing, to transfer to the new department any unit
> engaged in statistical or scientific work, together with their duties and
> authority.

Congress in this Act, as it had done in the case of civil service in the

Pendleton Act, created the new institution but delegated to the President the "politically hot" job of transferring to it relevant components in the departments. This "heat transference principle" became the undisclosed premise of subsequent reorganization acts. Among the units transferred by the President to the Department of Commerce and Labor were: the Bureau of Labor (first established in 1884 in Interior and which later became a "department without executive rank")—it was the predecessor of the Bureau of Labor Statistics; the Bureau of the Census; the National Bureau of Standards; and the venerable U. S. Patent Office dating back to 1790.

Theodore Roosevelt asserted his concepts in his Seventh Annual Message to Congress of December 1907 which embodied, as far as I can find, the first presidential request for continuing authority to adjust the executive structure. In referring to the studies of the Keep Commission, he said:

> I call attention to two government commissions which I have appointed and which have already done excellent work. The first of these has to do with the reorganization of the scientific work of the government which has grown up entirely without plan and is, in consequence, so unnecessarily distributed among the executive departments that much of its effect is lost for lack of proper coordination. The commission's chief object is to introduce a planned and orderly development and operation in place of the ill-assorted and often ineffective grouping and methods of work which have prevailed. *This cannot be done without legislation, nor would it be feasible to deal in detail with so complex an administrative problem by specific provisions of law. I recommend that the President be given authority to concentrate related lines of work and reduce duplication by executive order through transfers and consolidations of lines of work.*[6] (Italics added)

Congress did not act on this recommendation, but it was prophetic in respect to recommendations of subsequent Presidents and to the eventual series of reorganization acts in our time.

The work of the Keep Commission, known as the Commission (or Committee) on Department Methods (1905-1909) was a landmark of executive introspection. It stimulated management improvements in bureau after bureau and in such varied fields as accounting and costing, archives and records administration, simplification of paper work, use of office machinery, personnel administration, procurement and supply, and contracting procedures. It even investigated instances of corruption and devised methods for its prevention. All its members were young and vigorous full-time government officials who did much of their work outside official hours without additional pay. Its recommendations were often the precursors of later accounting and personnel reforms, including classification, preservation of historic archives, and the Federal Register, some of which were not adopted until thirty years later. Its history is vividly recounted in the scholarly essay of Professor Oscar Kraines: "The President Versus Congress: The Keep Commission, 1905-1909, First Comprehensive Presidential Inquiry Into Administration."[7] Congress, however, resented its activities because it threatened many vested interests and jobs and because it had only presidential sanction. President Roosevelt endorsed many of its legislative recommendations, none of which were enacted.

7. The Taft Commission and the Executive Budget

The Taft Commission on Economy and Efficiency was also a presidentially appointed commission which worked between 1910 and 1913. Its membership included such able administrative reformers and political scientists as Frederick A. Cleveland, its chairman; W. F. Willoughby; and F. J. Goodnow.[8] Its reports not only reasserted the continuing need for executive initiative in reorganizations but pointed out the importance of managerial research, by a competent survey staff, before reorganization decisions were arrived at. The Commission proposed that this staff should be part of the Bureau of the Budget which would report to the President, and which would become a center of information about all executive operations. The Bureau of Efficiency performed this function as an independent agency from 1916 until 1933, when it was abolished. Its director was Herbert Brown and its deputy director was William H. McReynolds, who became administrative assistant to the Secretary of the Treasury in 1933 and to the President in 1939. The Bureau was the initiator and incubator of continuing administrative research in the executive branch and recruited young administrative analysts from the universities, many of whom rose to important posts throughout the government. But it actually reported for many years to Senator Reed Smoot (Utah), chairman of the Joint Committee on Reorganization, and not to the President.

The other recommendations of the Taft Commission languished for eight years, including the interval of World War I, until the passage of the Budget and Accounting Act of 1921.

This Act is probably the greatest landmark of our administrative history except for the Constitution itself. It gave the President the indispensable managerial and fiscal controls of an executive budget which he had not had before and it supplied him for the first time with an executive staff in the form of a bureau headed by a director who, at the suggestion of Congress itself, was "his man" and was to be appointed by the President without Senate confirmation. It also authorized the Bureau of the Budget to make managerial studies but the Bureau, at the insistence of the Senate, remained housed in the Treasury Department. It was not until 1939 that it became the foundation stone of the new executive office of the President. Only then was it made the center of overall administrative management and executive organization studies (under the imaginative leadership of Harold D. Smith, who had been Budget director in the State of Michigan), which, in my view, it should continue to be.[9] One of its enthusiastic sponsors characterized the passage of the Budget and Accounting Act of 1921 as "the greatest measure of legislative and administrative reform in our history."[10]

8. Woodrow Wilson and the Overman Act

Woodrow Wilson's views of the role of the chief executive experienced a change in method but not in spirit between the time when, as a young professor, he had written *Congressional Government* until he became President of Princeton University, Governor of New Jersey, and President of the United States.[11] His early writings had pointed out the essentially irresponsible nature of administration by standing committees, but he was searching for a more responsible method of congressional participation rather than its elimination. He was influenced by the British cabinet model and in his youth had advocated that the President should select his cabinet from among the majority leaders of Congress.[12] Long after he had relinquished these early views including the one that the President, on a vote of no confidence, should be able to dissolve the Congress and appeal to the country in a special election, he still asserted the duty of the President to formulate policies and his right to appeal to the country to vindicate them.

Woodrow Wilson was one of the first scholars to say that public administration should be studied and could be taught.[13] He strongly favored an executive budget, but vetoed the first Budget and Accounting Act because he considered the provision for removing the Comptroller General by concurrent resolution of the two Houses an unconstitutional infringement of the executive power. After slight amendments, it was re-enacted and signed by President W. G. Harding, but the comptroller is still regarded as an officer of Congress. It is important to recall President Wilson's regular meetings with congressional leaders, the astonishing record of congressional support of his progressive legislative program during his first term, and his vigorous administration of World War I. His unwillingness to consult and to compromise with Congress on the ratification of the Covenant of the League of Nations was not, as generally supposed, typical of his relations with the legislative body.

The passage of the Overman Act, approved May 20, 1918 (40 Stat. 556-7), must be identified here as another landmark of reorganization. It was sponsored by Lee Slater Overman, for twenty-eight years (1903-1930) a respected and diligent senator from North Carolina, and chairman of the Senate Rules Committee. It was the first law that gave a president powers of reorganization by executive action in wartime. But its scope was severely limited. These were confined to "matters relating to the conduct of the present war." The authority was limited to consolidations and transfers of existing agencies and functions. No new agencies could be established by the President with the single exception (in Section 3) of an executive agency for the production of aircraft. It required that abolition of agencies had to be recommended to Congress for normal legislative action. The powers granted were to terminate six months after the end of hostilities, but provided that executive actions which had been taken under its provisions would also terminate and powers and functions would revert to their pre-existing status (Section 6). In order to make permanent the benefits of certain transfers, a very intricate piece of legislation had to be drafted and passed in 1920.

During World War I, in which American participation lasted only nineteen months, President Wilson had to go to Congress for legislation whenever he created a temporary war agency, among which one might mention the Council of National Defense (the first cabinet council created by statute), the National Defense Advisory Commission, the War Industries Board (of which Bernard Baruch became chairman), the Price Fixing Committee (Dr. Robert S. Brookings, chairman), the Fuel Administration (Dr. Harry A. Garfield, administrator), the War Trade Board, and others. The Taft-Walsh War

Labor Board had no legal powers and was established by executive action for purposes of industrial mediation and conciliation. American participation in World War II hostilities lasted almost forty-five months, but President Roosevelt had not only greater powers to organize temporary agencies but provisions for their oversight and coordination within the executive office of the President. The Overman Act of 1918, with many modifications, nevertheless became the precedent for subsequent executive reorganization legislation. On account of its historic importance, I have included its final text in Appendix III, Reorganization Acts.

In 1923, a Congressional Joint Committee on Reorganization, which had surveyed the executive structure, reported a comprehensive reorganization plan. Although Presidents Harding and Coolidge endorsed its proposals, which interestingly enough contained a provision for a Department of Education and Relief, Congress took no action on them.

9. *Herbert Hoover and the Legislative Veto*

To Herbert Hoover belongs the undoubted credit for the invention and espousal of the important peacetime reorganization device— presidential initiative subject to the legislative veto. I am supported in this assertion by the competent and massive unpublished doctoral dissertation, *A Study of the Legislative Veto*, by my friend Dr. Peter Schauffler of Philadelphia, to whom I am greatly indebted for clues to many of the statements and references in this chapter.[14] Louis Brownlow, who could admire some of Hoover's administrative insights while opposed to his political opinions, also sustains me in the following statement:

> Secretary of Commerce Hoover, in 1920 on the occasion of his testimony before the Joint Committee on Reorganization, suggested that Congress should give authority to the President to make such changes within the limits of certain defined principles as may be recommended to him by an independent commission to be created by Congress. President Hoover in his message to Congress of December 3, 1929, proposed that he be authorized to work out and effect reorganization measures, Congress to reserve to itself "powers of revision." This is the earliest reference found to the device of presidential action subject to rejection by Congress or requiring the approval of Congress.[15]

President Hoover, long before his election, had been a symbol of American management engineering in business and government. He was known as "the great engineer." As president, he believed that the cutting of governmental expenditures would solve the depression, that the President must take the initiative in respect to such reductions, but unfortunately he continued to rely too heavily on reorganization as a road to economy, as will be shown in Chapters V and VI.

President Hoover proposed that an executive order for reorganization be submitted to Congress to become effective within sixty days "unless Congress requested suspension of such action." He advocated the adoption of the general principle that executive and administrative functions should have single-headed responsibility, and that advisory, regulatory, and quasi-judicial functions should be performed by boards and commissions. He proposed to transfer regulatory functions from executive officials to commissions and executive functions from boards and commissions to executive officials.[16]

A further precedent for transfers by presidential action had reinforced the one established at the time of the creation of the Department of Commerce and Labor in 1903 mentioned above. It was contained in the Act of June 15, 1929 (46 Stat. 11, c. 24) which established President Hoover's Federal Farm Board. It authorized the President, by executive order, to transfer to or from the jurisdiction and control of the Federal Farm Board the whole or any part of any executive agency engaged in scientific or extension work or furnishing services with respect to the marketing of agricultural commodities, its functions, personnel, property, and unexpended appropriations. President Hoover in October 1929 transferred the Division of Cooperative Marketing in the Department of Agriculture to the Federal Farm Board pursuant to this Act. The Federal Farm Board was merged with the Farm Credit Administration in March 1933. Its stabilization functions were liquidated and twelve regional Banks for Cooperatives were authorized by Congress to finance farmer-owned cooperative marketing and purchasing associations.

Additional acts of this kind, none of which conferred general reorganization powers on the President but were restricted to certain agencies, are to be found in the Act of May 27, 1930 (46 Stat. 427) providing for the transfer to the attorney general of certain functions in the administration of the National Prohibition Act and the Act of July 3, 1930 (46 Stat. 1016) authorizing the President to establish the Veterans Administration by executive order and to transfer to it certain hospitals and administrative agencies related to the administration of laws concerning veterans relief and benefits.

As the depression advanced, Congress was finally persuaded to pass the Economy Act of June 30, 1932 (72nd Congress, 1st Session, 47 Stat. 413-415), which was the first instance of enacted law to provide for executive reorganization subject to congressional veto (Appendix III). The bill provided for transfers and consolidations, but abolitions of agencies had to be recommended to Congress for ordinary legislative action. An executive order providing for transfers or consolidations would become effective after sixty days, unless Congress approved it sooner by concurrent resolution, or unless it were vetoed *in whole or in part* by a simple resolution of either House. (A concurrent resolution, unlike a joint resolution, does not require the President's concurrence.)

As the depression and panic deepened, President Hoover's stock sank with it, and a Democratic Congress struck down the series of eleven reorganization orders he had sent up on the grounds that the wishes of the new President who would take office on March 4, 1933, should be considered. The legislative veto was thus applied to executive reorganization orders, ironically enough, the first time they were submitted, against the very President who had conceived the device. One should not, therefore, underrate the contributions made by President Hoover to the theory and practice of executive reorganization.

Chapter III

THE PRESIDENT'S COMMITTEE
ON ADMINISTRATIVE MANAGEMENT
(THE BROWNLOW COMMITTEE)

1. Origins

IN THE FIRST CHAPTER I HAVE DEALT WITH THE CONTINUING PROCESS of reorganization and the persistent pressures toward disunity and the impairment of integrated executive control. In the second chapter I recited some of the historical landmarks of administrative reform. In this chapter I turn to the first of three major efforts within the last four decades to examine and evaluate the organization and functioning of the federal executive establishment and propose measures of reform.

The *Report of the President's Committee on Administrative Management* in 1937 has become a classic paper on American administration. The *Report*, together with President Roosevelt's spirited letter transmitting it to the Congress, should be read and reread by all students of government. It is a reasoned critique of the executive branch and a bold effort to provide solutions for the complex problems of top administration. Furthermore, it is a model of clear and vivid English exposition.

The concern of the committee with the improvement of management reflected an uneasy awareness that throughout the world democratic government itself was on trial. The United States government had grown enormously and in haphazard fashion as we had been improvising ourselves out of the worst domestic depression in our history. Across the sea, Hitler defiantly taunted the democracies as impotent. Praise for the efficacy of the Fascist dictatorship in Italy was heard in surprisingly high places in the democracies. Some doubts were being expressed as to the ability of the American system to supply the bold dynamic leadership required for solution of the problems of modern government. The question was raised as to whether efficiency and democracy were compatible. Was constitutional government under a President and a Congress a luxury of an earlier age that could not be afforded in modern crisis government? The President, in appealing to the Congress to provide the assistance recommended by the *Report,* asked, "Will it be said, 'Democracy was a great dream, but it could not do the job'?"[1]

In an effort to meet the problems of unemployment, starvation, foreclosure, and bankruptcy, the country had become committed to a new concept of government. The sphere of the federal government had been extended not only to regulation of the economy with a view of correcting abuses, but also to its recovery and development. In addition, positive programs of social service and public works had been added to the national agenda. The New Deal was the answer to a demand for public action on many fronts, and new emergency agencies were improvised, field by field, without much regard to an administrative pattern.

Administratively, the President lacked the facilities to handle his vast job. A host of government corporations and other autonomous agencies had been added to the array that had already frustrated President Roosevelt's predecessor. Although many of these agencies needed a measure of operating autonomy in their early stages, the result was a widely dispersed executive function. Many of their functions impinged on each other, and as they began to acquire some muscle the need for coordination became increasingly acute. The President had scarcely any staff assistance with which to manage the federal enterprise. What staff aides and "brain trusters" he had were "detailed" to the White House but paid by other agencies and so were their stenographers. Over one hundred agencies presumably reported directly to him. It was "humanly impossible," he admitted, to handle the numerous contacts and the mass of detail that confronted him. His National Emergency Council, which included both cabinet members and heads of new agencies, was too large and unwieldy to be useful either for policy formulation or for operating coordination. It was, however, the forerunner of the series of smaller and more specialized series of cabinet councils used increasingly by subsequent Presidents. Louis Brownlow wrote that its able director, Frank C. Walker, became "the first of a long line of assistant presidents."[2]

How to manage the sprawling and brawling executive establishment and how to relate new and emergency agencies to the regular departments became an acute problem in the first year of the Roosevelt Administration. Action came slowly, however. In the summer of 1935, Charles E. Merriam took the initiative in bringing these twin problems before his colleagues of the National Resources Committee. In October of that year, Dr. Merriam reduced his proposals to writing in a memorandum on over-all management. He and his colleagues presented that memorandum to President Roosevelt. The proposal then made was to ask an independent nongovernmental agency to make a study and present recommendations that, if approved by the President, might be transmitted by him to the Congress. The particular private agency which, under this proposal, was to undertake the task was the Committee on Public Administration of the Social Science Research Council. During November and December, the President's interest in the study increased, and he decided that the matter was of such magnitude and importance that it should be undertaken by a governmental, not a private, body.

The Congress also was concerned at this time with the problems of executive organization. Early in 1936 the Senate, on motion of Senator Harry F. Byrd of Virginia, set up a select committee, of which Senator Byrd was made chairman, to study the organization of the executive branch, with particular emphasis on the discovery of overlapping and duplication and the reduction of costs. Several months later the House appointed a similar committee.

On March 22, 1936, the President announced the appointment of a committee which came to be known as the President's Committee on Administrative Management, composed of Louis Brownlow, chairman, Charles E. Merriam, and Luther Gulick, whose primary purpose was to consider the problem of overall management of the entire executive establishment, including the relations of the new and emergency agencies to the regular departments. Mr. Brownlow also was made chairman of an advisory committee to Senator Byrd's committee and Luther Gulick became one of its members.

The President and Senator Byrd, with Mr. Brownlow, worked out a plan for a division of labor under which the President's Committee was to consider the problems of overall management and the Senate committee was to consider the problems of detailed departmental organization. At the outset, the demarcation between the work of the two groups seemed quite clear. The Senate committee engaged the Brookings Institution to undertake its survey. Since the advisory committee to the Senate committee included two members of the President's Committee, it was assumed that the two projects would be continuously coordinated. The House created a select committee under the chairmanship of James Buchanan (Texas), who headed the House Appropriations Committee. He wanted no advisory committee and from the start differed with the objectives and methods of the President's Committee.

The staff of Brookings Institution had been critical of the Administration's program and the President had been critical of their views. Before their studies progressed very far, it became clear that there would be radical differences in the conclusions of the two reports. Unfortunately, as it turned out, each group went its own way almost from the start.

No funds were granted for the President's Committee until June, 1936, when the President was authorized to allocate not more than $100,000 from emergency funds for the study it was to undertake.[3] The President's Committee gave $10,000 to the House committee and assumed expenses of the staff of the Senate committee to the extent of another $40,000. This left $50,000 for the use of the President's Committee, of which it spent $45,000. The first Hoover Commission spent $1,907,600 on its more ambitious task of detailed investigation of department and agency activities, and the second Hoover Commission spent $2,848,334. Without even invoking the mystique of contemporary cost-benefit analysis, it is clear that the President's Committee was one of the greatest bargains Uncle Sam ever bought.

2. Method of Work and Orientation

The study carried on by the President's Committee was not to be a research project, but an original contribution arising primarily out of the background and experience of Committee members and staff. The President, it was reported, had expressed the hope the Committee would secure a staff that knew enough to "skim the cream off the top of their own experience." He wanted a report on principles, not details, lest disputes over specific details jeopardize public support of the broad principles of reform.

The research staff of 26 experts recruited to assist the Committee with the investigation of special problems reflected this aim. It was a scholarly group, composed largely of political scientists, well disposed to taking a reflective, conceptual approach to the problems of executive management. All had had valuable experience in or contacts with various parts of the federal establishment. A Washington columnist with a statistical bent calculated that over half of the group were Ph.D.'s, 70 per cent were currently in academic positions, practically all were academically oriented, and over half were under 40 years of age!

At the first full meeting of Committee and staff, the staff was instructed to refrain from all but the most necessary research. Mr. Brownlow urged the importance, rather, of placing their knowledge and experience at the disposal of the Committee. He suggested that the staff spend less time on surveys and more in group discussions of major problems and their possible solutions. Mr. Gulick expressed the hope that the staff would become "eyes and ears of the committee," and would make its contribution by helping the Committee to hammer out a program in final conferences.

The memoranda and reports of the staff were to be background for the Committee's consideration. In practice, they proved much less useful than the conferences between the Commission members and staff. Many of the memoranda were never printed; and, of the suggestions contained in the studies that were printed, many were disregarded in the Committee's *Report*. The real value of the research group was in their service as staff aides, advisers, and stimulators to Committee thinking. I was a member of the group and can bear witness to how productive this informal procedure was. I was particularly impressed with the energy, the research skills and coordinating ability of Dr. Joseph P. Harris, who acted as director of research for the Committee. Dr. Merriam always described the special studies of the staff as "non-supporting documents" for the Committee's *Report*. A list of the research staff appears at the end of this chapter.

The members of the Committee provided a rare combination of experience, knowledge, and brains. Mr. Brownlow, the chairman, was the least tainted by academic experience. At the time he was director of Public Administration Clearing House at Chicago and chairman of the Committee on Public Administration of the Social Science Research Council. These were culminations of his lifetime interest in government developed through wide experience in journalism, municipal government, and housing. Brownlow was a brilliant administrator, a man of action with a fabulous memory and a rare gift for synthesizing and generalizing his rich experience. He had been a commissioner of the District of Columbia during World War I under President Wilson and subsequently city manager of Petersburg, Virginia, and Knoxville, Tennessee.

As alderman and mayoralty candidate in 1912, Professor Charles E. Merriam, the dean of American political scientists, had seen the seamy side of Chicago municipal politics at its seamiest. He had been the adviser of mayors, governors, and presidents. He was the philosopher in the market place personified, and his contributions to both the theory and practice of government are too numerous to catalog here. Throughout the survey he protested that he was a mere political philosopher dragooned into a study of administration by his two colleagues. But his contributions to the *Report* were intensely practical, no less than those of his associates, and he was unable to escape responsibility for its contents.

Dr. Gulick had long been identified with administrative reform movements, particularly at the state and municipal levels. He had been director of research for the Commission of Inquiry on Public Service Personnel from 1933 to 1935. He had conducted the fact-finding studies on the basis of which the Virginia state government had been reorganized under Governor Byrd. He had made many other state and municipal studies. As president of the Institute of Public Administration, formerly the New York Bureau of Municipal Research, Gulick was a leading figure in governmental research. He brought to the Committee his unusual gift for the lucid and graphic exposition of administrative problems.[4]

With a common background in municipal and state reorganization, a profound knowledge of American history and politics, and a high mutual regard, it is not surprising that a fine rapport characterized the Committee's attack on the reorganization problem.

There was no question in the Committee's mind as to the criteria of reform. "Fortunately," their *Report* stated, "the foundations of effective management in public affairs, no less than in private, are

well known." The "canons of efficiency" they felt made self-evident
the needs of federal administrative management. "Stated in simple
terms," they said, "these canons of efficiency require the establishment of a responsible and effective chief executive as the center of
energy, direction, and administrative management; the systematic
organization of all activities in the hands of qualified personnel under
the direction of the chief executive; and, to aid him in this, the
establishment of appropriate managerial and staff agencies."

These "canons of efficiency" sound oversimplified today in the light
of the advancing complexity of national problems, of the tasks of
the government and, I might add, of the contemporary vocabulary
of political science. After World War II a number of political scientists
thought that the "love affair" with the executive branch had lasted
too long and began to pay more attention to Congress and to bureaucratic and voting behavior. But there have been no serious contributions from them which would give us an essentially amended doctrine.
Professor Mansfield is quite justified in his discussion of the proposals
for various means of overall program coordination when he asserts:

> And it does not seem too harsh a judgment to conclude that the recent
> academic literature on organization has been preoccupied with micro-
> rather than with macro-relationships, and is hardly relevant to the prob-
> lem here.[5]

This view of the Presidency was the essence of the Committee's
distinctive approach to the problem of reorganization. Effective administrative management was their guidepost; the concept of the
Presidency as a unique American institution was their touchstone.
The study, as Brownlow pointed out, was to be guided by the basic
understanding that in the American scheme the President was *in fact*
responsible for all of national administration. The Committee attributed the failure of previous efforts at federal reorganization to
concentration on "bureau shuffling" directed to the limited objectives
of eliminating overlapping and duplication and effecting consolidation. They were convinced that the basic problem was administrative
management and that it could be solved only by equipping the
President with means of controlling and directing administration to
the extent necessary to discharge his broad responsibility. They believed that by staffing the Presidency with effective tools of overall
management it would be possible to resolve the subsidiary problems
of organization. Reorganization, as they understood it, was not to be
a "one-time shot," but a continuous process.

The Committee was not preoccupied with expectations of large-scale economies to be effected through reorganization. Its members frankly faced the fact that experience in the states and municipalities had demonstrated that relatively small savings could be attributed to reorganization. They were concerned almost exclusively with "making democracy work" by equipping the President with the tools for the effective direction and supervision of the executive establishment. They thought economies would ensue from reorganization but they doubted that they could be accurately measured. Economies, moreover, were a by-product and not the main objective.

3. Proposals of the Committee

The sweeping nature of the proposals of the President's Committee on Administrative Management, strongly endorsed by the President's messages, may best be depicted by its own summary at the end of their *Report:*

1. Expand the White House staff so that the President may have a sufficient group of able assistants in his own office to keep him in closer and easier touch with the widespread affairs of administration and to make a speedier clearance of the knowledge needed for executive decision. (In an earlier section of the *Report*, the Committee had asserted that "they should be possessed of high competence, great physical vigor, and a passion for anonymity," a phrase borrowed from the characterization of the secretariat of the British War Cabinet, and uttered by Thomas Jones, the late Chancellor of the University of Wales, who had been private secretary to Prime Minister Lloyd George.) [5-A]

2. Strengthen and develop the managerial agencies of the government, particularly those dealing with the budget, efficiency research, personnel, and planning, as management arms of the Chief Executive.

3. Extend the merit system upward, outward, and downward to cover all non-policy-determining posts; reorganize the civil service system as a part of management under a single responsible administrator, strengthening the Civil Service Commission as a citizen Civil Service Board to serve as a watchdog of the merit system; and increase the salaries of key posts throughout the service so that the government may attract and hold in a career service men and women of the highest ability and character.

4. Overhaul the 100 independent agencies, administrations, authorities, boards, and commissions and place them by executive order within one or the other of the following 12 major executive departments:

State, Treasury, War, Justice, Post Office, Navy, Conservation, Agriculture, Commerce, Labor, Social Welfare, and Public Works; and place upon the Executive continuing responsibility for the maintenance of effective organization.

5. Establish accountability of the Executive to Congress by providing a genuine independent post-audit of all fiscal transactions by an auditor general, and restore to the Executive complete responsibility for accounts and current financial transactions.

At various parts of the *Report* the Committee further defined its proposals in the following selected areas:

1. The presidential assistants, probably not exceeding six in number, would be in addition to his present three secretaries who deal with the public, with the Congress, and with the press . . . they would remain in the background, issue no orders, make no decisions, emit no public statements.
2. The three managerial agencies—the Civil Service Administration (personnel), the Bureau of the Budget (finance), and the National Resources Board (planning)—should be a part and parcel of the Executive Office.
3. Administrative research should precede reorganizations and should be a major function of the Bureau of the Budget.
4. Congress to authorize the twelve major executive departments and to delegate to the President continuing authority by executive order to transfer, consolidate, and abolish functions, including those of emergency agencies, and within the twelve departments.
5. Department heads to be given stronger managerial powers and staffs, including a single executive officer who should be a career official.
6. The administrative functions of the independent regulatory commissions to be assigned to the executive departments, under single administrators, with independent boards, attached to departments for housekeeping purposes, to perform the quasi-judicial functions and to hear appeals.
7. Government corporations to be placed under departments acting as "supervisory agencies," with semi-autonomous status and suitable control of policies, finance and personnel.
8. New and special agencies to be given varying degrees of temporary autonomy, in their initial stages, within the twelve departments.
9. A strict separation to be made between accounting and control, and audit, the former two reverting to the Treasury Department, and the latter to be in a new independent office of Auditor General, performing continuous decentralized field audits. The auditor general to report to Congress cases in which he and the secretary of the Treasury are in disagreement.
10. The President to be given a contingent fund to enable him to bring in persons of high competency for specific purposes for short periods.

4. The Rising Storm of Flak

Not only was the President's plea ignored as the opposition substituted the criterion of money savings for his expressed objective of better management,[6] but his motives were misrepresented in an anti-reorganization campaign marked by distortions and falsifications. The effectiveness of that campaign was shown by the change in public temper from unruffled neutrality in January, 1937, to a frenzied public outcry against the reorganization bill rising to a climax in March, 1938. The early calm had but presaged the rising storm of flak to come.

The President had sufficient grounds to feel secure that the public would accept his program. Just nine weeks before he submitted the *Report* to the Congress he had been re-elected with the endorsement implied in carrying all but two of the forty-eight states, with an unprecedented 75 per cent Democratic majority in the House and Senate. But if he felt vindicated politically, he was nevertheless frustrated administratively. Moreover, his victory was tempered by the series of vetoes his program had sustained at the hands of the judicial branch. The Supreme Court in its previous session had invalidated the Agricultural Adjustment Act and the Bituminous Coal Act; and in the Humphrey case it had taken away one of his few controls over the regulatory commissions.

Although the President's reorganization message was reported to have "stunned" the capital, shaken Washington officialdom, and roused the Congress, the public first greeted the President's proposals with apparent indifference.[7] The tone of the initial press reaction ranged from enthusiastic to mildly sympathetic.[8] Editorials lauded the work of the President's Committee. *The Washington Post* wholeheartedly agreed with the President's characterization of the *Report* as a "great document of historic importance," because of "the scope of its consideration, the clarity of its reasoning, and the logic of its conclusions."[9] Another metropolitan daily welcomed the unequivocal proposals of the Committee and acclaimed "the thoroughness and boldness of research and recommendations."[10] Editors approved of this timely effort to bring order to the sprawling executive establishment, and the President was accorded much praise for his "forthright attack on the problem."[11] One editorial, however, saw the reorganization bill as not much of a reform except of the President's own abuses.[12]

And the interesting view was advanced in the leading midwestern anti-Administration daily that better business management was not in any case an appropriate objective. "It is not always a virtue," it pointed out, "in a system of government, that it is to be able immediately and completely to get things done."[13] Another opponent perceived an attempt to preserve New Deal agencies and activities and increase the President's powers through reorganization, but levied no charges of "dictatorship."[14]

After a few days the question of reorganization was relegated to the back pages of the daily papers. The introduction a few weeks later of the Administration bill to reform the Supreme Court effectively sidetracked reorganization and removed it from the focus of public and congressional attention. When it emerged again in August of 1937, speedy enactment of most of the reorganization proposals appeared likely.[15] The reaction engendered by the stormy controversy over the court bill soon began to be felt, however, and seriously impaired the prospect of early passage of reorganization legislation.

The imminence of passage in the spring of 1938 of the substituted omnibus Byrnes bill signalled the attack against reorganization by anti-Administration forces: Father Coughlin, the National Committee to Uphold Constitutional Government, and the Republican opposition in Congress. The campaign of distortion and intimidation that swept the country was spearheaded by a now excited press. The boldface type used to spell out "dictatorship" in headlines across the nation's front pages during the Court fight was resurrected for the attack on reorganization. The Hearst and Gannett chains chorused the dictatorship theme. With one exception, Chicago papers referred to the Byrnes bill as the "Dictatorship Legislation." In the words of one paper, "the bill offers a greater menace to Free Government than the discredited plot to control the Supreme Court. . . . The present reorganization bill stems directly from the infamous Brownlow Report which frankly sought an executive dictatorship. . . ."[16]

With the fears of many successfully aroused, with group pressures activated, with an avalanche of inspired telegrams engulfing the Capitol, the President's disclaimer of any inclination to be a dictator was of no avail, and the bill was recommitted as two thousand "Paul Reveres" rode in from the East and Midwest to save the nation.[17]

5. *Legislative History—Ashes into Phoenix*

But even more than in the case of the Court reform bill, the President had lost a battle and won a war. The most basic of the reorganization proposals were achieved in 1939 when the Seventy-sixth Congress adopted legislation that enabled the President to realize the substance of most of his reorganization objectives.

A parliamentary obstacle of no little importance to the consideration of the recommendations of the *Report* of the President's Committee was the fact that its scope was so great that it touched the jurisdictions of many committees of the House and Senate. A special Joint Committee on Reorganization, in addition to the select committees under Senator Byrd and Representative Buchanan (Texas), had to be authorized to consider the legislation. The original co-chairmen of the joint committee were Senator Joseph T. Robinson (Arkansas), majority leader, and Representative John J. Cochran (Missouri), chairman of the House Committee on Expenditures, both of whom died during the course of the hearings. Representative Buchanan died shortly after. Special honorable mention is due to them as well as to the men that succeeded as co-chairmen: Senator James F. Byrnes (South Carolina) and Congressman Lindsay Warren (North Carolina) for their valiant efforts to carry on the battle in a cause which had no great popular appeal.

A more detailed chronology will show how close the Congress came to giving the President his entire reorganization program at the height of the opposition and how much was accomplished by the legislation that finally emerged. Virtually all the major proposals of the President's Committee were included in bills introduced in the first session of the Seventy-fifth Congress in 1937. In the House the proposals were embodied in four separate measures;[18] in the Senate, in a single omnibus bill.[19] In this session the House passed two of its bills. One provided for six administrative assistants to the President;[20] another granted the President reorganizational powers similar to those granted in 1933 and created a Department of Welfare.[21] In this session the Senate held hearings on its bill but took no action. In the special session in the fall of 1937, attention was largely concentrated on the farm bill and the anti-lynching measure, but it appeared likely that the Senate would complete action successfully when the Congress met again.

Early in the third session of the Seventy-fifth Congress, Senator Byrnes introduced a new omnibus bill[22] which included the provisions of the two bills that had passed the House and the more controversial provisions reorganizing the Civil Service Commission and the General Accounting Office. This bill was reported and passed the Senate.[23] In the House the combined resistance to several aspects of the omnibus bill was decisive, however; and the adoption, by a margin of only eight votes,[24] of a motion to recommit buried the reorganization bill.

The bill which was enacted into law was introduced in the House in February 1939 and included only two types of reform recommended by the President's Committee, but they were major ones. One provided a method whereby the President would have continuing authority to initiate reorganization plans, albeit the exact formula for doing so was a congressional invention. The other provided administrative assistants to the President. The bill was introduced by Representatives Warren and Cochran and was obviously a compromise measure. Debate was largely partisan. Although some amendments were adopted, the bill emerged from conference with its basic provisions intact, and became law April 3, 1939 (53 Stat. 561). (See Appendix III.)

6. Accomplishments

It would seem profitable at this point to attempt some summary appraisal of the accomplishments resulting from the 1937 effort. Clearly the most original contribution of the President's Committee, and perhaps the most profound contribution in that generation to the progress of administrative science, was the formulation of a new concept of the administrative position of the Chief Executive. Up to this time it had been assumed that the President would supervise his subordinates as he was able, and if things went wrong (and he found it out) that he would replace them. It was not ordinarily thought that he should provide continuous management of the executive establishment or that his office should be institutionally equipped for that purpose. The *Report* of the President's Committee set forth a concept of positive management, as distinguished from sporadic supervision.

Merriam and Brownlow invented the phrase "administrative management" which has now so thoroughly saturated the literature of administration that we assume it was always used; actually, it never was before 1935 and was formally approved by President Roosevelt in April of 1936. A corollary of the Committee's concept of administrative management was its view of personnel, budget, and planning functions as staff arms of the Executive.

Another contribution of lasting importance, which stemmed directly from the Committee's distinctive view of the President's administrative position, was its affirmation of the principle of broad presidential authority to initiate executive reorganization. The responsibility for administrative management was necessarily the President's; integral to that responsibility, it pointed out, was control over reorganization.

Up to this time the Congress had delegated substantial reorganization authority to the President[25] only in emergency periods of war and depression. Normally, the Congress jealously retained its control over the administrative structure. Although the record clearly indicated its inability and unwillingness to accomplish reform, the Congress would not ordinarily grant the President broad reorganization authority. The President's Committee advanced the proposition that reorganization was essentially an executive function. Contending that the "division of work for its effective performance is a part of the task of doing that work," the Committee concluded that the "task of reorganization is inherently executive in character and must be entrusted to the Executive as a continuing responsibility."[26] Only the broad outlines of departmental design, it maintained, were to be determined by the Congress. The continuing process of internal distribution of activities was a function of the Executive.

The refinement of the principle in the provisions of the reorganization bill of 1939 for presidential plans and the legislative veto was not a product of the President's Committee or of the White House. To the admission on the House floor that the bill "had never been profaned by coming before the eyes of Mr. Corcoran or Mr. Cohen,"[27] Mr. Brownlow subsequently added that "neither the text of the bill nor its substance was profaned by any suggestion made by me or either of my colleagues. . . ."[28] The substance of the bill nevertheless conformed to the principle enunciated by the President's Committee two years earlier. Although the device of the legislative veto of plans submitted by the President provided a practical means for ultimate congressional control,[29] the Reorganization Act of 1939 was yet an avowal by Congress of its own inhibition in this area and a recognition of the propriety and practical necessity of presidential action. It established the principle that the President should be given authority to initiate and provide the detailed prescriptions of administrative reorganization in times other than wars and economic crises.

The Committee's *Report* was instrumental in restoring the President to the position of administrative leadership envisaged by the Constitution and the "decision of 1789." Integral to the principle of presidential responsibility for administrative reorganization was the view of reorganization as a continuing process. The *Report* contended that reorganization would require not only painstaking initial research but continuing experimental adjustment. Mr. Brownlow sketched the problem in the hearings before the Joint Committee of Congress. "If the Archangel Michael," he conjectured, "could come down and arrange it perfectly by the 1st day of March 1937 by the 1st day of March 1938 you would need another Archangel to come down and adjust it."[30] The Committee proposed a *continuing* presidential authority over a *continuing* problem. This view of reorganization as a "continuing task growing out of and intimately related to the day-to-day work of the executive agencies"[31] provided an important new perspective for the consideration of the old problem of federal executive reorganization.

The establishment of the Executive Office of the President in 1939 stands as one of the most notable achievements of this era. The creation of a central staff office for the White House in which were placed the agencies of overall management equipped the President for the first time with tools commensurate to his task. The Office for Emergency Management in the Executive Office of the President provided a critically needed instrument for the fast-changing needs of emergency organization in the period before World War II—an instrument which helped us reach an advanced state of preparedness before actual hostilities and much longer ahead than had ever been possible in our history. While most of the agencies created by the President in the Office for Emergency Management within the Executive Office ultimately received specific congressional sanction through appropriations, and in some cases by legislation, the existence of the overhead structure or tent device provided a legal basis for the establishment by the Executive of defense and war agencies. Moreover, the President was equipped for the defense and war responsibilities with administrative assistants, a military Chief of Staff, and an Executive Office that included managerial units for planning, for personnel administration, and for fiscal control. It was the first time we ever went into a war with a general staff for the Commander-in-Chief.

One of the wisest reflections, in the best spirit of American institutions, on the significance of the legislative result of the *Report* of the President's Committee was uttered shortly after the passage of the 1939 Act by Professors John D. Millett and Lindsay Rogers:

> To students of political science and public administration a nice balance between legislature and executive has seemed a philosopher's stone for which they should search. In actual practice, a lack of balance between the two powers has not infrequently been a stumbling block in the way of legislative and administrative efficiency. That the two instruments of government should not and do not operate in separate and distinct fields of competence has long been obvious. . . . .
> Recently, as the complexity of problems and the drain on legislative time have increased, a new device has been invented: a mandate to the executive to act, and, if the result is not liked, a *legislative veto*. It is this we propose to discuss with particular reference to the Reorganization Act of 1939.[32]

THE PRESIDENT'S COMMITTEE ON ADMINISTRATIVE MANAGEMENT

Louis Brownlow, chairman   *Charles E. Merriam   *Luther Gulick

Research Staff
Joseph P. Harris, Director of Research

G. Lyle Belsley	James Hart
A. E. Buck	Arthur N. Holcombe
Laverne Burchfield	*Arthur W. MacMahon
Robert H. Connery	Harvey C. Mansfield
*Robert E. Cushman	*Charles McKinley
Paul T. David	John F. Miller
William Y. Elliott	John D. Millett
Herbert Emmerich	Floyd W. Reeves
*Merle Fainsod	Leo C. Rosten
James W. Fesler	Spencer Thompson
Katherine Frederic	Mary C. Trackett
Patterson H. French	Schuyler C. Wallace
William J. Haggerty	Edwin E. Witte

* President, American Political Science Association

Chapter IV

ADMINISTRATIVE LEGACY
OF FRANKLIN D. ROOSEVELT

1. Depression, Recovery, and Reform

THE POLITICAL ENVIRONMENT OF THE FOUR TERMS OF THE ADMINISTRA-
tion of President Franklin D. Roosevelt (actually, his death on April
12, 1945, cut short his fourth term to eighty-two days) was one of
successive crises: from depression to recovery, from recovery to reform, from reform to war, and from war to peace. During these
convolutions, his long-term interest in handing to future presidents
a more manageable executive establishment was constantly in conflict
with his tendency to administrative improvisation to meet the recurring crises. His own inclination to administrative experimentalism
to meet immediate needs as he saw them continually diverted him
from his awareness that a more orderly executive apparatus was
imperatively required. But I think it is a fair statement that he was
the president who institutionalized the presidency. In spite of having
sired and aborted more agencies than all his thirty-one predecessors
put together, he bequeathed to his successors a major legacy in the
form of permanent vehicles of administrative management. It is for
this reason, and because my period of fulltime government service
took place during his presidency, that I devote this chapter to my
impressions of his administrative performance. These impressions are
derived from my occasional direct contacts with him and with his
staff, from serving under men who reported to him frequently, and

from a sampling of the growing collection of documents and other people's memoirs. My conclusions deviate from the inherited stereotype about his administrative weaknesses, but I hope they will be found to be neither too critical nor too adulatory.

It is difficult for this generation to reconstruct the image of the situation in which the country found itself on March 4, 1933, the day that Franklin D. Roosevelt took office. It is dramatically summarized by Arthur M. Schlesinger, Jr.:

> It was hard to understate the need for action. The national income was less than half of what it had been four short years before. Nearly thirteen million Americans—about one-quarter of the labor force—were desperately seeking jobs. The machinery for sheltering and feeding the unemployed was breaking down everywhere under the growing burden. And a few hours before, in the early morning before the inauguration, every bank in America had locked its doors. It was not just a matter of staving off hunger. It was a matter of seeing whether a representative democracy could conquer economic collapse. It was a matter of staving off violence, even (at least some thought) revolution.[1]

The situation called for drastic and immediate action on many fronts. In the first one hundred days, Congress gave Roosevelt everything he asked for. The desperate need was for restoration of the economy and of public morale. All kinds of hare-brained proposals were circulating with the country in a mood of utter panic. The high priority need was for reversing the catastrophic downtrend rather than for stopping to work out a tidy organizational pattern. Some of the actions taken were of a stop-gap nature; others had long-term objectives. It is remarkable that they were not more disorderly than they were and that during that period only three permanent agencies were created.

The day before Roosevelt took office, on March 3, 1933, Congress had granted the President the most sweeping reorganization powers ever enacted in peacetime in the form of another reorganization act contained in a rider to the Treasury-Post Office Appropriation Act (47 Stat. 1517-20). This Act amended the Act of June 30, 1932 and empowered the President to submit reorganization proposals to become effective within sixty days without any provision for a veto power in Congress (Appendix III). It added broad powers to abolish agencies but not entire executive departments. Congress thus gave the incoming President legislation approaching war powers in response to the desperate mood of the times. This was the same Congress that had given President Hoover weaker reorganization powers but had stricken down his proposals.

During the first one hundred days of the New Deal only three permanent agencies were created, two of which had had the benefit of previous planning and study: the Farm Credit Administration and the Tennessee Valley Authority. The third, the Federal Deposit Insurance Corporation, sprang out of the urgent necessity to restore confidence in the commercial banking system. In the case of Farm Credit, Roosevelt had a plan ready before inauguration. It was prepared by Henry Morgenthau, Jr., his friend and neighbor from Dutchess County, New York, who had been his conservation commissioner at Albany. Morgenthau was assisted by William I. Myers, Dean of the New York State School of Agriculture at Cornell University, a brilliant agricultural economist, a specialist in agricultural credit, and an academe who later dynamically disproved the rule that a professor could not administer. I served as executive officer and deputy governor under these two able men who became the first and second governors of Farm Credit Administration (F.C.A.).

Farm Credit Administration was established by executive order 6084 on March 27, 1933, twenty-four days after the wide powers of the Reorganization Amendments of March 3 had been enacted. It succeeded both the Federal Farm Board and the Federal Farm Loan Board which had supervised the cooperative system of Federal Land Banks as well as the Federal Intermediate Credit Banks. Many New Dealers considered the agency to be excessively "sound" and insufficiently "sympathetic" with the small and impoverished farmer and with the new farm subsidy programs. They underestimated, I believe, its innovative contributions both to the immediate crisis and to the building up of long-term credit institutions. The setting up of Production Credit Associations to be cooperatively owned and managed by farmers and which in many areas have replaced or supplemented private country banks was a more radical step than any that was tried in the field of commercial banking. The Farm Loan Associations, many of which were insolvent, were reorganized and enlarged to extend long-term cooperative credit through the Federal Land Banks. Regional banks for cooperatives were established for the special purpose of lending to farmers' marketing and purchasing cooperatives. Farm Credit undertook the initial administration of the Federal Credit Union Act of June 26, 1934 (48 Stat. 1216) although it was designed more for urban than for rural people because it was also based on cooperative credit principles. The emergency functions of Farm Credit were conducted with considerable courage and great celerity. Its commissioner's loans, later taken over by the Federal Farm Mortgage Corporation, prevented literally hundreds of thousands of farm foreclosures and the government got its money back. Its emergency crop loans enabled many small farmers to carry on in the face of adverse prices and crops. It also was assigned the job of winding up the ill-fated stabilization operations of the Federal Farm Board, and of liquidating the Regional Agricultural Credit Corporations and the Joint Stock Land Banks. It should be recalled that the farm depression had started long before the industrial one and commodity prices had fallen during the twenties when everything else was booming. Many country banks had closed permanently. Farm Credit Administration, which started as an independent agency, and then in 1939 was placed uncomfortably in the Department of Agriculture, is today an autonomous agency supervising and examining the series of twelve regional credit banks in four fields, and hundreds of cooperative farm credit associations.

The Tennessee Valley Authority was a successful innovation in the creation of a regional agency for the development of a river valley, for power development, for flood control, for navigation, for the development of fertilizer, and for the reclamation of an eroded region. It had been the subject of years of national controversy, debate, and study. The bill for its creation was drafted and strongly espoused by Senator George W. Norris (Nebraska) and was practically ready at the time of Roosevelt's inauguration. It was approved May 18, 1933 (48 Stat. 58). Henry Steele Commager, the historian, has this to say about it:

> During the First War the federal government had built two nitrate plants at Muscle Shoals on the Tennessee River, and to provide power for them it undertook the construction of the Wilson Dam. Peace found this great dam unfinished, and as soon as the Harding Administration came to power it moved to stop further construction and then to turn the dam over to private enterprise. . . . . Twice Senator Norris was able to get through Congress a bill providing for the construction and operation of the Muscle Shoals hydroelectric plants by public authority. Twice the bill was vetoed, first by President Coolidge, and then by President Hoover. . . .
> Even before he took office Franklin Roosevelt had toured the Tennessee Valley with Senator Norris as his guide. No sooner was he President than he proposed not merely government ownership of Muscle Shoals but the comprehensive development of the whole Ten-

nessee Valley—a vast area of some forty thousand square miles spreading into seven states. . . . The T.V.A. became not only the most spectacularly successful of all New Deal enterprises; it was also the most influential, for it inspired emulation, symbolically or literally, in Europe and eventually in all the continents of the globe.[2]

T.V.A. is unique both in respect to its structure and its administration. It is a corporate authority, which now has power to issue its own bonds for development purposes. It is an independent establishment of the federal government with a board of directors of three men and a staff headed by a general manager who reports to the board. Its multipurpose aspects cut across the functions of many federal agencies and state and local ones, but over the years it has established a modus vivendi with them. T.V.A. in its power functions is a wholesale supplier to one hundred and sixty local electric systems: one hundred and eight municipalities, fifty cooperatives, and two privately owned utilities. It supplies federal installations and industries whose power requirements are large or unusual. Power to meet these demands is supplied from twenty-nine dams and eleven steam plants operated by T.V.A., six U.S. Corps of Engineers' dams in the Cumberland Valley, and twelve Aluminum Company of America dams whose operation is coordinated with the T.V.A. system. Today, its electric power production from steam plants exceeds the power generated by hydroelectric stations.

The Federal Deposit Insurance Corporation (F.D.I.C.) was established June 16, 1933 (48 Stat. 162) as an independent government corporation under authority of Section 12-B of the Federal Reserve Act. Its present status is prescribed by the Federal Deposit Insurance Act of 1950 (64 Stat. 873). Its income is derived from assessments on insured banks and from interest on its investments in government securities. Its immediate influence in 1933 was to restore public confidence in the commercial banks of the nation, and its long-term influence has been to strengthen the banking system of the United States. The Comptroller of the Currency sits on its board, and for a time at least a joint plan was in effect to compose jurisdictional controversies over standards of bank examinations between the Comptroller, the Federal Reserve System, and the F.D.I.C.

I shall not try to describe the bevy of agencies that were created to meet the contingencies of depression, recovery, and war. Gone with the wind is the big parade of New Deal agencies or "alphabet soup" such as N.R.A., A.A.A., F.E.R.A., W.P.A., P.W.A., C.W.A.,

R.F.C., the last actually having been created in the Hoover administration. Gone are such wartime establishments as N.D.A.C., O.E.M., O.P.M., O.P.A.C.S., W.P.B., W.L.B., W.M.C., N.H.A., F.E.A., and O.W.M.R. The last was the Office of War Mobilization and Reconversion, headed by former Senator James F. Byrnes (S.C.), who resigned as associate justice of the Supreme Court to accept a position which held more statutory authority than had ever been granted to an executive establishment. As for my younger readers who may not be able to identify this array of acronyms, I refer them for translation purposes to the *United States Government Organization Manual*.[3] My apologies are offered to the alumni of agencies whose initials I may have inadvertently omitted!

2. *Roadblocks to War Administration*

In the words of the late Fritz Morstein Marx, for years the gifted analyst of the Bureau of the Budget, "World War II was our first administered war." Before launching into some of the legislative technicalities which made this possible, a word is in order on the political and administrative background in which President Roosevelt had to work before the attack on Pearl Harbor actually brought the United States into combat.

Four factors stand out as having had special influence on the series of rather inhibited administrative arrangements contrived by the President during the so-called "defense period." First, was the fact that the country had just been grappling with the difficult problems of recovery and reform, and the administrators of the New Deal were intensely preoccupied with internal crusades and unbelievably insular in respect to the outside world. Second, in Congress and in the country generally there was a wide-spread spirit of isolationism and antimilitarism. Many Americans did not want to get involved in a second European conflict. The "America First" movement was attracting a surprising amount of support, some of it among political and intellectual leaders. Senators were still investigating the industrial-military complex of World War I under the name of "merchants of death." The spirit of non-involvement and minding our own business was rampant. There was resistance to preparedness moves and to aid to the allies, who seemed to be losing the war to the dictators. In this atmosphere, a good deal of our early steps for preparedness had to be sugar coated and coaxed through a reluctant Congress. The short-lived "non-aggression" treaty between Hitler and Stalin in August 1939 had stunned and further confused American public opinion. Eyes were focused on Europe. The possibility of an attack by Japan on our own territory was not conceived of until it occurred.

The third factor was the antipathy felt by President Roosevelt, partly as a result of his service as assistant secretary of the Navy in World War I, to the kind of industrial mobilization or M–Day plans that were being developed by the general staff of the Army. These were modeled rather closely after the designs of the War Industries Board in World War I, and called for a war mobilization of industry, in close relationship to the military, under the complete coordination of an industrialist. President Roosevelt greatly respected the sagacity of Bernard M. Baruch, who favored these plans and frequently consulted him in World War II, but could not accept this amount of delegation of the President's political and administrative authority to industry and to the military. This situation is thoroughly treated in the volume edited by Harold Stein on *American Civil-Military Decisions* and particularly in the essay by Albert A. Blum on the "Birth and Death of the M–Day Plan."[4]

In August 1939, Roosevelt appointed a War Resources Board, chaired by Edward R. Stettinius, Jr., who was then chairman of the board of the United States Steel Corporation, to advise him on the organization of industrial mobilization in the event of war. Roosevelt was so disturbed by the Board's recommendations, which resembled the Army's M–Day plans, that for a long time the report was suppressed. Louis Brownlow's memoirs give us a graphic and first-hand view of the quandary in which the President found himself.[5]

The fourth factor was the almost unbelievable hostility between management and labor, the deep suspicions of businessmen of the New Deal, and the divisions among the ranks of organized labor itself. During the defense period, industry had prospered and for the first time in our history big business did not want to or need to take on munitions contracts. When war came they had to be compelled to do so. The rise of the power of the Congress of Industrial Organizations, the United Automobile Workers, and the United Mine Workers threatened the traditional supremacy of the American Federation of Labor and of the powerful railroad unions. Labor leaders eyed with profound distrust the recruitment of hundreds of industrialists in the defense and war agencies, but could rarely agree among themselves on what positions to take or who was to represent them.

It is my considered opinion, based on statements made to me by leaders from both camps, that William S. Knudsen (management) and Sidney Hillman (labor) were displaced because of pressure from their own constituencies. These two patriotic naturalized Americans put their interests, of the country and loyalty to the government ahead of their group interests, and were eventually superseded by men of smaller calibre. All these tensions and animosities were contributing factors in the organization of the government's war machinery. And although not explicitly stated, the thorough exposition contained in the volume on *Industrial Mobilization for War,* prepared under the supervision of James W. Fesler, War Production Board historian, does, I believe, support these observations.[6]

The upshot was the creation of a strange series of administrative monstrosities, in which known administrative concepts were jettisoned in order to contrive agencies, however unorthodox, which could advance our preparedness without abdication of presidential powers. On May 29, 1940, foundations of the national defense program organization of World War II were laid by the reactivation of the Advisory Commission to the Council of National Defense provided for in Section 2 of the Act of August 29, 1916 (39 Stat. 649) which was still in effect. The President approved a regulation of the Council (its only act) that the Advisory Commission was to be composed of advisers: (1) Industrial Production (William S. Knudsen); (2) Employment (Sidney Hillman); (3) Industrial Materials (Edward R. Stettinius, Jr.); (4) Farm Products (Chester C. Davis); (5) Price Stabilization (Leon Henderson); (6) Transportation (Ralph Budd); (7) Consumer Protection (Harriet Elliott); (8) Purchasing (Donald M. Nelson). Quarters were furnished this stellar group in the handsome building of the Board of Governors of the Federal Reserve System, and the commission was informed that the President would be their "boss"; but they usually met without a chairman, with increasing internal differences and confusion.

Next there was the Office of Production Management (O.P.M.) with a director general from industry, William S. Knudsen, a deputy director general from labor, Sidney Hillman, and the secretaries of War, Henry L. Stimson, and Navy, Frank Knox. The creation in August 1941 of the Supply Priorities and Allocations Board (S.P.A.B.) confused matters further. After Pearl Harbor, the War Production Board (W.P.B.) was founded. It at first looked like a general industrial mobilization board under a one-man administrator from industry, Mr. Donald M. Nelson, but he was soon surrounded by a series of overlapping agencies and "czars" that steadily eroded his supremacy. All these agencies were under the constant surveillance of the Office of Emergency Management, the Bureau of the Budget, and Mr. Harry Hopkins, the expediter without portfolio. Mr. William S. Knudsen, one of my bosses in the Office of Production Management, used to tell me: "In Washington they call them 'coordinators' but in Russia they are called 'O.G.P.U.'" I have often wondered how this bizarre series of structures ever managed to accomplish the extraordinary mobilization of World War II, which was much more efficient than that of World War I. For a time at least these executive heresies rocked my sense of administrative orthodoxy. I believe Churchill and Stalin were even more astonished, not to mention Hitler and Hirohito.

To illustrate the extent to which labor-management distrust and general diffusion had gone in the National Defense Advisory Commission (N.D.A.C.), I cite the impasse which had been reached in February 1941, when the Office of Production Management was established to replace it, regarding the posts of General Counsel and Executive Secretary. There was heated controversy on whom to appoint to these two positions and on what their duties should be. In the N.D.A.C., each commissioner had had his own battery of lawyers. Mr. John Lord O'Brian, on the advice of Secretary Stimson and the recommendation of President Roosevelt, was appointed General Counsel. His insistence on a unified legal division, as well as his ability and wisdom, contributed greatly to the morale and coordinated administration of the industrial mobilization effort. My own appointment to the then undefined post of Executive Secretary, first of O.P.M. and later of S.P.A.B. and W.P.B., was also a result of the impasse. President Roosevelt wrote Messrs. Knudsen and Hillman suggesting my name because of my government experience and for the further reason that I "would not entirely agree with either of them." In my first interview, the disarming "Bill" Knudsen said: "I don't know you, Mr. Emmerich, but I am not such a big man that I cannot listen to a suggestion from the President of the United States." Mr. O'Brian also honored me with his confidence and friendship and an excellent rapport was established between the office of the Executive Secretary and the Legal Division.

3. The Office of Emergency Management and the War Powers Act, 1941

President Roosevelt had new tools and powers that no previous president had been given on the eve of a global involvement which was infinitely greater than had been expected. A week after Hitler invaded Poland and started the European front of World War II, an ingenious and far-sighted provision had been written in Executive Order 8248 of September 8, 1939. Professor Clinton Rossiter wrote: "Executive Order 8248 may yet be judged to have saved the Presidency from paralysis and the Constitution from radical amendment."[7] This order, which was drafted by the Bureau of the Budget, with the advice of Louis Brownlow, established the internal divisions of the Executive Office of the President, which had been created by Reorganization Plan 1 under the provisions of the Reorganization Act of 1939.[8] (Also see Appendix III.) The provision was to the effect that there should be contained in the Executive Office "in the event of a national emergency or threat of a national emergency, such office for emergency management as the President shall determine." After Hitler's invasion of Norway, Denmark, the Netherlands, and Belgium in May 1940 and with the impending fall of France, the President issued a proclamation declaring a total national emergency and on May 25, by administrative order, established the Office for Emergency Management. William H. McReynolds of the White House staff was named the first liaison officer for emergency management, and was later succeeded by Wayne Coy.

The Office for Emergency Management became a kind of overall tent and service agency for defense and war establishments and gave immense flexibility, as conditions changed, to constitute and reconstitute units of government. It had a special advantage during the "defense" period. The Reorganization Act of 1939 expired on January 21, 1941, and thereafter the President had no authority for eleven months on government reorganization until the passage of the First War Powers Act on December 18, 1941 (55 Stat. 838). In the meantime, such defense agencies as the Office of Production Management, Office of Price Administration and Civilian Supply, Office of the Coordinator of Inter-American Affairs, Office of Scientific Research and Development, Office of Lend-Lease Administration, and Office of

Facts and Figures could be and were created by executive order as parts of the Office of Emergency Management (Appendix III).

The Senate sub-committee on Appropriations did not like this method of creating new agencies, and senators, at a hearing in the spring of 1941, raised sharp questions as to whether they had been legally authorized. I attended the hearing as executive secretary of the Office of Production Management and, seeing that we were in great trouble, telephoned Mr. Knudsen, its director general, to come up quickly. He was then at the height of his prestige as ex-president of General Motors Corporation and when he entered the room the senators rose to greet him, forgot their inhibitions, and passed the appropriations for the whole array of emergency agencies. They even told Mr. Knudsen that if the funds proved insufficient to come back and ask for more. If there had been any doubt about the authority for creating these agencies, the act of appropriating funds gave a sanction to their legality and we were in business.

The First War Powers Act, 1941, was approved December 18, 1941, just eleven days after Japan's attack on Pearl Harbor catapulted the United States into World War II. Compare this interval with the thirteen months it took to pass the Overman Act of 1918 after our declaration of war on the German Empire. Title I authorized the coordination of executive bureaus and agencies "in the interest of the more efficient concentration of the government." The powers granted to the President were to be exercised only "in matters relating to the conduct of the present war." He could make "such redistribution of functions of agencies as he may deem necessary." However, if statutory bureaus or functions were to be abolished, the President was to make a recommendation to Congress for its approval. Six months after termination of the war the authority under Title I would cease, and all the agencies were to resume the exercise of duties, powers, and functions "as heretofore or hereinafter by law provided." It was Overman over again, but there was no time to quibble over bill drafting with the Japanese fleet approaching Manila, and Hitler's submarines heading for the Florida coast (Appendix III).

By the end of 1945, most of the war agencies were liquidated, and in 1946 authority under Title I of the First War Powers Act, 1941, lapsed. Special legislation once more had to be passed to preserve some of the wartime mergers and transfers that were deemed to be of permanent value. In fact the Reorganization Act of 1945 included the conversion as one of its purposes.

No attempt will be made here to list the numerous defense and war-time agencies. Those wishing to pursue this matter should examine "The War Agencies of the Executive Branch of the Government."[9] Its list of defense and war agencies covers fifteen pages of fine print and describes one hundred and fifty-six agencies not all of which, for-tunately, functioned at the same time. A list of major war agencies terminated by executive order in 1945 will suffice for purposes of illustration:

> Office of Civil Defense, Office of War Information, War Refugee Board, War Manpower Commission, Office of Economic Stabilization, Office of Strategic Services, Foreign Economic Administration, War Production Board, Smaller War Plants Corporation, National War Labor Board, and War Food Administration.

In 1946, the Office of Price Administration, which had become in-creasingly controversial, was abolished and a few of its functions were temporarily vested in other agencies. Some of the combined and inter-national programs were taken over by the United Nations Relief and Rehabilitation Agency (UNRRA), other United Nations bodies, and later by NATO. Title I had bestowed no regulatory authority on the President and special legislation had to be enacted in the fields of price control, priorities, war mobilization, foreign trade, and recon-version when it was needed.[10]

The last and most powerful war agency was concerned with recon-version to peace as well as with war mobilization, the Office of War Mobilization and Reconversion. The President finally had to yield to the pressures for overall coordination of the huge establishment, but when it came the war was beginning to be won, the mobilization was in being, and Mr. Justice Byrnes, the administrator, was a politician the President trusted, not a general nor a big name industrialist.[11]

4. *Administrative Profile of Franklin D. Roosevelt*

POLICY AND SPENDING

F.D.R. was a gregarious patrician, travelled and literate, with a first-rate inquisitive and acquisitive mind. His associates, both on the left and on the right, deplored his lack of a formal ideological system. Consistency, to paraphrase Emerson, was not one of his vices, and his pragmatism and experimentalism seemed to many of them as sheer opportunism. They forgot that he was not primarily an intellectual but first and foremost a politician, who saw his major function as gaining support of the American people for programs designed to see them through a series of successive crises and for reforms to prevent their recurrence. Early associates, such as Lewis W. Douglas, Raymond Moley, George N. Peek, and Donald Richberg, turned away from him because they could not adapt to his changing policies. Staunch New Dealers were unable to adjust to the needs of a war economy in 1942, and he had to remind them that "Dr. New Deal was out and Dr. Win-the-War was in." At the risk of oversimplifying the philosophy of this complex man, I incline to the view that he was basically conservative as to the preservation of the system of a capitalist federal democracy and radical as to the means of its preservation, which he sensed could only be safeguarded if government controlled its excesses, supplemented its deficiencies, and extended its benefits more widely and deeply.

F.D.R.'s spending policy changed during his first year in office. He was accused of being a great spender, but his pre-war budgets never exceeded $10 billion, which seems miniscule compared to his own wartime budgets, or the 1971 budget of $200 billion, and was actually less than the Eisenhower deficit for fiscal year 1959 and the Johnson deficit for fiscal year 1968. He insisted that the social security system be placed on a contributory, self-liquidating basis, and he turned over the administration of public assistance and unemployment insurance to the states. He strongly opposed inflationary nostrums for debt refinancing and monetary policy, such as those advocated by Senator Huey Long (Louisiana) and the two North Dakota radicals, Senator Lynn J. Frazier and Representative William Lemke, in 1936. He depended greatly on the advice of his shy but able secretary of the Treasury, Henry Morgenthau, Jr., whose innovative staff was not reckless, even if they occasionally gave him some unfortunate advice on tax legislation. F.D.R. reluctantly adopted deficit financing, but even during World War II relied greatly on the scrutiny of expenditures and performance of the war agencies by his skillful Director of the Budget, Harold D. Smith.

LEADER OF MEN

Franklin D. Roosevelt was person-minded. He liked to deal with people and even tended to personify institutions. In spite of his liking for people and his cordiality, there was always a certain detachment which caused Cordell Hull to record in his memoirs that he acted more like a spectator than a participant at cabinet councils. He identified with the many different people he had to see, and with their subject matter, and listened attentively to each visitor. If he found their views completely unacceptable, he artfully diverted the conversation to other channels. His manner inspired confidences, and these interviews stocked his retentive memory with quantities of intelligence. His cordiality and attention often led his visitors to conclude that he had accepted their formulas verbatim, and some of them reacted violently when they did not like what finally came out of the hopper.

He never committed himself entirely to one man, not even to Harry Hopkins. People he invited to explore a subject were often disconcerted to discover that he had one or more other parties looking into it. He thus deliberately fostered options. He eventually became aware of the strengths and weaknesses of his appointees, but not always soon enough. He inspired loyalty and gave his subordinates considerable rope which he could suddenly pull taut when he felt they were letting him down. He sometimes did this without warning and faithful officials were injured as a result. His reproofs were no less painful for being subtle and courteous.

F.D.R. roared at a good story and relished, almost excessively, an aptly turned phrase. He had his own nicknames like "Henry the Morg" and "Tommy the Cork" for half of his entourage, and was probably the first president to call people by their first names, a mode of address which very few ventured to reciprocate.

HIRING AND FIRING

Roosevelt's enormous acquaintanceship and catholicity of interest enabled him to recruit people of the most varying types. Hundreds of bright, highly motivated young people were attracted to government service by the aura of idealism and innovation of the New Deal. Conservative businessmen were abundant in the National Recovery Administration (N.R.A.) and heavily populated the War Production Board (W.P.B.). Although several tried, none of them was permitted to control the government. He demanded loyalty to a program rather than to himself or to the Democratic Party. Even his first cabinet was not composed entirely of party regulars, and after the election of 1940 he went so far as to include two prominent Republicans in the cabinet,

Henry L. Stimson and Frank Knox, in order to unite the country with war threatening. This was a transaction in which Louis Brownlow assisted, for once stepping out of his apolitical role.[12]

F.D.R.'s reluctance to fire people has been exaggerated although he preferred to induce their resignations, to transfer them, to circumnavigate them, or to reorganize their agencies. But other presidents have been known to follow these patterns. Executives from industry in the War Production Board told me that these patterns were also prevalent in the business world. As assistant secretary of the Navy during World War I, F.D.R. helped establish the austere system of "selection-out" providing for the compulsory retirement of naval officers who had been passed over three times for promotion, a system which has since been adopted by the Foreign Service. As Governor of New York he had, after the findings of the investigation of Judge Samuel Seabury, removed Jimmy Walker, the venal playboy mayor of New York City. He discharged Arthur E. Morgan, chairman of the Tennessee Valley Authority, on the grounds of "contumacy," although one year before, in 1937, he had told me and two other members of the committee which he had appointed to make a confidential survey of the internal organization of the T.V.A., that "Arthur Morgan was a national resource whose services should be saved for the nation." He had three vice-presidents in his four terms and many new faces in each one of them.

STAFF WORK

Even before the Executive Office of the President was created, he "borrowed" from sundry agencies the services of people to act as his "brain trust." Raymond Moley and Rexford G. Tugwell were among the earlier ones, followed by Benjamin V. Cohen and Thomas G. Corcoran. In 1941, Harry Hopkins forsook his emergency relief duties and became the gray eminence of war mobilization and personal emissary to Churchill and Stalin, living for a time in the White House and performing brilliantly without an assigned office and with no portfolio except his battered briefcase. Mrs. Eleanor Roosevelt was the only First Lady to have served as a full-fledged White House staff member, even though it is recorded that Dolly Madison and Edith Bolling Galt Wilson played important policy roles. As Federal Public Housing Commissioner, I received a number of cases to investigate from Mrs. Roosevelt marked: "E.R. please look into this one, F.D.R." She was the President's surrogate and conscience in such fields as housing, welfare, and above all race relations, in which area she could take positions far in advance of those he was politically prepared to espouse. In her staff role, Lady Eleanor was no dilettante and outdid the "pros" in seeing her cases through to a conclusion. Her other public roles of course went way beyond the scope of a White House staff aide and she became an American symbol of humanitarianism throughout the world.

INTEREST IN DETAIL

One of his associates said that at times F.D.R. would go into "fly-speck detail." I was present in his office the day that Harold D. Smith was sworn in as Budget Director and the President insisted on being informed as to whether the commission should be handed to Smith before or after the oath was taken. He once stopped to draw me an architectural profile for the temporary dormitories for government girls in Washington, at the height of the war, while "Pa" Watson, his appointments secretary, with a long waiting line of dignitaries, was verging on apoplexy outside the door.

It is interesting to note that this President of the United States, having after one hundred and fifty years accomplished the feat of establishing an executive office, thereupon had to intervene personally in breaking down resistances to releasing the necessary office space next to the White House to accommodate it. Budget Director Harold D. Smith told me the story of how Mr. Roosevelt, who rarely visited the departments, was wheeled into the old State, War, and Navy building accompanied by Smith and Under Secretary of State Sumner Welles, to inspect the space situation personally. When told that certain space was needed for active files, the President actually began pulling out file drawers. The first file he came to was labelled "Wild Horses in China!" The Under Secretary of State could not maintain that this was a current or urgent matter and so F.D.R. got the space he needed to house his staff and the staff of presidents to come.

Since 1939, presidents have gradually taken over the entire building and their staffs have even overflowed into new federal brick structures of the Kennedy period. The grand old pile, now known as the Executive Office Building, is a unique relic of the reconstruction style of architecture. The State and Defense Departments, which had occupied it beginning in 1875, have long since been ensconced in the great edifices of Foggy Bottom and the Pentagon.

He remembered where he had left off the last time you saw him, and always began taking up at that point. His interest in detail often proved to be surprisingly related to main political and administrative issues. He had the executive gift which Paul H. Appleby, in not the best of his puns, called "the art of making a mesh of things."

IMPROVISATION

His weakness for administrative improvisation had elements which Harry Hopkins called "puckishness." This took the form of his uninhibited creation of agency after agency during the New Deal and wartime periods. He often gave them overlapping missions, and seemed to delight in giving them similar initials, such as W.P.A. and P.W.A., or O.P.M. and O.P.A. In spite of his announced desire to keep a "happy ship" these improvisations, many of which did their jobs, fostered inter-agency competition and exacerbated the internecine warfare among the agencies and their prima donna chiefs. When various untried and experimental programs were launched, he did not put all his eggs in one basket and acted on the theory that, by fostering a little inter-agency competition, the better program headed by the abler chief would win out.

OLD LINE DEPARTMENTS

F.D.R. doubted whether the old line bureaus could rise quickly and energetically enough to cope with the urgent need for innovative action in recovery, reform, and war. He knew their shortcomings from his World War I experience and in 1933 to 1945 the civil service had not attained the quality it has today. Even so, many of the New Deal administrations, while autonomous, were closely linked to large departments as in the case of Agricultural Adjustment (A.A.A.) with Agriculture, National Recovery (N.R.A.) with Commerce, and Public Works (P.W.A.) with Interior. He held the prevalent belief that formally placing temporary agencies in permanent departments would make it more difficult to change, transfer, or abolish them later. A number of the temporary agencies, such as N.R.A., conducted programs which were discontinued but others became the basis for permanent legislation.

CAREER OFFICIALS

In spite of F.D.R.'s skepticism concerning the old line bureaus, he made frequent use of the services of career officials, at various levels of competence. He had a high regard for modest Rudolph Forster, the long time executive clerk of the White House. He appointed shrewd William H. McReynolds his administrative assistant for personnel liaision and with the defense agencies. "Mac" had entered the civil service as a stenographer in the Post Office Department, rose to inspector, then had served many years as deputy director of the Bureau of Efficiency and, upon its dissolution in 1933, became administrative assistant to Henry Morgenthau, Jr., first in Farm Credit Administration and then in the Treasury. After the resignation of Lewis W. Douglas, President Roosevelt appointed as acting director of the budget from 1934 to 1939 Daniel W. Bell, whose brilliant and unprecedented career in the Treasury began with entrance as a messenger and ended as under secretary. Bell was a rare expert on the fiscal side of the Budget and carried everyone's estimates in his head. In a professional sense, Harold D. Smith, who succeeded Bell, was a career man; for he had been director of the budget for the State of Michigan, as was Surgeon General Thomas W. Parran, who had been health commissioner in the State of New York.

On the diplomatic and military levels, F.D.R. relied too heavily to suit Secretary Hull on Sumner Welles, a career man, who became under secretary of State. He appointed distinguished military professionals such as General George C. Marshall and Admiral William D. Leahy. In lesser civilian posts he often appointed admirals and generals of demonstrated ability. He respected "know-how" regardless of its source.

5. F.D.R's Long-time Bequests to the Presidency

In spite of his tendency for improvisation in the case of the crisis agencies, Franklin D. Roosevelt had a long-time view of the presidency and its baffling problems of relationships with the Congress, and with the departments, agencies, and bureaus. As revealed by his talk with congressional leaders in January 1937 (Appendix I), he was keenly aware that the presidency needed staff assistance, and that the departmental structure required simplification and delegation, lest the

President's task should become even less manageable than he had found it. The report of the President's Committee on Administrative Management and the passage of the Reorganization Act of 1939 (which was discussed in Chapter III) gave him the opportunity for contrition and expiration of his improvisations and became the basis for his more lasting reforms. The needs of the administration of World War II once more called forth another rash of administrative improvisation and proliferation of temporary agencies, but it gave him a chance to exercise the muscles of his newly created Executive Office (Appendix III). After 1939, he became increasingly interested in leaving the presidency more adequately staffed and in handing over to his successors a more orderly executive establishment. He was less successful in rationalizing the permanent organizational structure than in creating new tools for administrative management. No new independent regulatory commissions were created after 1939 unless A.E.C. is included in this category. He left his successors a number of long-time bequests. He institutionalized the presidency, founded the Executive Office of the President—including the White House staff—and, starting with the Reorganization Act of 1939, set the pattern for the series of similar acts which gave to presidents, with only brief interruptions, continuing authority to initiate reorganization plans which Congress could defeat, but not amend, by legislative veto. He reestablished continuing overall administrative research, as an executive function, in the Bureau of the Budget as a condition precedent to executive reorganizations and to stimulate intradepartmental management surveys.

At the same time the policy instruments of the presidency were sharpened. On the insistence of Congress, he began a central clearance system, also in the Bureau of the Budget, of the opinions of department heads on proposed legislation so that Congress could be informed which of their diverse views were "in accordance with the program of the President." He established central points of initiative and coordination in the executive office for the numerous scientific programs and statistical activities of the government. He made "brain trusting" a continuing staff arm of the presidency as a basis for policy formulation. He set up the National Resources Planning Board for this purpose, with authority to retain temporary outside consultants, which produced such farseeing reports as the one on urbanism called "Our Cities" and numerous prophetic conservation papers. Although N.R.P.B. was abolished by Congress in 1943, the pattern established in F.D.R.'s time of giving the White House previously unavailable authority and unearmarked funds was continued, enabling each subsequent president to develop the executive office and to appoint ad hoc task forces and temporary advisory commissions to investigate emergent problems of national policy. But a number of the present-day components in the executive office of the President came to have permanent policy planning assignments such as the Bureau of the Budget, the Council of Economic Advisers, the National Security Council, the Office of Emergency Preparedness, and the Office of Science and Technology, in addition to the growing number of councils advising in other major problem areas. Professor Rossiter comments as follows: "For some years now, it has been popular, even among his friends, to write off Mr. Roosevelt as a second-rate administrator. In the light of Executive Order 8248, an accomplishment in public administration superior to that of any other President, this familiar judgment seems a trifle musty."[13]

Each of his successors has found the vehicles of administrative management and organization that he bequeathed to them indispensable for the related tasks of policy formulation and control of the gigantic executive establishment. Each one of them has utilized these vehicles for which Roosevelt laid the foundations and has adapted them to the ever changing needs of the times and to his own style and method.

Chapter V

HOOVER I

1. Background and Orientation

IT IS IMPRACTICABLE TO REPORT IN DETAIL ON THE WORK OF THE FIRST
Hoover Commission in this brief treatise. The variety and scale of the
Commission's studies were vast and each one of its reports would
require concentrated attention. Moreover, it would be difficult, if not
presumptuous, for one person to attempt to do justice to all the subjects treated in the reports. It is my intention, therefore, to concentrate
on the major organizational aspects in the reports of the Commission
that may be of interest to the generalist and to attempt to appraise the
significance of this monumental effort in the continuing process of
structural adjustment and management in federal administration.

The Commission on Organization of the Executive Branch of the
Government (hereinafter referred to as Hoover I or simply, as it deserves to be called, the Hoover Commission) was established in part
to bring into an integrated organization structure the numerous agencies left in the wake of war and demobilization. The origins of the
commission may also be found in the temper of the Eightieth Congress.
The Congress was concerned with the problems arising out of a 250-
billion-dollar national debt and an unprecedented peacetime budget
of 40 billions. It was torn between its desire to reduce the debt and
balance the budget and its urge to encourage private investment by
tax reductions. The second urge was irresistible and there followed a
series of efforts to reduce expenditures.

The first postwar Congress was in a mood for deflation of the executive establishment. There had been agitation since the war for return of the public payroll and executive activities to prewar proportions, but the Congress had lacked the data needed to make informed cutbacks and the will to eliminate any substantive program. The Eightieth Congress was the first Republican Congress in sixteen years, moreover, and was in a vindictive mood. It was eager to take stock of the accumulated New Deal, war, and postwar programs and their administration. In the spring of 1947, with widespread expectations of the election of a Republican President the following year, the time seemed ripe for a thoroughgoing examination of the federal enterprise. It was expected that such an audit would reveal vast areas of waste and large opportunities for what Rowland Egger called "painless economy." It was expected to provide a convenient guide for a program of retrenchment that would result in enormous savings in the new Republican administration. Congressional prerogatives, always restricted in wartime, would be restored. The Lodge-Brown Act stated specifically that one of the objectives of the examination should be "to define and limit the executive branch."[1]

In the light of the temper of the Congress and the times, the restraint exercised by the Congress in passing the law which authorized the establishment of the first Hoover Commission, approved July 7, 1947 (61 Stat. 246), was astonishing. It provided for a commission that was to be mixed in several respects. It was to consist of twelve members, six of whom should be Republicans and six Democrats. Four of its members were to be chosen by the President, four by the Speaker of the House, and four by the Presiding Officer of the Senate. The members eventually chosen were Herbert Hoover (chairman), Dean Acheson (vice chairman), George H. Mead, Joseph P. Kennedy, Professor James K. Pollock, and James H. Rowe, Jr., from private life; Senators George D. Aiken and John L. McClellan, and Representatives Clarence J. Brown and Carter Manasco, from the legislative branch; and Arthur S. Flemming and James V. Forrestal from the executive branch.

The Congress was generous in its financing of the commission. At a time when the appropriations committees were paring down every item they could, Congressman John Taber of New York, the chairman of the House committee, gave assurance that there would be no lack of funds forthcoming, and the original appropriation was doubled before the commission finished its work. President Truman expressed his interest in the project from the very beginning. There is reason to believe not only that he gave encouragement to the adoption of the legislation establishing the commission but that he was among the first to suggest that the commission be headed by our only living ex-President, whose name continued to be a symbol of managerial efficiency, despite the economic and political disasters of his single term as President.

Throughout the study, even at the height of the political campaign in the fall of 1948, a most remarkable relationship existed between Chairman Hoover and President Truman. The President had instructed James E. Webb, the director of the Bureau of the Budget, and all federal executive agencies and departments to cooperate with the study in every possible way; and this cooperation, particularly on the part of the Bureau staff, continued when Frank Pace, Jr., became the director of the Bureau. This cooperative relationship between the commission and the executive branch persisted throughout and even, in spite of some rankling on both sides, survived the unexpected reelection in 1948 of President Truman.

The formula for the commission's composition was unique in its painstaking provision for the representation of outside interests. The commission, fortunately, was less delicately balanced than the formula. Although the appointments were to be made equally from public and private life, one of the private citizens turned out to be an ex-President and all the rest had had governmental experience of a high order. Yet half of the commission had backgrounds in business and professional fields. In all, the appointments brought an extremely high level of ability and experience to the study of federal reorganization. The Congress was well represented by the ranking majority members of the House and Senate Committees on Expenditures in the Executive Departments, the ranking minority member of the Senate committee, and the House sponsor of the reorganization study. This representation, it may be noted, was not so successful in facilitating congressional passage of the commission's proposals as had been hoped.[2]

The low proportion of academicians on the Hoover Commission contrasts markedly with the composition of the President's Committee on Administrative Management. The Hoover Commission included a lone professor. Many scholars served on the task forces, but most of the larger committees were headed by non-academes. "Men of action," recruited from the business world, were prominent on committees and staffs. Their employment of a larger number of management and accounting consultant firms inevitably brought to the project much of the perspective of private business administration. The result may be seen in a general efficiency engineering approach in the task force reports. Paul M. Appleby suggests, however, that the commissioners had an entirely different approach, and that their reports reflect the "political officer" character of the members of the commission rather than the efficiency engineering approach of the task force staffs.[3] This points out the need to distinguish clearly between the reports of the commission and of the task forces.

2. *Method of Work*

The strong leadership of Mr. Hoover was in evidence throughout the work of the commission. His prestige as an ex-President naturally assured this leadership. After all, he had experienced the problems under consideration; it would not be easy to challenge his point of view. His recommendations, therefore, frequently prevailed on disputed points.[4] The Commission on Organization of the Executive Branch became the "Hoover Commission" both in name and in spirit. Such leadership was indispensable for the commission. Without it a twelve-man body of heterogeneous composition would at many points have found agreement extremely difficult to achieve. It might have broken down altogether if any other than an ex-President had run the show.

Mr. Hoover, on taking the chairmanship of the commission, assumed an identification with the fate of reorganization and viewed the entire project very much as his own. Announcing this to be his "last public service," the only living ex-President at 73 performed prodigious feats of hard labor in developing the reports and later in formulating specific reorganization proposals.

It is almost ungenerous, in view of the good work that was accomplished, to comment on how his method of organizing the work served to increase Mr. Hoover's burdens. He not only presided at commission meetings; he also directed the staff work in the greatest detail. He was executive director as well as chairman of the enterprise. He selected the task forces personally, often with only pro forma approval of the commission, arranged for survey contracts and kept in touch with the chairmen of the major projects. He insisted on writing many of the early drafts of the commission reports himself; and, if they suffer from certain awkwardnesses of style, his was nevertheless the principal influence for decisiveness and brevity. It is not generally realized that he constituted himself the task force for the treatment of the Presidency in the report on *General Management of the Executive Branch*. Before the staff work began he told me, "I guess I'll take that one myself. Who is there who ought to know more about it?"

The most distinctive aspect of this comprehensive study of the executive branch of the federal government is the dimension in which it operated. Unlike earlier efforts, the Hoover Commission thought of its project not only as a job of mobilizing information but also as a job of mobilizing influential leaders behind the idea of reorganization. Recruiting to its task forces influential leaders both inside and outside the government, it automatically created important pressure groups for reorganization. The commission viewed its task from the outset largely as one of securing public acceptance. The study of the President's Committee on Administrative Management had been a confidential inquiry concerned with advancing a new theory of executive management. This was exactly the opposite—a much heralded project of surveys presented in a fashion calculated to secure support for the recommendations of the Commission. In fact, the complete silence of the Hoover Commission concerning the earlier study forces one to conclude that it was a deliberate element of its strategy not to impair the possibilities of acceptance of its recommendations by any reference to the controversies and unfair interpretations that followed the work of President Roosevelt's Committee. If Congressman Dirksen could declare that the 1939 reorganization bill had not been profaned by the eyes of Messrs. Corcoran and Cohen,[5] so the Hoover Commission could contend that its work had not been sullied by the hands of Brownlow, Merriam, and Gulick. But before the Hoover Commission was through it found itself compelled, in the words of Rowland Egger, "to read the minutes of the previous meeting."

The style of the reports is similarly distinctive; the paucity of verbiage explaining and interpreting the recommendations of the Hoover Commission is remarkable. The style is Mr. Hoover's own, brief and terse. The similarity of the reports to press releases reflected the intent that each be short enough to appear in *The New York Times*, which they usually did, and which explains their often incomplete character. These were to be action documents. Publication of the reports in sequence was similarly contrived; thus each set of proposals, individually released, could command attention it could never have received as part of a single comprehensive report.

Publicity considerations are reflected, also, in the extensive use of charts in the reports. Over one hundred adorn the task force studies and commission reports. An excellent device for "selling" reorganization, the "before and after" organization charts were an integral part of the commission's recommendations. Charts, moreover, fitted well with the commission's concept of reorganization, particularly that of its chairman. Mr. Hoover was extremely interested in the movement, transfer and consolidation of agencies and units. The President's Committee, pointing out that "a nice blueprint, an attractive-looking chart, is not the end of reorganization,"[6] had restricted its designing to a single rough outline of the twelve proposed departments. The Hoover Commission was far more concerned with the blueprints of reform. The concern, for example, with the consolidation of lesser agencies like the National Archives and the American Battle Monuments Commission reflects this preoccupation. The emphasis on graphic presentation of "bureau shuffling" was evident also in the two summary charts of the *Concluding Report.*

The treatment of the Hoover Commission by the press is particularly noteworthy. In contrast to the editorial hostility that attended the effort of the President's Committee twelve years earlier, the tone of the press coverage of the commission's reports was highly favorable. The association of ex-President Hoover with the project evoked the plaudits of some partisan sectors; and the approval of some anti-Administration journalists betrayed satisfaction with the commission's portrayal of government gigantism and its findings of overlapping and duplication in many federal agencies.

The reaction of most leading newspapers and periodicals was consistently favorable. Charges of "dictatorship" and "executive domination" were conspicuously absent. Editorial columns that had opposed the 1938 reorganization attempt as an "aggrandizement of the President's constitutional powers" now considered a strong, unified Executive to be "a prime requisite of republican institutions."[7] Papers that had labeled the 1938 legislation the "dictator bill" considered the Hoover Commission recommendations a "monumental effort to bring order out of chaos" and recommended their prompt enactment into law.[8] The small minority who remained opposed to reorganization were less apoplectic in their reactions. One leading critic of the President's Committee scoffed at the ineffectiveness of this bipartisan effort, viewing its emphasis on improvement rather than elimination of functions as begging the whole question.[9]

3. *Principles of Overall Management*

The philosophy and principles of administration on which the commission proceeded appear in its opening report on *General Management of the Executive Branch* and in its *Concluding Report*. These two reports are the high points of the entire study and alone would have given the Hoover Commission work great significance. The report on *General Management* fortunately was finished fairly early, and once its main outlines had been approved by the commission it provided a general point of view which became a connecting thread in the subsequent work. The commission could screen the highly diversified, autonomous task force studies in the light of a body of doctrine which it had hammered out for itself. Thus it made its job feasible and gave greater coherence and unity to the reports that followed.

The first report asserted that ". . . we must reorganize the executive branch to give it the simplicity of structure, the unity of purpose, and the clear line of executive authority that was originally intended under the Constitution."[10] The commission's first recommendation to the Congress was that it should give to the President continuing reorganization powers not restricted by limitations or exemptions. It recognized at the outset the continuing nature of the reorganization function and the need for executive initiative subject to congressional review for its effective operation. In the second place it found that as a result of poor structure and weak lines of authority, the President and his lieutenants, the department heads, could not control the work of the bureaus and operating agencies. It recommended a more orderly grouping of the functions of the government into major departments and agencies under the President, the establishment of clear lines of control, the provision of stronger staff services for the President and the department heads, the development of a greater number of capable administrators, broader patterns of control to replace the detailed laws and regulations that destroy executive initiative and responsibility, and decentralization to the departments and agencies of routine administrative services under high performance standards and effective supervision.

The key to the approach of the Hoover Commission is found in the treatment of the problem of presidential management in the introductory report, where the influence of Chairman Hoover was most conspicuous.

The specific recommendations in this area are really the further development of a trend. For the most part they reaffirm the importance of equipping the President with effective staff arms for overall management. The recommendation that the National Security Council and the National Security Resources Board be elevated to the Executive Office formalized existing procedure. The proposals for unrestricted presidential discretion in staffing and organizing the Executive Office, for an office of personnel, and for a staff secretary provided new devices to meet presidential needs that had long been sensed but had not been defined. The Council of Economic Advisers was to be replaced by an office of the economic adviser under a single head. The work of interdepartmental committees was to be better integrated and there was to be an annual inventory of such committees in order that those whose work had been completed might be terminated. The office of the budget was to be kept in the Executive Office, reporting directly to the President, and its work in the field of administrative management was to be strengthened. An office of general services was to be created to provide supply, records management, and public buildings operation and maintenance services for all departments. Thus the responsibility of the Presidency for administrative management of the executive branch was reaffirmed. The Executive Office of the President, which came into existence in 1939, was to be strengthened for the effective discharge of that responsibility.

The commission went further in pointing up the line of command in its recommendations on departmental management. Not only were the 65 departments and agencies to be regrouped by major purposes into one-third that number, but within each department the bureaus were also to be regrouped. No subordinate was to be given authority independent of his superior. Budgets and assignments of functions were to be under the flexible control of department heads. Department heads were to operate under common standards their administrative services of accounting, budgeting, personnel, and procurement. An administrative assistant secretary, presumably a career man, was to supplement the political under and assistant secretaries and give continuity to the administration of management services. Each department was to have such staff assistants as a general counsel, a financial officer, a personnel officer, a supply officer, a management research officer, an information and publications officer, and a congressional liaison officer. Staff officials and bureau chiefs were to be appointed by department heads and wherever possible they were to be career officials. General suggestions were made for the simplification of the federal field establishment.

These recommendations constitute the most significant lesson of the entire effort. Created in an atmosphere strikingly at variance with New Deal concepts, headed by a Republican ex-President who had been a leading figure at his party's recent convention, the Hoover Commission concluded with the same general theory of the Presidency and presidential management that the President's Committee had elaborated in 1937. In the words of Herman Finer, "The Hoover Commission, and many of its collaborators are Mr. Brownlow's children."[11] Right down the line the commission gave wholehearted endorsement to a strong executive, effective tools for executive management, and continuing presidential authority over reorganization—principles that had called forth charges of "executive usurpation" from anti-New Deal sources throughout the preceding twelve years. Citing Alexander Hamilton as authority, the commission saw no dangers in an energetic, integrated executive and stressed the necessity of granting the President the means for giving "firm direction to the departments and agencies."[12]

In its statement of the problems and needs of the American Presidency at midcentury, the commission reasserted the principle of overall management and disappointed some of its congressional sponsors. Appleby pointed out that *"The crucial significance of any large effort towards reorganization lies in its view of the relationship between structure and control."*[13] At the conclusion of a comprehensive study this bipartisan commission, composed of men of wide experience and varied talents, provided the American institution of the Presidency with a highly respectable and knowledgeable endorsement of the need for continuing reorganization powers and administrative leadership.

4. Centralization of Policy and Delegation of Operations

The major emphasis of the reports of Hoover I was on centralization of responsibility for policy making and setting of standards and on delegation and decentralization of operational decisions. These recommendations had a great influence in reestablishing the authority of department heads over their subordinates based upon the principle of decentralization of operations with standards and supervision centrally supplied. Impressed by the size and rigidities of the federal leviathan, the commission aimed consistently at the amelioration and reduction of bottlenecks caused by centralization of services. Decentralization was a particularly notable feature of the recommendations relating to the "housekeeping" activities of the federal government. In the reports on personnel, management services, supply activities, and budgeting and accounting, the commission proposed substantial decentralization to the operating agencies. In the case of the personnel function, it recommended further delegations within the agencies themselves. The commission sought thus to strengthen the managerial position of the operating heads, recasting the role of the central service agency to make it a policy-formulating, standard-setting, and inspectional body.

Without in any way disparaging the value of the commission's work as a whole, it appears to me that many of the subsequent reports failed to fulfill the high hopes engendered by the first document, and a large number of the task force reports, although useful because of the rich store of materials and suggestions provided, are decidedly disappointing in quality. The suggestion of decentralization, for example, raises questions as to standards and scope that are left unanswered as a result of the generalized nature of the commission's recommendations. This shortcoming is particularly evident in the case of the personnel proposals. As Commissioner Pollock's dissent pointed out, the standards of decentralization, left unspecified by the commission, were likely to turn out to be inflexible, artificial, centralizing procedural standards that would effectively "produce a dead hand in personnel administration."[14] Some critics also raised the question whether the commission's formula for insuring compliance would be effective.[15]

In the brief report on *Federal-State Relations,* as in other reports, attention is directed toward a shift in emphasis from control to operations, from center to periphery, from the federal government to the states, that reflects the commission's antipathy to bureaucratic concentration at the top and its desire to stimulate initiative and independence at subsidiary levels. While applauding the affirmation of these principles, one could wish that the huge quantity of research performed for the commission might have led to more penetrating and precise prescriptions.

The report on *The National Security Organization* and the competent task force study were of particular interest to me. I was among those who strongly urged Mr. Hoover to include this topic when he

consulted me on the draft agenda. He told me it had been omitted on
Secretary Forrestal's advice that it was premature. The secretary
withdrew his objections when an excellent task force headed by
Ferdinand Eberstadt was appointed. Defense expenditures amounted
to approximately one-third of the federal budget. The heated question
of unification of the defense department had for some time projected
the technical issues of federal management into unprecedented public
notice. The findings and recommendations of this report of the commission laid the groundwork for the National Security Act Amendments of 1949 (63 Stat. 578) which established the Department of
Defense. It may be noted that in the report on *The National Security
Organization* the commission had an opportunity for full application
of its across-the-board recommendations for departmental management.

The report on *Foreign Affairs* was of high quality, although some
able observers feared that its main recommendation may have unduly
subordinated the functional desks to the geographical. I myself believe that a fair balance was maintained and that the provision for
regional assistant secretaries has made it possible to exploit and at the
same time coordinate the contribution of the specialists.

The commission's proposals for the independent regulatory commissions constituted reappraisal of a central problem of the President's
Committee on Administrative Management. The Committee's recommendation that these agencies be merged in the departments but retain
autonomy in their quasi-judicial functions had encountered strong
opposition and had failed of acceptance. The Hoover Commission favored continuing the independence of the regulatory commissions,
although it recommended that the administrative functions of several
of them be transferred to related departments. It proposed, in fact, to
extend to all the commissions the limitations now restricting the President's power to remove members of most of them.

In the proposals for transfer of the administrative functions of the
Interstate Commerce Commission, the Maritime Commission, and the
Civil Aeronautics Board to the Department of Commerce, the Hoover
Commission moved significantly in the direction of a unified transportation department. Although it rejected the task force suggestion that
regulatory functions dealing with transportation be grouped in a new
transportation regulatory commission, the Commission's elaboration of
a proposed transportation service[16] in the Department of Commerce
was an important step toward the unification of federal transportation
activities.

5. Policy Areas and Dissents

At a number of points the Hoover Commission and its task forces departed from the restraint of earlier studies, crossing administrative boundaries and entering policy areas. In several places thinly veiled attacks on New Deal programs reflected attitudes in agreement with those of the Eightieth Congress that established the commission. The outstanding example of uninhibited intrusion into policy areas was the Task Force Report on Revolving Funds and Business Enterprises prepared by Haskins and Sells. The Brookings Institution study of federal welfare activities similarly ranged far into policy matters remote from problems of organization, particularly in its evaluation of the old-age and survivors insurance program.[17] The report of the Task Force on Agriculture Activities included specific policy recommendations to curtail farm home lending operations and to effect a more conservative program on the part of the Rural Electrification Administration.[18]

Although the commission rejected some of the more obvious programmatic recommendations of its task forces, it also trespassed on the realm of policy. For example, a majority of the commission clearly entered the policy field in recommending a solution of "the Indian problem." In the area of federal-state relations, the commission rejected the detailed proposals of its task force studies but undertook, over the dissents of Commissioners Acheson and Forrestal, to state some general views on the redistribution of governmental functions. These excursions into policy, it may be noted, split the commission, and the report on *Federal Business Enterprises* was the high point of explosiveness in the attempt to bridge the gap between policy and administration.[19]

An extremely valuable part of the reports of the Hoover Commission were the dissents and the several varieties of separate statements of views of individual commissioners. Representing disagreements that could not be reconciled through debate and efforts to obtain consensus, these separate opinions provide a wealth of insight into the problems treated. Significantly, the commission achieved considerable consensus in its treatment of problems of organization and structure. Its cohesion was progressively dissipated, however, as it moved into areas of policy, and the commissioners finally split in all directions over the controversial issues of electric power production and transmission and the activities of federal lending agencies.

The independence of the commissioners is revealed by the fact that each of them dissented at least once from a recommendation of the majority. It would be interesting to trace the pattern of dissents by the method recently applied to the decisions of the Supreme Court.[20] But even a cursory review shows the frequent joint dissents of Commissioners Rowe and Acheson. The four members who filed the smallest number of dissents were Kennedy, Flemming, Hoover, and Mead; the four who filed the largest number were Rowe, Acheson, Forrestal, and Pollock.

The deviation of the commission from the recommendations of its study committees merits analysis. In significant instances, the commission declined to follow the advice of its task forces. In virtually all these instances the task force recommendations had involved policy considerations. The programmatic proposals of the Brookings study and the substantive recommendations of the task force on federal-state relations were conspicuously ignored. The power proposals of the Haskins and Sells firm elicited no consensus on the part of the commission. Considerably less disagreement with the staff arose out of purely organizational recommendations. Except for its failure to endorse a transportation regulatory commission, the commission substantially followed the recommendations of its staff with regard to overall structure, auxiliary services, and departmental management. This result probably owes much to the fact that Chairman Hoover personally supervised the task force work in these cases.

6. Controversy over Savings Effected

The commission's treatment of the economy aspects of reorganization has been overpublicized, largely as a result of unofficial statements by members of the Citizens Committee on the Hoover Report rather than of the conclusions of the reports themselves. In answer to a Senate committee question as to whether he believed reorganization would "substantially reduce the cost of government," Mr. Hoover replied that the "savings ought to amount to billions."[21] The first report similarly suggested that "the savings to the American taxpayer can amount to billions."[22] Succeeding reports indicated the expectations of specific savings in particular areas by citing the estimates ventured by the task forces in these areas. A totaling of these yielded an over-all estimate of three billions in savings and this was the figure that was publicized.

There was some debate in the commission as to its position on savings. Disagreement flared into print as Commissioners Acheson and Rowe appended a dissent to the agriculture report. They criticized the estimates made by the task forces as unrealistic, undocumented, and frequently mere guesswork; their use by the commission, they felt, gave them authenticity in the eyes of the Congress and the public. The commission's explanation that the estimates were not its own but those of the task forces did not avoid the appearance of commission endorsement of figures that were largely unsubstantiated and often plain conjecture.[23] It may be noted that the commission made no summary statement of total savings to be expected. The *Concluding Report* was eloquently silent on the economies to be realized from the commission's recommendations.

After the publication of the reports there appeared more realistic statements on the dollars-and-cents potential of reorganization. To be sure, the estimate of savings of three billions continued to be cited. Chairman Hoover mentioned an increased "ante" of "about four billion a year"—again as an aggregate indicated by "an inventory . . . made of the views of the heads of our task forces as to the amounts they thought could be saved in their special fields."[24] But others stated the limited economies they expected to be derived from reorganization. Even Commissioner McClellan, in his capacity as chairman of the Senate committee holding hearings on reorganization, admitted that economies would not come immediately or directly. In the hearings on Reorganization Plan I, he stated that he had never considered the proposals as promising specific dollar economies. "The only hope," he conceded, "is that if we get a better-organized government, a better-integrated government, we can get better government; at least better government for the same money we are now spending."[25] Budget Director Pace similarly described the main purpose of the Hoover Commission: "to establish a more effective form of government, which will establish economies. . . . It is generally recognized," he pointed out, "that better government means more economical government; and that is the purport of the Hoover Commission operation."[26]

7. Extraordinary Results

The record of results achieved after the commission submitted its recommendations was extraordinary. Substantially following the suggestions of the reports, the Congress established the General Services Administration[27] and passed the Military Unification Act[28] and the State Department Reorganization Act.[29] In the Reorganization Act of 1949[30] the President was given continuing reorganization authority, although of a more restricted nature than had been recommended by the commission. Under the authority of this act, President Truman effected many of the commission's proposals—strengthening the Executive Office, strengthening the positions of the chairmen of the Civil Service Commission and the Maritime Commission, reorganizing the Post Office Department, and transferring the Employment Service to the Department of Labor and the Public Roads Administration to the Department of Commerce.[31] In the closing days of its first session, the Eighty-first Congress raised the federal salary ceiling in the direction urged by the commission.[32]

Changes that could be accomplished through administrative action were effected in great number. An important example was the decision to include a performance type of budget for fiscal year 1951. Manifold changes in structure and procedure were made within the departments and agencies. In all, the steps toward administrative reform surpass in number those of any year in the history of the executive branch of the federal government. After the passage of the Reorganization Act of 1949 (Appendix III) President Truman submitted eight reorganization plans, of which six became effective. In 1950, he submitted twenty-seven reorganization plans, of which twenty became effective. Most of these were in accordance with the recommendations of Hoover I. There was also enacted a series of legislative bills affecting organization, notably the National Security Act Amendments.

The emphasis on public relations, on "selling" reorganization, was a basic part of the planned Hoover strategy. An important instrument in this achievement were the citizens committees for the Hoover Report. Hundreds of distinguished leaders representing diverse interests were recruited into a national committee under the chairmanship of President Robert L. Johnson of Temple University; they lent nonpartisan prestige to the Hoover Commission proposals. Dr. Johnson, who had served as a member of the Task Force on Personnel, later organized a committee at Temple University to draft a sequel to the reports of Hoover I; the Temple University Study of Reorganization was presented to President Eisenhower and became a curtain raiser to Hoover II. Thirty-two state committees were formed and they stimulated widespread interest in and pressures for enactment of reorganization measures. Specific endorsement of the proposals of the commission was thus obtained from numerous citizen groups. Reorganization was in a sense packaged and sold. Even if many more people subscribed to the pamphlets than read them, and only a few understood their significance, the total effect was an educational one for citizen understanding of big government. The public relations of Hoover I was a serious professional job, a job which the Brownlow Committee had neglected, and which the supporters of Hoover II pushed beyond the limits of credibility.

President Truman through Executive Order 10072 stepped up the program of internal management improvement in the federal agencies. He appointed an Advisory Committee on Management Improvement, of which I was a member, consisting of twelve persons, seven from outside the federal service and five from within. (See Chapter VII.)

A stimulus was also given by the work of the Hoover Commission to state reorganization. Almost half of the states created commissions or special committees to make comprehensive surveys of their administrative apparatus. Unfortunately, relatively little action was taken at the state level on these recommendations.

The acceptance by the press and by radio commentators of the first Hoover Reports was unprecedented. The printing presses continued to pour out untold pages of material concerning them. This material varied from packaged propaganda promising vast and undocumented savings to the excellent appraisals by publicists and the more penetrating and objective analyses of scholars in the scientific journals. References to good summaries of the Hoover I recommendations and to one of the best appraisals will be found in the notes.[33]

This Niagara of material was in scale with the gigantic dimensions of the commission's own output. The nineteen reports of the commission and the printed and unprinted findings of its twenty-four task forces contain approximately 2,000,000 words, produced at a cost of about $1.00 a word. In this vast endeavor three hundred persons, many of great distinction and talent, from many walks of life, aided the bipartisan mixed commission headed by the only living ex-President of the United States. A list of the chairmen of task forces and other staff personnel is appended here.

Stimulated by the remarkable entente between ex-President Hoover and President Truman, an astonishing number of the recommendations of the commission were put into effect. It was estimated that over 100 of the 277 specific suggestions have been effected by congressional or executive action although this kind of tabulation means little in view of the dissimilarity in kind and importance of the enumerated recommendations. Hoover I will go down in history as the greatest show on earth in the field of applied government research. And appropriately so, for the commission was looking into the biggest tent on earth and the one on which the safety, health, and welfare of this planet greatly depend.

TASK FORCE CHAIRMEN AND PRINCIPAL RESEARCH GROUPS OF THE
FIRST HOOVER COMMISSION

I. *General Management of the Executive Branch*
*The Office of the President and its Relation to the
Departments and Agencies:* Don K. Price, Stephen K.
Bailey, H. Struve Hensel, John D. Millett.
Federal Field Offices: Klein and Saks (Management
Consultants), Dr. Julius Klein, project director.

II. *Budgeting and Accounting*
John W. Hanes. Accounting Phase: T. Coleman Andrews,
T. Jack Gary, Jr., and Irving Tenner.
Budgetary Phase: Institute of Public Administration,
New York, A. E. Buck, project director.

III. *Statistical Services*
National Bureau of Economic Research, Frederick C. Mills,
project director.

IV. *Records Management*
National Records Management Council, E. J. Leahy,
project director.

V. *Federal Supply Activities*
Russell Forbes, project director.
Staff assistants and an advisory committee drawn from
industrial purchasing executives.

VI. *Personnel Management*
John A. Stevenson, president, Penn Mutual Life Insurance
Company, chairman of Task Force; Cresap, McCormick and
Paget (Management Consultants), Richard Paget, project
director.

VII. *Foreign Affairs*
Harvey H. Bundy and James Grafton Rogers, committee
Henry L. Stimson, adviser
John F. Meck, Jr., staff director.

VIII. *National Security Organization*
   Ferdinand Eberstadt, investment banker, and former vice chairman, War Production Board, chairman of Task Force (with civilian and military advisory committees).

IX. *Treasury Department*
   A. E. Buck, Montgomery B. Angell, Daniel W. Bell, and William T. Sherwood.

X. *The Post Office*
   Robert Heller & Associates, Inc., Management Engineers, F. L. Elmendorf, project director.

XI. *Department of Agriculture*
   H. P. Rusk, Dean of Illinois College of Agriculture, chairman of Task Force.

XII. *Department of Interior*
   Natural Resources: Leslie Miller, former Governor of Wyoming, chairman of Task Force. Public Works: Robert Moses, chairman of the New York State Council of Parks, and of the Triborough Bridge Authority, chairman of Task Force and director, with a staff of consultants from state and local public works agencies.

XIII. *Department of Commerce*
   Regulatory Commissions: Robert H. Bowie and Owen D. Young, committee. Robert R. Bowie, project director, Harold Leventhal, executive officer.

   Transportation: The Brookings Institution, Charles Dearing, project director, Wilfred Owen, assistant project director.

XIV. *Department of Labor*
   George W. Taylor, consultant
   Public Welfare, The Brookings Institution
   Research directors: Lewis Meriam and Avery Leiserson
   Committee: Robert R. Bowie and Owen D. Young

   Departmental management: H. Struve Hensel and John D. Millett

   Statistical Services: National Bureau of Economic Research, directors: Frederick C. Mills and Clarence D. Long with an advisory committee.

XV. *Medical Activities*
   Medical Services: Tracy S. Voorhees, chairman of Task Force, Howard M. Kline, project director, and specialist consultants.

Welfare Activities: Dr. George W. Bachman and Lewis
Meriam.

XVI. *Veterans' Affairs*

Franklin D'Olier, first national commander, American
Legion, and former chairman, Prudential Life Insurance
Company, chairman of Task Force.
Valentine Howell, project director, and special consultants
from the insurance and other industries and professions.

XVII. *Federal Business Enterprises*

Federal Business Enterprises and Revolving Funds: Major
General Arthur H. Carter, project director, and Colonel
Andrew Stewart, research director (Haskins and Sells,
C.P.A.'s).

Lending Agencies: Paul Grady and Theodore Herz (Price,
Waterhouse & Co., C.P.A.'s), and an advisory committee.

XVIII. *Independent Regulatory Commissions*
(see report on Department of Commerce)

XIX. *Social Security and Education*
Lewis Meriam, Hollis P. Allen, and Avery Leiserson.

XX. *Indian Affairs*
George Graham, professor of Political Science, Princeton
University, chairman of Task Force.

XXI. *Federal-State Relations*
Thomas Jefferson Coolidge, chairman, United Fruit Company,
and former Under Secretary of the Treasury, chairman of
Task Force.

Project undertaken by the Council of State Governments,
Frank Bane, project director.

The Task Forces, advisory groups, and special consultants are all
listed in the McGraw-Hill volume (Note 33-A). They are too numerous to list here but most of the names were distinguished in government, business, the professions, including law, education, engineering,
and the social and physical sciences. They were fairly well balanced
politically and geographically with a possible, but understandable,
weight in favor of the Northeast. The absence of women and of blacks
was conspicuous. Nevertheless, if there is such a thing as "the establishment," Mr. Hoover, with few exceptions, enlisted the cooperation of
many of its most enlightened, experienced, and public-spirited members.

Chapter VI

HOOVER II

1. *Philosophy of the Commission*

FOR THE SECOND TIME IN SIX YEARS CONGRESS, IN 1953, BROUGHT FORTH another Commission on the Organization of the Executive Branch of the Government, hereinafter referred to as the second Hoover Commission or simply as Hoover II.

The full title was in fact a misnomer. The director of the budget had vainly suggested that a different name be adopted to distinguish it clearly from its predecessor. In its 600,000 words and 1,162 pages, and the 3,300,000 words of its staff, 19 task forces, and a number of special committees, it dissected a large miscellany of governmental functions and activities which were to be abolished, simplified, restricted, mutualized, or transferred to private ownership and operation. The subject matter treated ranged from such minutiae as the shipment of ping pong balls to Berlin and of canned tomatoes from coast to coast, and the details of bureau letter writing and paperwork, to problems at the highest level of public policy with profound implications for national security and prosperity, such as public generation and distribution of electric energy, government lending and insurance of loans and deposits, scientific research and development, civilian control of procurement and budgets in the Department of Defense, the operation of huge military transport systems, and the complexities of foreign aid. The bulk of this enormous inquiry, the appropriations for which amounted to $2,848,534, was devoted either to detailed studies of operations or to the broadest questions of policy and function, and only a relatively small part of the study was devoted to the problem of the organization of the executive branch.

Executive organization, which in my view was exemplified in the reports of the Brownlow Committee and of the first Hoover Commission, concerns those elements of structure, personnel, budgetary, and other systems of a government which produce an energetic and viable administrative management, capable of responding to the needs and the will of the country and of its citizens. The administrative management has to be adjusted continually as conditions change to be flexible and effective in the rendering of public services. It must have the ability and will to identify the need for new arrangements in these elements and to discover lapses, deficiencies, and waste in existing ones. Above all it should be expert in the art of relating the objectives of public policy to the hard realities of feasibility and implementation. The President, as chief executive, and the department heads, as his responsible advisors and administrators, need to have the authority, the staff, the data, and the facilities compatible with their large responsibilities to enable them to formulate sound policies and to defend them. They need the means to see that their huge and complex establishments are conducted efficiently and in accordance with policy determinations, and to adjust them from time to time to changing conditions. Good administrative management at the top levels requires excellent channels of two-way communication to help department heads receive information and advice and to create an environment and atmosphere of morale and reasonable certainty in which their bureaus and administrations can do their work. But these high officials also need to have assistants capable in liaison work for activities that go beyond those embraced in even the biggest department. The need for and means of coordination of overlapping policies and programs, which will continue to exist under the best organization obtainable, must be a special part of high level concern. Whereas these elements had always been important, they had become indispensable in the second half of the twentieth century, a time of an accelerating rate of technological change, of social unrest and population movement, of urbanization, of economic fluctuation, of vast external responsibilities and an international situation in a chronic state of revolution and violence; a time fraught with unprecedented dangers, recurrent crises, and great opportunities. In broad terms these are the needs of executive organization for the governing of the republic which has been catapulted into the responsibilities of the world's first power and which is the international symbol of democracy cum efficiency.

But Hoover II became to a large extent an exercise in the audit of operating methods rather than another and profounder look at executive organization. It was moreover an unprecedented mandate by Congress for an inquiry into its own legislation, not only of the Roosevelt and Truman periods, but going back in some cases four decades to the genesis of activities begun by the Federal Reserve and Farm Loan Acts. This aspect of its work has been understressed in the growing collection of political commentary. No terms of reference so sweeping and covering so many areas of activity had previously been given by Congress to a mixed commission half of whose members were neither members of Congress nor of other branches of the government.

"The philosophy of the commission" was a phrase frequently used by Mr. Hoover, never with great precision, but it referred to the ultimate major premises of Hoover II. These were concerned with the reduction of governmental functions, not only to save money and to reduce taxes, but primarily to eliminate competition with private enterprise—to restrict and abolish many of the programs which had been adopted to regulate, stabilize, supplement, and assist the private sector during World War II and when the years of the great depression of the 1930's had revealed its deficiencies. The enormous scope of Hoover II and the remarkable labors of Mr. Hoover in his eightieth year, in once more personally supervising every detail of so large an effort, were predominantly concerned with what the government should not do rather than how it should be organized and managed.

Mr. Hoover's "philosophy of the commission" was entirely consistent with the terms of reference enacted by Congress and with the record of the debates on the 1953 bill. Their origins can be understood if the prevailing climate of opinion is recalled. With the first Republican President in twenty years, as a result of General Eisenhower's victory in 1952, and with Republican majorities in the House and the Senate, the trends under two decades of Democratic rule, which many conservatives believed to be a threat to American free enterprise, were to be audited, arrested, and reversed. The business and propertied classes were deeply disturbed over these trends. They were concerned with the growth of the intervention in the economy, the invasion of state and local prerogatives, the regulation of business and finance, the protection of labor and agriculture, the growing number of persons dependent on government insurance, health and welfare payments, the peace-time size of the military establishment, the growth of executive authority and initiative, and above all by the competition of public enterprises with business. They were appalled by a 1953 federal budget of $75 billion and a public debt of $266 billion, and by the continuing high rates of federal surtaxes on incomes and estates. In the words of James Wechsler, it was "The Age of Suspicion" and the growth of social legislation was equated with the fear of the spread of world communism. The extent of the hostility to this trend was expressed in such hyperbole as the demagogic phrase "twenty years of treason." Hoover II was created to arrest and reverse this trend, to cut big government down to size and to restore what many people considered to be "the American way-of-life" and what President Harding after World War I had simply designated as "a return to normalcy."

2. Terms of Reference

In Section 1 (Declaration of Policy), of the 1953 Act creating the second Hoover Commission,[1] the following terms of reference are enumerated. All the wording except that in italics is identical with the 1947 Act which had created Hoover I.[2]

It is hereby declared to be the policy of Congress to promote economy, efficiency, and improved service in the transaction of the public business in the departments, agencies, boards, commissions, offices, independent establishments, and instrumentalities of the executive branch of the government by—

(1) recommending methods and procedures for reducing expenditures to the lowest amount consistent with the efficient performance of essential services, activities, and functions;

(2) eliminating duplication and overlapping of services, activities, and functions;

(3) consolidating services, activities, and functions of a similar nature;

(4) abolishing services, activities, and functions not necessary to the efficient conduct of government;

(5) *eliminating nonessential services, functions, and activities which are competitive with private enterprise;*

(6) *defining responsibilities of officials;* (N.B. The language of the

1947 Act ended with "(5) defining and limiting executive functions, services, and activities.")
(7) *relocating agencies now responsible directly to the President in departments and other agencies.*

The crucial clauses of the 1953 Act (Ferguson-Brown bill) which gave Hoover II a clear mandate for inquiries far beyond those of its predecessor are of course paragraphs (5) and (6). These declarations left no doubt that it was intended to go much further than what is ordinarily thought of as "reorganization" and to launch a broad inquiry into major functions of governmental activity, with large policy implications. Item (7) seems to aim at shortening the span of control resulting from the number of agencies reporting directly to the President, and although vague and somewhat elliptical, was a bow to the theories expounded or assumed in the two predecessor reports.

There is, remarkably enough, some evidence that a broad construction of the 1947 statute creating the first Hoover Commission could also have provided a basis for so wide an inquiry. Its point 5 (supra) called for the commission to engage in "defining and limiting executive functions, services, and activities" which could have been construed as a mandate to examine questions of policy and function, and which was in fact stronger language than point 6 of the 1953 Act.[3] Indeed, in a policy statement adopted at a meeting of the commission, on October 20, 1947, it declared that it was not confined to recommending management or structural changes which improve the efficiency or performance of the executive branch, but [had been] "clearly directed to explore the boundaries of government functions in the light of their cost, their usefulness, their limitations, and their curtailment or elimination."[4] Professor Fesler has pointed out that President Truman's unexpected victory in the 1948 election may have caused a modification of this view, for on November 11, 1948, Chairman Hoover announced that the job of the commission was to make "every government activity that now exists work efficiently. I take it that major functions of the government are determinable as needed by the Congress."[5] To paraphrase Mr. Dooley's famous dictum, it would appear that a commission as well as a Supreme Court will follow the election returns.

The Senate and House committee reports recommending the 1953 statute, however, leave no room for doubt as to the purposes intended in the case of the second Hoover Commission. The report of the Senate Committee on Government Operations states, inter alia:

Although the proposed commission would be similar in composition to the earlier Commission on Organization of the Executive Branch of the Government . . . it would have added authority to study all activities of the federal government, and to make recommendations to the Congress and the President relative to changes in federal programs and policies.[6]

Similarly, the House Committee on Government Operations reported that:

The proposed commission would have the purposes and duties of the Committee on Organization of the Executive Branch of the Government established under Public Law 162, 80th Congress, . . . with some very important additions . . . .[7]

The committee reports, then, provided the major justification for Mr. Hoover's statement that:

The Ferguson-Brown bill looks to the reestablishment of such a commission . . . as that over which I presided from 1947 to 1950 with powers to investigate and recommend policies as well as administrative methods. That former commission was unable to report on policy questions.[8]

There were, then, important differences in approach between the two Hoover Commissions, particularly with respect to the second commission's conception of its role and to the intention of influential members of Congress. A review of the legislative history of the statute creating Hoover II indicates that the motive force behind the bill was supplied by congressional Republicans. President Eisenhower had, upon taking office, appointed the President's Advisory Committee on Government Organization consisting of Milton Eisenhower, Nelson A. Rockefeller (succeeded in 1958 by Don K. Price), and Arthur S. Flemming. This productive committee which lasted throughout President Eisenhower's two terms was in the process of submitting its initial reports when Congress began its consideration of the Ferguson-Brown bill. And while the administration raised no objection to the idea of a new Hoover Commission, it evidenced little enthusiasm for its creation and it was clear that Hoover II was conceived of as essentially a congressional commission.

At the same time, Congress was debating a bill to establish a Commission on Intergovernmental Relations to investigate invasions of federal power into the realm which was "the primary interest and obligation of the several states and the subdivisions thereof." As the hearings and debates took place simultaneously it is sometimes difficult to identify which measure senators were speaking to.[9]

Further, the chief advocates of a second Hoover Commission, Senator Homer Ferguson (Michigan) and Representative Clarence J. Brown (Ohio), were determined that Hoover II should serve the purposes of the conservative Republicans in Congress. Senator Ferguson, who had never suppressed his suspicion of and hostility to Democratic policies of the previous twenty years, noted that the declaration of policy in section one of the bill which he had introduced was intended to look at more than "reorganization";

> to make certain that this commission has full power to look into the activities of the federal government from the standpoint of policy and to inquire: Should the federal government be performing this activity or service and if so, to what extent? . . . The cost and size of our federal government can best be reduced by cutting down the things which the government does. . . . Reorganization cannot strike at the root of the problem of big government.[10]

Representative Brown made it equally clear that Hoover II would not suffer from the same restrictions which had hampered the first Hoover Commission:

> The thought behind the legislation Senator Ferguson and I have introduced has been not only to carry on the work of the Hoover Commission . . . but to go into certain fields that the Hoover Commission itself could not go into. In other words the Hoover Commission was limited . . . [it] did not have the power to recommend a complete elimination or abolishment of an activity. . . .[11]

It was clear, then, that Hoover II was in no sense a "neutral" commission. Rather, it was established on the firm premise that the federal government had grown far beyond any reasonable limits under President F. D. Roosevelt's New Deal and President Harry S. Truman's Fair Deal and that this growth would have to be reversed. If there was any doubt that Hoover II would confirm this belief, the membership and orientation of the new commission and even more so that of its "task forces" dispelled it.

3. Membership and Orientation

Not only were the terms of reference of the two Hoover Commissions different but there were marked differences in the character of their membership. Both were "mixed" commissions of twelve members, with four members appointed by the President, four by the president of the Senate, and four by the speaker of the House. Of the twelve members, six were from private life, two from the executive branch, two from the Senate, and two from the House. While the statute creating the first Hoover Commission specified that both major parties were to be represented equally, the second Hoover Commission had no such restriction, and of the members appointed seven were Republicans and five were Democrats. On this point, however, William R. Divine observed: "A review of the commission reports and dissenting opinions does not indicate that partisan politics has played a major role in the reports. For example, . . . in no instance does a report show a split along strictly party lines."[12]

The members of the second Hoover Commission were, on the whole, more conservative than their counterparts on the first commission. Roscoe Drummond, the experienced political commentator, in analyzing the membership of the second commission, noted that "The full membership of the commission has been completed and shows that Mr. Hoover will be assured of a commission membership warmly sympathetic to his views."[13] This was certainly the prevailing assumption at the time of the appointment of the commission. But as its work and that of its task forces proceeded, this characterization proved to be too dogmatic. Surprises were in store for the chairman, the Congress, and the press in the increasing number of independent views expressed by commissioners.

It is worth noting that the five carry-overs from the first commission—Hoover, Flemming, McClellan, Brown, and Kennedy—did not include its three leading dissenters, Dean Acheson (its vice chairman), James Rowe (Democrat), and James K. Pollock (Republican). Surely James A. Farley, New Deal postmaster general and chairman of the Democratic National Committee, who had turned against Roosevelt in 1940, and who had become head of the Coca-Cola Export Corporation, and Joseph P. Kennedy, Sr., multimillionaire and "founding father" and Roosevelt's chairman of the Securities and Exchange Commission and Ambassador to the Court of St. James, not to mention Senator John L. McClellan of Arkansas, the last two having been Democratic members of the first commission, might have been counted upon to go along quietly with the new terms of reference. But they were men of years of experience in dealing with questions of public policy and when the chips were down frequently found it impossible to support the reports of their private-business-oriented "task forces" and from time to time were supported by Republican members Arthur S. Flemming and Attorney General Herbert Brownell, and occasionally even by Chairman Hoover himself. But for the most part it was Representative Chet Holifield (California), the fifth Democratic member of Hoover II, who found himself the frequent and lone dissenter.

A much greater imbalance characterized the composition of the task forces and special committees of the second commission. Perhaps the Brownlow Committee erred on the side of appointing too many political scientists on its staff, and Hoover I had a good many of them in key positions, but Hoover II was practically uncontaminated in this respect. Out of 150 persons I can identify only 6 in this category. Its task forces were heavily weighted with representatives of business and the professions who could hardly have been called "disinterested" on problems so largely concerned with business and government.[14] The task force which presented the report on Water Resources and Power consisted in large part of industrialists, lawyers, accountants, and engineers who were identified with private utilities. The result was a report that was so hostile to public power and river control that the commission felt obliged, in making its own report, to modify the task force recommendations.

Fesler pointed out that the second commission often appeared to be confused about the role of its own task forces. In some reports it is not evident whether the recommendations are the commission's own or are merely endorsements or recommendations for consideration of task force reports.[15] Even where the commission makes this distinction clear, however, it often places itself in "the odd position of endorsing task force recommendations that are so detailed and specialized that the commission can only be expressing its blind faith in the task force's judgment."[16]

Moreover, the contrast between the preoccupation of the two Hoover Commissions is striking. The first commission was essentially concerned with providing the President and department heads with the authority, structure, and methods needed for effective administrative management accompanied by political accountability. Its recommendations reflected the necessity for clear-cut lines of authority, control, and assignment of functions in the executive branch. Very few of the recommendations of the second commission on the Organization of the Executive Branch ever got around to the topic implied in its name.

There were, thus, in terms of both membership and orientation, profound differences between the two Hoover Commissions. Moreover, these disparities magnified the contrast in their conception of their terms of reference. Their reports accordingly differ sharply both in respect to subject matter treated and to the nature of recommendations made. The first commission was interested in efficiency, economy, and responsibility by a reform of structure and method of the executive branch; the second commission, while even more concerned with economy, was preoccupied with the shrinkage of governmental functions ranging from the highest questions of public policy and function to minute questions of operational methods. It was dealing with what the *Wall Street Journal* called "a revolution in Washington's way of governing."

While the contrast with Hoover I is marked, the basic viewpoint of Hoover II, to limit governmental functions and to restrict and restrain the President, is completely opposite to the assumptions of the Brownlow Committee report as asserted in the following excerpt:

> Too close a view of the machinery must not cut off from sight the true purpose of efficient management. Economy is not the only objective .... ; the elimination of duplication and contradictory policies is not the only objective . . . ; a simple and symmetrical organization is not the only objective . . . ; higher salaries and better jobs are not the only objectives . . . ; better business methods and financial controls are not the only objectives. . . . There is but one grand purpose, namely, to make democracy work today in our National Government; that is, to make our Government an up-to-date, efficient, and effective instrument for carrying out the will of the nation.[17]

The end of reorganization for Hoover II was, according to the commission's report, "to recommend methods by which savings could be made in the expenditures of the executive branch without injury to the security or welfare of the country."[18] And, indeed, the reports of Hoover II were replete with estimates of the savings which would result from the implementation of their recommendations. The estimate of these annual savings ranged from $5 to $8 billion, but it was aware that not all would be realized. Nevertheless, the commission asserted the hazardous prophesy that "with all such discounts there are enough possible savings left to enable the balancing of the budget and reduction of taxes."[19] Even more extravagant claims as to economy and savings continued to be made by the Citizens Committee for the Hoover Report. Congress, the press, and the public evinced an astonishing gullibility concerning these claims for savings, in the face of the continuing rise in government expenditures, in budget deficits, and in increases of the public debt. The danger of such forecasts lies not only in the extreme difficulty of accurately allocating savings attributable to any single factor but in failing to take into account what new burdens may be placed on the budget by unforeseen demands arising from new national and international situations. One can fault Hoover II for venturing such rash predictions even if one cannot hold it responsible for the increase in expenditures as shown in the following table:

GROWTH OF UNIFIED FEDERAL BUDGET AND GROSS FEDERAL DEBT
(*billions of dollars*)
From *Federal Budget in Brief, 1971*

Fiscal Year or June 30	Incidence	Receipts	Outlays	Surplus+ Deficit−	Debt
1954	Report of Hoover II	69.7	70.9	−1.2	270.8
1962	Last full year of Eisenhower Budgets	99.7	106.8	−7.1	303.3
1970	Last full year of Johnson Budgets (est.)	199.4	197.9	+1.5	374.7

Even less plausible was the *Memorandum to the President* in 1958 which attempted to compute the percentage of implementation of the 497 recommendations of Hoover II.[20] It reported in all seriousness that 42.3 per cent of the recommendations had been accepted wholly (or with minor modifications) and that 34.8 per cent had been accepted partially (or as to basic objectives). The recommendations were neither identified nor grouped by categories. When one considers the wide disparity in the nature and importance of the many proposals, such "pseudometrics" cannot be taken seriously any more than an addition of random items ranging from peanuts to elephants. The use of such oversimplified "numbers games" in assessing the results of efforts at government reorganization has at least the one virtue that nobody can either prove or disprove the assertions.

4. Reorganization Aspects of Commission Report

The major portions of the reports were devoted to an examination of approximately 3,000 establishments in the government which were "competitive" with private enterprise. Most of these were military operations, such as post exchanges, commissaries, and the large military, sea, and air transport services. The commission recommended that these activities be curtailed or returned to private enterprise. President Eisenhower, a soldier's general, perceived the values of post exchanges and similar services to military morale and opposed their "privatization". Some of these services were, pursuant to Hoover II, transferred to "private and cooperative associations" exempt from Army controls and audits. Their management fell into the hands of a group of professional non-commissioned officers whose peculations, exposed in 1969, had assumed the proportions of an international scandal.

As for nonmilitary business activities—such as the postal savings system, the Tennessee Valley Authority fertilizer program, public generation and distribution of power, the lending, guaranteeing, deposit and mortgage insurance activities, farm credit and housing— the commission again challenged the necessity for many of these operations and recommended their curtailment or abolition, gradual devolution to private ownership, or at the very least their "mutualization" or incorporation. Only two activities, the services of which were no longer deemed necessary, were eventually liquidated: The Postal Savings System and the Reconstruction Finance Corporation.

Given the growth of governmental business-type activities, particularly in the military services during World War II, the need for an objective review and appraisal of such activities was apparent by the early 1950's, and many viewed the commission's inquiry as well suited to such an examination. Nevertheless, the commission's studies went far beyond this scope. Its call for elimination of so numerous and varied a range of permanent governmental services, many of which had come to be accepted even by the financial community, cast doubt upon the validity and objectivity of any single proposal, whatever its merits might have been. As Commissioner Holifield stated in one of his numerous dissents, ". . . the incidence of opportunity for private enterprise cannot be determined by adherence to some simple formula that government enterprise is inherently bad and private enterprise is inherently good."

In this brief treatment it is impossible to treat fully a report covering 20 different fields and making almost 500 recommendations, many of them of an operational nature.[21] There were, however, a number of important recommendations dealing with reorganization of the executive branch and with improvements in administrative management. I shall confine myself here largely to these aspects of the Hoover II reports.

In an extraordinarily brief (one page) treatment of agency control in its final report to the Congress, the commission recommended that 33 of the 64 agencies which it had studied be directed to report to *an official in the executive office who would be designated by the President.* The remaining 31 agencies in which he had "an unavoidable direct responsibility" would continue to report to the President. Unfortunately, the commission had no task force or staff report on this recommendation and did not reveal its criteria for deciding when the President had direct responsibility and when such responsibility could be delegated to an untitled official whose status would have had to be nothing less than that of an "assistant president" or "administrative vice president" of super cabinet rank. Since one of the tasks assigned to the second commission by Congress was "(7) relocating agencies now responsible directly to the President in departments and other agencies" it is hard to explain such a cavalier, curt, and imprecise last-minute treatment of this major and complex problem which radically affects the political and administrative structure at the apex of the executive branch. The Brownlow Committee had faced this problem head-on with its recommendation to relate every operating activity to 12 major departments of government each headed by a cabinet officer, and to provide the President with central services in regard to financial management, planning, and personnel administration. The first Hoover commission approached the problem differently but advocated a large measure of decentralization to departments and agencies of operational functions, once general policy had been determined at the center, and provided for a concentration of scattered government-wide business services. The greatest short-fall in the performance of the second commission was its failure to deal seriously with this, by all odds its most important, organization assignment.

In an effort directed toward the coordination of many conflicting and competing programs, the second commission suggested the creation of two bodies in the executive office of the President. First was a Federal Advisory Council of Health "comprised of members of the medical profession and distinguished laymen." The duties of this advisory council of part-time men from outside the government were to review medical policies and activities "to further coordination, eliminate duplication, and develop overall policies."[22] A Water Resources Board was to be transformed from the President's present Committee on Water Resources and The Interagency Committee on Water Resources. This board was to be created from among the cabinet members, together with five public members, presided over by a nongovernment chairman, and the public members were to be recruited from engineers, economists, and others of recognized abilities. The board's primary purpose would be "to determine the broad policies for recommendation to the President, and with his approval, to the Congress. It would have the further duty to devise methods of coordination of plans and actions of the agencies both at the Washington level and in the field. With the resources of the government agencies available for data, the board would require but little staff."[23]

Two questions might be raised about these two top-level recommendations in the field of governmental reorganization. The minor question is whether the commission was not really throwing its hands up in the case of these two complex fields and, instead of recommending new policies and a rearrangement of agency functions and structures, was simply passing the buck to two coordinating councils. But the more important question was whether these bodies, consisting of a large number of part-time outsiders, were intended to assist the President in the coordination of many scattered and conflicting programs, or whether they were really meant to surround the President in fields in which the commission believed there was an excess of governmental activity. Given the orientation of the commission and its task forces, it is hard to avoid the conclusion that the two recommendations were essentially devices to place the public business of water resource and health policy in private hands.

The commission's recommendations for the Water Resources Board were in sharp contrast to those of the Brownlow Committee, which advocated a national resources planning board. But they must be read in the light of many other comments and recommendations which were both dogmatic and controversial, sharply criticizing existing power policies and procedures. Commissioners Brownell and Flemming filed a statement of general dissent from this report, a critical separate statement was filed by Commissioner Farley, and Commissioner Holifield filed an 84-page separate statement and dissent in which he blasted the accuracy of the facts, the validity of the conclusions, and the soundness of the recommendations of the entire report.[24]

In an interview on June 29, 1955, Mr. Holifield charged that the commission had deliberately sought to play down dissenting views in its report, particularly by putting the dissents in a separate volume.[25] In fact, in the astonishingly frank separate statement by Chairman Hoover at the beginning of this volume, he unconsciously revealed his dim view of the competence of some of his fellow commissioners:

> The members of this commission are of course free to record their separate views which depart from the recommendations of the majority of the commission. However, in respect to the dissents recorded here, some of them ignore the fundamental purposes for which the commission was created and the directive which the commission received from the Congress. Some others indicate a misunderstanding of the recommendations or their implications.

Throughout the separate statements and dissents, the prevailing view was that in order to control and limit public power generation and distribution the commission was preventing the nation, through its government, from adequate action as to water resources for purposes of flood control, navigation, irrigation, water supply, and conservation. In a criticism echoed by many congressional Democrats and representatives of conservation and public power areas, Holifield declared that the commission's proposals were "carelessly thrown together" in an apparent attempt "to stop federal power development for the sake of private utilities." Other critics charged that the commission failed to do its job by neglecting to submit concrete proposals for streamlining the twenty-five or so federal agencies which deal with water resources.[26] And further, the commission's analysis was viewed as faulty:

> These reports will probably fail to be of help because they are not sufficiently broad in scope to settle policy controversies, and because they are too easily penetrated on a superficial level. This penetration appears likely to be based on a failure of the commission to establish facts; its inclination to jump to conclusions as a technique for arriving at basic premises; and its lack of clear analytical reasoning.[27]

STRENGTHENING MANAGERIAL AND ACCOUNTING FUNCTIONS
OF THE BUREAU OF THE BUDGET

Much more relevant to government organization, and much less controversial, were the recommendations of Hoover II that the Bureau of the Budget's managerial and budgetary functions be strengthened and expanded, particularly so far as they related to agency performance, and that the Bureau was to receive annual reports on the conduct of agency operations. It was also recommended that a staff office of accounting be established under the Director of the Budget with the responsibility, among others, of developing overall plans for accounting and reporting in the executive agencies; correspondingly, each agency and major agency subdivision was to set up a position of comptroller. The commission also proposed that all obligational authority arrangements be replaced by accrual and cost accounting methods in both the executive budget and in congressional appropriations.

Considerable improvement in governmental accounting had already been effected by means of informal cooperation between the Treasury Department, the Bureau of the Budget, and the General Accounting Office starting with the time in 1947 when James E. Webb was budget director and began taking lunch with O. Max Gardner, under secretary of the treasury, and with Lindsay Warren, the comptroller general. As all three men were friends from North Carolina, it became possible for the first time for these three agencies to talk to each other reasonably on accounting matters. The Budget and Accounting Procedures Act of 1950 was a direct result of these conversations and provided for a continuous effort known as the Joint Financial Management Improvement Program under the cooperative auspices of the three agencies which has resulted in effecting an important series of improvements in the general accounting of the government, in agency managerial accounts, and in auditing procedures.

The trend today is less in the direction of cost accounting in the business sense than towards new methods of program planning and performance budgeting systems which had been foreseen in Hoover I. In 1967 a special committee appointed by President Johnson made a strong proposal for accrual accounting as opposed to the obligational method—the government had already been moving in that direction. As of the time of writing, the indications are that the economists have prevailed over the cost accountants; but the appetite of the appropriations committees for program, planning, and budgeting systems and for accrual accounting has not yet been fully tested.

<h3 align="center">LEGAL SERVICES AND AN ADMINISTRATIVE COURT</h3>

In a thinly disguised attempt to curtail the power of certain regulatory and quasi-judicial agencies, and to remove them still further from executive influence, Hoover II recommended that an administrative court be established outside the executive branch to take over the adjudicatory functions of the National Labor Relations Board, The Tax Court, and a number of regulatory commissions and agencies. The court was to have three parts: (1) a tax section, (2) a trade section, and (3) a labor section, which would replace the National Labor Relations Board. The trade section was to have limited jurisdiction in trade regulation now vested in the Federal Trade Commission, the Interstate Commerce Commission, the Federal Communications Commission, the Civil Aeronautics Board, the Federal Reserve Board, the United States Tariff Commission, the Federal Power Commission, and the Departments of Interior and Agriculture. Hearing commissioners were to be completely independent of the agencies whose cases they investigate. Such an administrative court would have had a resemblance to the Conseil d'Etat, which has evolved as an able and useful institution under French law and administration; but its full application to the American system is almost inconceivable.

These recommendations called for a complete judicialization of these regulatory bodies in the interest of protecting the private undertakings that were regulated, and entirely overlooked the original national needs and abuses which had given rise to their creation. In calling for still further independence of these highly autonomous commissions, they were a move for a complete divorcement from presidential influence and control, the need for which the Brownlow Committee had emphasized and Hoover I had acknowledged. There was no apparent recognition of those functions of these bodies which are related to national development or the need for coordinated executive direction of both the communications and transportation systems of the country, for which latter purpose a Department of Transportation had to be created in 1967. Nor was there any attempt made to reconcile the inconsistencies between the proposed administrative court and the recommendations made in regard to "Reduction of Number of Agencies Reporting to the President."

Certain other proposals were contained in the commission's report on the subject of legal services and procedure, although several separate statements and dissents were filed and the commission transmitted proposals 29-48 to the Congress without recommendation as they were highly technical suggestions for amendment of the Administrative Procedures Act. A proposal calling for the centralization of legal services, including litigation, in the Department of Justice for all agencies would appear to run counter to the formula of the first Hoover Commission to decentralize authority to the departments and to strengthen managerial powers of their heads. A career corps for lawyers was probably one of the most constructive parts of this report even if it was not entirely convincing on the reasons why lawyers needed a system separate and apart from the regular civil service.

FOREIGN AID

In a report on overseas economic operations, the commission presented a dissent-filled brief in which several commissioners attacked the very concept of foreign aid. A number of the recommendations indicated a lack of understanding on the part of the commission of the purposes of foreign aid as an instrument of American foreign policy. In these policy areas the commission introduced a variety of specifics, some of them sensible and some in the nature of "hobbies." Hobbies and styles have plagued the foreign aid programs from the outset. Among these suggestions were the ones that all technical assistance to NATO countries be discontinued; that technical assistance projects in other areas be based upon joint local and United States funds; that, where repayment was not a real prospect, assistance be in the form of outright grants; that special emphasis be placed upon agricultural and irrigation projects; that with certain limited exceptions manufacturing plants be built in the "Asian-African" arc.

On the side of administrative reorganization, the major proposal called for further decentralization of foreign aid operations to the regular departments, such as Treasury, Agriculture, Interior, Labor, and Health, Education, and Welfare, leaving the International Cooperation Administration (the predecessor of AID) only some vague

duties of policy formulation of non-military aid, subject to the control
of the Secretary of State. Such dispersion ignored the painful administrative history of foreign aid, the necessity of relating it more closely
to foreign policy, the imperative need for the formulation of integrated country programs, and programs of a regional nature, all of
which tendencies were to take an entirely different direction under
President Kennedy's reorganization on regional and country lines of
the Agency for International Development in 1961. Dean Acheson,
one-time Secretary of State and vice chairman of Hoover I, on more
than one occasion has testified eloquently to the unsoundness of the
scatteration of foreign aid which Hoover II had proposed. It would,
indeed, be a step backward from the present emphasis on increased
participation and determination of priorities by the host countries in
planning their own needs for foreign loans, grants, and technical assistance.

BUSINESS ORGANIZATION OF THE DEPARTMENT OF DEFENSE

A major portion of the second commission study dealt with business operations in the Defense Department, such as procurement,
supply, storage, accounting, and general management. Many of the
studies on this subject were highly specialized and competent, and
indeed, Defense was the only department which received a systematic
and thorough examination. The emphasis throughout was on divesti-
ture of business operations and on modern business management and
methods under civilian heads of activities retained. In a determined
effort to insure civilian control, and to avoid going into the military
aspects, there was again a preoccupation with method and system,
often unrelated to major purpose, which characterized so many of
the Hoover II reports. The most difficult and still unsolved problem
of how to elicit and how to evaluate and utilize military advice on
military, naval, and aerospace hardware and weapon systems with
reasonable efficiency and economy in the procurement and maintenance of these costly items, was not tackled. But many of the steps
recommended were implemented and have led to considerable progress
toward a method of dealing with such questions. Constructive suggestions were made to improve the pay of scientific and professional
personnel and to make more effective the research work in Defense
and other departments.

The commission recommended that the Secretary of Defense create a new civilian position which would be responsible for planning and the review of military requirements. It proposed that assistant secretary positions for applications, engineering, properties and installations, and health and medical affairs be replaced by four management assistant secretaries with responsibility for logistics, research and development, personnel, and financial management. These slots at the Defense Department level would have their counterparts in each of three services, and these positions were to be primarily responsible for budgetary review and policy formulation. In addition, common supply and service activities were recommended, with their administration being placed in a new Defense Supply and Service Administration.

Subsequently, under the vigorous administration of Secretary Robert S. McNamara, the Department of Defense carried these trends considerably further and achieved a high degree of coordinated civilian control of research, development, and procurement of weapon systems. What had been, in the early days of "unification," a loose federation of military departments and services began to be a unified military establishment.

But the provisions of the Department of Defense Reorganization Act of 1958 (72 Stat. 514) which gave the Secretary of Defense increased authority to transfer, reassign, consolidate, and abolish functions can be only partially attributed to the recommendation of the second Hoover commission.

PERSONNEL AND CIVIL SERVICE

On the subjects of personnel and civil service, the second commission probably produced its most distinguished report. The task force on whose report the commission's recommendations were based was markedly different in its composition from most of the others. Headed by a university president and political scientist, Dr. Harold W. Dodds of Princeton, its membership included men who had been active students and practitioners of personnel administration in the public service, in foundation administration, and in large private business corporations. They were Frank W. Abrams, Chester I. Barnard, Lewis B. Cuyler, Devereux C. Josephs, Don G. Mitchell, General Willard S. Paul, Robert Ramspeck, William Hallam Tuck, and Professor Leonard D. White. Professor George A. Graham of Princeton University was its staff director.

The commission's report was mostly concerned with the problems of the high-level executives in the federal service, their responsibilities, their status and interchangeability, their compensation, opportunities for advancement, and their training. It recommended steps to increase the quality of the career services as well as of the officials in policy posts often referred to as temporary or "political executives."

Although never formally implemented, gradual steps have been taken to carry out the recommendation that Mr. Hoover said was the single most important one made by the commission. This called for the creation of a senior civil service, with rank in the man rather than in the post, and with opportunities for transfer and for interchangeability throughout the service.

Other major recommendations of the report called for salary increases in the top scientific, professional, and executive posts of the federal service, for both career and non-career officials, to attract and retain a higher grade of personnel. By the passing of successive salary acts and by the adoption, in principle, of a policy that salaries should have some relation to those paid in educational and business enterprises, these recommendations have had a considerable influence on governmental pay rates. The ridiculously low scales of the 1950's and before have been revised, the $20,000 barrier has been pierced for the career service, and the $30,000 barrier for cabinet and sub-cabinet officers and more recently for the "super grades." Furthermore, "fringe" benefits for the federal service have been steadily improved from the olden days although they still, at the executive echelons, lag behind those of competing occupations.

Perhaps the greatest progress has been made in the recommendation that each department foster the training and development of its personnel, largely as a result of the passage of the U.S. Government Employees Training Act of 1958.

A number of the recommendations have not been implemented, such as the one calling for simplification of the classification system and reducing the number of grades to six from the present G.S. 1–11 categories. Another suggestion was that rural letter carriers, U.S. marshals, and field officials of the Bureau of Customs and the United States Mints be appointed without political clearance. It has taken over ten years to begin to carry out this proposal in regard to the Bureau of Customs, and only small progress has been made in the other units. In regard to the difficult problem of conflict of interest, the Senate continues to tailor the ground rules to each high political nomination made by the President and it is just possible that this case law procedure is better than the adoption of a new statute that makes no sense. Revisions of conflict of interest orders and statutes governing other categories of positions have been enacted.

Perhaps the most controversial of the proposals was the one that career administrators should be relieved by non-career executives of responsibility for the advocacy or defense of policies. In this connection it was suggested that additional non-career executives should be added and that the schedules of positions exempted from the competitive civil service be revised. With the growth of the number of bureaus and administrations whose able chiefs had come up through the career service it is difficult to see how this policy could have been implemented. The congressional subcommittees expect to hear from the administrative chief who is expert in his calling and who knows what is going on. In the American system it is doubtful whether this immaculate separation of the civil service from policy advocacy can be maintained as it is for example in the British, although it must be admitted that it leads to some of the difficulties described in Chapter II.

This view of the role of the career civil servant drew a sharp criticism from Professor Wallace S. Sayre who called the report "unrealistic." He stated that, "The political executive who is all policy and politics, the career executive who is all competence and neutrality are not portraits from real life."[28] A similar view had been taken by me and G. Lyle Belsley earlier in an examination of the use of Schedule C:

> Most career officials deal in confidential matters of many kinds and participate in the policy-forming process when in the ordinary course of their duties they make recommendations to their superiors. Employees far down the administrative line are performing functions of this kind all the time; they should not be obliged to occupy excepted positions in order to do so. If policy determination is construed too inclusively, then this approach threatens to place beyond the reach of career workers too many of the positions of responsibility, interest, and importance which must be in the career service if it is to attract and hold competent personnel. In fact, the career service can be seriously stunted through such an approach.[39]

LENDING AGENCIES AND THE TREASURY

Another area in which the Hoover Commission was concerned with the competition between government and private enterprise was dealt with in its report on lending, guaranteeing, and insurance agencies. While acknowledging that the agencies involved in these activities had made significant contributions, the commission recommended that two important changes be made. It proposed that certain agencies, such as the Rural Electrification Administration and the Federal Housing Administration, be "mutualized" and recommended that the activities of certain agencies be made subject to the Government Corporation Control Act. The first recommendation in particular stirred up considerable controversy, with relatively strong dissents coming from Commissioners Brownell, Farley, Flemming, Kennedy, and Holifield.

An astonishing and frequently overlooked recommendation was the one numbered 47 (under Lending Agencies, Page 110):

> That a representative of the secretary of the Treasury sit ex-officio on all boards and commissions having the power to affect the fiscal policy of the United States. His major function when serving in this capacity would be to convey to such agencies the credit policy of the federal government.

This recommendation was as naively radical as it was imprecise. Did it mean to include the proposal that the Secretary of the Treasury should be put back on the Board of Governors of the Federal Reserve System from which he had, along with the comptroller of the currency, been ejected by the Banking Act of 1935? On what other boards would his representative sit? Does "credit policy" also mean "fiscal" or "monetary" policy and is this the only topic on which he could speak or would he be a first-class member of such boards with full right of voice and vote on all topics? Once more the commission, in its preoccupation with the details of operations, treated a major organizational proposal of considerable importance in a superficial and slipshod manner.

A number of devices were recommended by the commission to place the operations of revenue-producing agencies on a "business-like basis," to reveal and eliminate both direct and indirect subsidies, to charge them with interest at the going Treasury rate, and to compel them to pay taxes to local governments. They were no longer to be permitted to invest their working capital in interest-bearing government bonds. All these steps were designed to make their costs and their rates more comparable with those of private lending operations. Certain agencies were to be made self-supporting and autonomous as corporations subject to the provisions of the Government Corporation Control Act of 1945, which required a business type of accounting and auditing. In other cases they were to be "mutualized," by which is meant joint ownership by government and private interests with an eventual goal of becoming entirely privately owned. My own experience in the Farm Credit System made me sympathetic to this kind of participation in ownership and management, but here again Hoover II tended to overlook the broad public purposes which these instrumentalities were created to serve. The recommendations of the commission went so far that their complete adoption would have negatived such purposes and would have impaired the operations of their services which the commission found to its evident surprise had been conducted, in the main, with efficiency and integrity.

Finally, greater corporate autonomy deprives both Congress and the President of effective supervision and control of these agencies and the coordination of their activities with national policies.

5. Disappointing Results

While it must be acknowledged that Hoover II had a considerable influence on reforms of an operating nature, its larger effects were disappointing, particularly to its enthusiastic sponsors. Four general reasons for its shortcomings can be cited: (1) its terms of reference were too broad and ill defined; (2) its method of work caused it to concentrate on the details of business operations and to ignore the major purposes of governmental programs; (3) it failed to enlist the participation of the executive branch in its studies; and (4) the political timing for rendering its reports was miscalculated.

The second commission covered entirely too much ground in too many fields and had to rely on reports of its many business-oriented task forces and their subcommittees which were too numerous, voluminous, and detailed to permit of more than the most superficial consideration by the busy members of many task forces and particularly of the commission itself. Furthermore, it violated the pretty well established principle that in government and business enterprises involvement and participation from the outset of the chief executive officer and his staff are indispensable to the success of a reorganization exercise. Paradoxically enough, although it had received lip service support from the White House, the staff of the second commission and Chairman Hoover had less communication and rapport as time went on with Republican President Eisenhower, his White House staff, and executive office than there was under Democratic President Truman and his associates with Mr. Hoover as chairman of the first commission. The formalities of the White House staff under the ministrations of Governor Sherman Adams, the assistant to the President, tended to act more as an insulator of the President than as a conductor. This "apartheid" grew as the work of the second commission proceeded, and ex-President Hoover had increasing difficulty in making appointments to see President Eisenhower.

The political timing of Hoover II reports also was miscalculated. The commission's reports did not emerge until 1955 and were made not to the 83rd which had created it but to the 84th Congress which was considerably less receptive to its "philosophy," as was reported in an article entitled, "Hoover Policies: Commission has Stirred Congressional Wrath by Seeking Changes in Federal Programs."[30] The prognosis for the implementation of its findings was subsequently verified by events, even had its recommendations been less controversial on the policy level.

In at least one respect I must agree with the "philosophy" of the second commission, for I believe that large savings and reduction in expenditures cannot be achieved just by executive reorganization, and in fact are not its main objectives. Some economies can be effected by better organization, but they are impossible to measure and at best are small in size. Governmental expenditures can only be cut in large amounts by eliminating activities and functions, and when this is done just for the sake of economy the question still remains whether it has not injured the prosperity and well being of many segments of the population and regions of the country. Moreover, these are questions for the President and Congress to decide and cannot be delegated to an ad hoc commission.

In spite of objectives and methods which now seem dated, Hoover II raised important questions of policy and operation, many of which had been hastily improvised in times of war and depression, on which review, public debate, and reconsideration were not inappropriate. As a result of its labors, the Government of the United States was left stronger, not weaker, not only by reason of the recommendations it made which were carried out by the President and the Congress, but also as a result of the many, once the issues were re-raised, that were rejected and filed.

But in terms of the newer political economy even more basic questions must be raised as to the "philosophy" of Hoover II. If government activities in areas in which private enterprise had been unable to venture are compelled to pay all the charges of a private business, will they be able to continue and to provide electric power, mortgage lending, low rent housing, soil nutrition, and other services to regions and income levels previously deprived of them? Is the reduction of public expenditures regardless of their purposes and effect a good in itself? Perhaps the newer approaches in measuring the "input-output ratios" of governmental programs will give us a sounder basis for what should be continued and what abandoned, particularly in the case of such undertakings as large public works and procurement of costly military hardware.

The enthusiasm in conservative quarters for the second Hoover Commission must be understood in the light of a cumulative hostility to big government and the hopes of those who thought the opportunity had come at long last to revert to a former era of small government. Hoover I had, in their view, only grazed the surface, and Hoover II was expected to dig deeper in what they believed to be a rich vein of bureaucratic and socialistic waste and extravagance. In view of this background, the reports of the second Hoover Commission revealed a moderation which must have disappointed its progenitors.

Uneven and unbalanced though its final reports proved to be, this vast and microscopic examination of a myriad of public activities yielded considerable tangible value to the government and the country. Exaggerated claims have been made for these accomplishments, particularly by the Citizens Committee for the Hoover Report, and for the savings that could be effected; but even so the reports of Hoover II pointed out many wasteful practices left over from the improvisations during depression and war and even in the policy areas raised questions worthy of debate. Readers who may deplore my many omissions of the vast compass of governmental endeavor of Hoover II or who find my evaluations over-critical will find a useful corrective in the volume, *"The Hoover Report—1953–1955— What It Means to You as Citizen and Taxpayer,"* which is the most sympathetic and complete summary of the work of the commission.[31]

Chairman Hoover himself wrote the introduction and praised it because it presents the philosophic background enunciated by the commission which he characterized as being "indeed the background of our government and our way of life"; and because of its skillful reduction to 100,000 words of the 3,300,000 words in the documentation of the commission and its task forces.

The composition and method of work of Hoover II, nevertheless, calls into question the efficacy of a mixed part-time commission, with excessive terms of reference and largely autonomous task forces, to deal with such a profound range of problems. The remarkable fact emerges, moreover, that not a single major permanent program resulting from the years of depression, recovery, war, and reform was abolished as a result of this prodigious inquiry. The basic programs adopted in the last thirty years have been carried on and added to in the administrations of President Eisenhower and his successors.

6. Commission Members and Task Force Chairmen

I. Commission Members
  A. Appointed by the President (Dwight D. Eisenhower)
    1. Herbert Hoover, chairman (Republican)*
    2. James A. Farley, business executive and former Postmaster General (Democrat)
    3. Herbert Brownell, Attorney General (Republican)
    4. Arthur S. Flemming, director, Office of Defense Mobilization (Republican)*
  B. Appointed by the president of the Senate (Richard M. Nixon)
    1. Senator Homer Ferguson, Michigan, replaced by Senator Styles Bridges, New Hampshire, in 1955 (Both Republican)
    2. Senator John L. McClellan, Arkansas (Democrat)*
    3. Solomon C. Hollister, dean, Cornell University School of Civil Engineering (Republican)
    4. Robert G. Storey, president of the American Bar Association and dean of the Southern Methodist University Law School (Democrat)
  C. Appointed by the speaker of the House (Joseph M. Martin)
    1. Representative Clarence Brown, Ohio (Republican)*
    2. Representative Chet Holifield, California (Democrat)
    3. Joseph P. Kennedy, financier, former ambassador to Great Britain (Democrat)*

4. Sidney A. Mitchell, investment banker, executive director
   of the first Hoover Commission (Republican)* [served
   full time and acted as chairman's deputy]

   * Denotes members who served on the first Hoover Commission.

II. Task Force Chairmen
   Personnel and Civil Service: Harold W. Dodds, president of
      Princeton University
   Paperwork Management: Emmet J. Leahy, management consultant
   Federal Medical Services: Dr. Theodore G. Klumpp (replaced
      Chauncey McCormick, September 26, 1954), pharmaceutical
      executive
   Lending Agencies: Paul Grady, partner of Price Waterhouse and
      Company, accountants
   Transportation: Perry M. Shoemaker, president of Lackawanna
      Railroad
   Legal Services and Procedures: James Marsh Douglas, former
      chief justice, Supreme Court of Missouri
   Surplus Property: General Robert E. Wood, former chairman of
      Sears, Roebuck and Company
   Food and Clothing: Joseph P. Binns, managing director of the
      Waldorf-Astoria Hotel
   Business Enterprises: Charles R. Hook, chairman of the board,
      Armco Steel Corporation
   Depot Utilization: Clifford E. Hicks, president of New York
      Dock Company
   Research and Development: Marvin J. Kelly, president of Bell
      Telephone Laboratories
   Overseas Economic Operations: Henning W. Prentis, Jr., chairman
      of the board, Armstrong Cork Company
   Real Property: John R. Lotz, former chairman of the board,
      Stone and Webster Engineering Corporation
   Budget and Accounting: J. Harold Stewart, partner of Stewart,
      Watts, and Bolling, accountants
   Business Organization of the Department of Defense: Charles R.
      Hook (see Business Enterprises)
   Intelligence Activities: General Mark Clark, president, The Citadel
   Water Resources and Power: Admiral Ben Moreell, chairman,
      Jones and Laughlin Steel Corporation

Chapter VII

AGENCIES, FEDERALISM, AND CONGRESS

1. Reorganization Act of 1939

A STRANGE PARADOX OF AMERICAN GOVERNMENT IS SEEN IN THE SPEC-tacle of legislators chronically exhorting the administration to stream-line its policies and its operations, to consolidate and coordinate agencies by "major purpose," to eliminate "duplication and over-lapping," and to simplify the executive structure for the sake of "economy and efficiency." In fact, these vague exhortations are carried over into the language of every reorganization act. But when steps are taken to accomplish any of these fine purposes, members of Congress tend to run to cover, prefer to be "included out" on the roll call, and often oppose the action proposed. They are even more loath to initiate specific actions in this domain. They are in favor of reorganization in principle but are opposed to it in the specific case.

In spite of the early warning signals given us by Luther Gulick against "chartism" and the tendency "to place the chart before the horse," the chart continues to be equated in importance with the horse, judging by the footpounds of emotional energy generated by even the hint of a change.[1] A change as minor as the relocation in the hierarchy of a library can lead to an astonishingly heated con-troversy.[2] The symbolism of such transfers, combined with vague fears of loss of authority and prestige rather than concern for the actual effect on operations (which in the case of departmental libraries has produced some magnificent controversies) seems to be capable of arousing strong emotions in the minds of professional public

129

servants. To the outsider, this emotional output seems quite out of proportion to the importance of the change. But the insiders transmit their anxieties to their subcommittees and pressure groups, and the effect on interested congressmen seems to be paralyzing. Members of Congress are frank to state that the penalties from constituents and interest groups for espousing transfers and consolidations are often too heavy to be worth the political investment involved. When they advocate such a change it is likely to be of a kind that will upgrade a favored agency with the ardent support of interest groups or to downgrade an agency which has no such support. The latter situation has characterized the insecure parade of agencies which has administered the program of foreign aid. There seems to be a special form of resistance to putting new and emergency programs into one of the major departments of government even though there is a growing body of evidence that the support of a cabinet member would enhance its prestige. The pressures are usually for placing such activities directly under the President, either as an independent establishment or as a part of his executive office.

Congressmen have given tangible recognition to these facts of political life in two ways. They have delegated power to initiate reorganization plans to the President as indicated by the series of reorganization acts they have enacted beginning with the one in 1932. And they have referred reorganization bills to the Committees on Government Operations in the House and the Senate, which in itself is an indication of their awareness that reorganization problems had best be considered in a body presumed to have less agency loyalties than the substantive committees.[3]

The powerful chairmen of substantive committees exhibit a chronic form of allergy to structural change. The transfer of a bureau may deprive a committee of jurisdiction over it and the jurisdictional sensitivities of committees of Congress are at least as intense as are those of the agencies of the executive branch. Time and again the agricultural committees have shown their strong opposition to the transfer of the Forest Service from the Department of Agriculture to the Department of the Interior or to a proposed Department of Conservation, although strong rational arguments can be made for having all agencies with functions primarily concerning the custody and conservation of public lands in the same department. In spite of the contention of the U.S. Forest Service that it has a conservation rather than a recreation mission as well as responsibility for fostering good forestry practices on private lands, it is difficult for the outdoor bound citizen to understand why adjoining national parks and forests have separate sets of rangers or why "Smoky the Bear" protects trees in national forests but dares not roam in a national park.

Congressional committees express their jurisdictional predilections in a number of other ways. These may take the form of specific exemption of a favored agency, such as the Army Corps of Engineers, from the terms of a reorganization bill. Or they may take the form of turning down a reorganization plan until special immunities are granted to a protected bureau. The exemption of the Office of the Comptroller of the Currency from the plan which proposed to put all the bureaus of the Treasury Department under the supervision of its secretary was a case in point.[4] In that instance, the American Bankers Association strongly opposed the subordination of the Office of the Comptroller of the Currency (which no longer controls any currency but which regulates and examines national banks) to the "political influence" of the secretary, and by implication, of the President. The ablest program administrators are the most protective and contumacious. They are prone to suspect that the motivations of the temporary and inexperienced political officers and the pressures upon them are a threat to the purposes and integrities of their hard won, long term programs. But if political officers take pains to win their respect and loyalty, the professionals can become invaluable allies in implementing new policies.

In the light of these resistances, the passage of the reorganization bills in different forms by both houses in 1937, then their reintroduction in the Senate as an omnibus bill and passage there, only to be defeated in the House in April 1938 by the narrow margin of 204 to 196, remains one of the legislative marvels of President F. D. Roosevelt's second term.[5] This was the Executive Reorganization Bill which emerged as a result of the report of the President's Committee on Administrative Management and which had been strongly endorsed by the President in his special message of January 12, 1937.[6] It was the most comprehensive administrative management and executive reorganization reform proposal in our history. In fact, its sweeping nature would have prevented its consideration at any other time, for in one measure it pinched every sensitive nerve in the bureaus, raised the jurisdictional hackles of committees of Congress, and outraged each major organized lobby.

Although the President disarmingly admitted his own guilt in creating too many independent agencies during his first term, which former Governor Alfred E. Smith of New York had castigated as "The New Deal's Alphabet Soup," he took a long view of the dangers of proliferation. He warned the Committee on Administrative Management that during the next century fifty or more independent commissions might be established, resulting in a complete splinterization of the executive branch.

President Roosevelt was fully aware of the resistances he would encounter in the Congress to his reorganization proposals. He had told the committee that the year 1937 might be the only time in a century that such sweeping reforms could be enacted, right after the extraordinary Democratic victory in the 1936 elections. He had refused to consider the committee's findings during the heat of the election campaign; but, when he received them in mid-November of 1936, he accepted a surprisingly large part of them. His subsequent tactics indicate that by January 1937 he had decided that only a surprise assault and a kind of shock treatment could win the approval of Congress, a technique he invoked only in exceptional cases.

While the report was being hammered out, Louis Brownlow had frequently cited an old Austrian proverb, "Soup is not eaten as hot as it is cooked," and the committee had expected the President to cool it off much more than he did. All concerned were aware that it would be a scalding potion for congressional palates.

Only two days before it was sent as a message to Congress, on Sunday afternoon, January 10, 1937, the President invited the majority leaders of the House and Senate, members of the committee (Louis Brownlow, chairman, Charles E. Merriam, and Luther Gulick), and certain staff members to meet with him for a preview of its contents.[7]

Immediately after attending the meeting, I prepared an extended note in my dairy of its extraordinary proceedings during which the President himself, not the members of the committee, expounded the theory and proposals of the report and administered the shock treatment. Louis Brownlow, whose years in journalism had made him an exacting editor, wrote me that the note was both accurate and complete. He later referred to it several times in his autobiography.[8] My diary notes were usually terse, but I wrote this one out at length because I had a hunch that this meeting might prove to be of historic importance in the annals of federal executive organization and administrative management. It is more revealing of President Roosevelt's blitz tactics and of congressional stunned reactions than anything I could say today. I, therefore, venture to include it in this volume precisely as I wrote it thirty-three years ago. (Appendix I: *Meeting of the President and his Committee on Administrative Management with the Majority Leaders of the House and Senate at the White House, Sunday, January 10, 1937.*)

The defeat in the House of the Reorganization Bill of 1938[9] can largely be ascribed to the storm aroused by the President's proposal for enlarging the Supreme Court, pejoratively referred to as "the court packing bill."[10] On February 5, 1937, I noted in my diary "evening papers announce President's message on Supreme Court and the judiciary. A pretty sweeping issue has now been raised. What will it do to the reorganization plan?", and again on February 20 "President's judiciary proposals have taken the front stage." The court bill was made to order to arouse conservative forces of the country, supported by a good deal of the American press, to make an all-out attempt to undo the national mandate of the 1936 election. They saw their chance to raise the cry of "dictatorship" as a convenient cover for their resentment to the reform and recovery legislation of the Roosevelt first term, some of which a conservative court had struck down. The very powerful interests which had demanded vigorous federal action and executive initiative in 1933, when, as a result of the great depression they were panic-stricken, had now become alarmed by such action and initiative and at the same time were emboldened by their own survival and recovery. Before the court message was sent up, the reorganization proposals had had a fairly favorable reception by the press. But thereafter the cry of "dictatorship" was extended to the reorganization measure as well, and fell on anxiously receptive ears in view of the prevailing anxiety concerning the escalating power and aggression of Hitler in Europe, not to speak of the continuing dictatorships of Franco, Mussolini, and Stalin.

The Reorganization Bill of 1938 could only by a paranoid stretch of the imagination have been equated with dictatorship. In a low keyed reply to such allegations, the President said he had not the slightest wish to have dictatorial powers bestowed upon him. The measure, while sweeping and an abrupt departure from long encrusted habit patterns, today seems more technical than revolutionary. Many of its provisions have been adopted over the years. The opponents to it were the "economic royalists" who later wildly cheered the first and second Hoover Commission reports because they were told that their acceptance would restrict the sphere of government and would reduce taxes, failing to perceive that in many respects they were but sequels to the Brownlow Committee report. The two Hoover Commission reports reinforced this illusion by rigorously suppressing any reference whatsoever to the report of the President's Committee on Administrative Management, although Hoover I was heavily influenced by its findings and a microscopic inspection of Hoover II discloses some of its fingerprints. The most charitable interpretation of this tabu that I can find is that the two Hoover Commissions did not want to arouse the opposition of the sleeping knights errant that had gone forth to slay the dragon of Brownlowism.

The story of the unprecedented mobilization of pressure groups against the reorganization proposals of 1937 is now available in Professor Pollenberg's lively book.[11] He describes dramatically how the preoccupation of Congress with debates on the court bill played into the hands of opponents of reorganization by providing the necessary time to get mobilized. He shows how this delay prolonged consideration of reorganization issues into 1938, by which time Roosevelt's popularity and prestige had taken one of its periodic nosedives as a result of economic recession at home and the growing rumbles of a war in Europe, after Hitler's Austrian *Anschluss* in March. Furthermore, the reorganization proposals were necessarily technical, not generally understood, and had no support from an organized lobby of their own. And Roosevelt steadfastly refused to promise immense savings as a result of reorganization. His self-denying ordinance in respect to savings should be contrasted with the reckless claims made in this regard by the two Hoover Commissions and the even less inhibited promises of the Citizens Committee for the Hoover Report.

In retrospect it may be said that the Reorganization Bill of 1938 was too broad in its scope and too precise in its terms. In spite of all the hullaballoo the bill had created, the Reorganization Act of 1939, which was both more limited and vaguer, passed by large majorities with little opposition.[12] It did not reorganize anything but gave the President the authority to initiate reorganization plans, subject to a sixty-day legislative veto which will be discussed later. It thus allayed congressional anxieties and resistances. Its passage converted the immediate 1938 defeat into a victory over the long term and laid the basis for the extraordinary series of administrative management reforms of the last thirty years. It made possible the creation of the executive office of the President. It provided the tools for flexible and successful administration of World War II. Most important of all it opened the way for continuing initiative on the part of the President to adjust the structure of the executive branch of the government to the ever-changing needs of the nation.

2. New Departments and Agencies

Structural reorganization in the executive branch since 1945 has responded more to the special requirements of the vast new functions and programs that have accrued to it than to any rational organization pattern. In spite of its resistances to transfers and consolidations of existing agencies, Congress seems willing and able, when convinced of their necessity, to create new ones—which is a paradoxical exception to the paradox I have been describing. Although there are now twelve major cabinet departments, they do not correspond to the twelve recommended by the Brownlow Committee, nor has its recommendation to place all executive functions under twelve departments been carried out. However, the general principle asserted in its report, which had support of both Hoover Commissions, to reduce the number of agencies reporting directly to the President, has influenced the formation of large new departmental conglomerates. The tendency toward fractionalization of new agencies persists, however. When a new need arises, programs are devised which focus on single objectives, and new agencies tend to be created within or without departments with narrow missions which frequently impinge on those of existing ones. The problems of inter- and intra-departmental coordination are thus compounded and often transcend the power of the President and his departmental heads to cope with adequately. Citizens, local authorities, and other potential beneficiaries of federal largesse are left paralyzed by the mounting array of programs and the complex variety of procedures.

The official chart of the government of the United States in the *U.S. Government Organization Manual for 1969–1970* lists twelve executive departments and thirty-three independent offices and establishments. (See Appendix II, Exhibit D.) The independent agencies vary greatly in respect to their relations to the chief executive, and a simple line chart cannot give a true picture of this complex array of symbioses. The chart also lists thirteen separate groups in the executive office of the President which will be discussed in Chapter VIII. Those who put their trust in the necromancy of chartism should not be misled that there are thus fifty-eight agencies actually reporting to the President although forty-three are enough even if one excepts those that are borderline cases in a mystical "fourth branch." Hoover II claimed there were sixty-six in 1954 and there may be more now depending on who does the counting. Even the theorists who assert that the latter-day criticism has completely demolished the "span of control" theory would admit that such a reach would exceed one's grasp. It is probably fortunate that most of these units respond to "the law of the situation rather than to final authority," as Mary P. Follett long ago discovered was the case in regard to organizational units in industry.[13]

As to the thirty-three independent agencies and establishments, the structure and powers of fifteen of them make them no more than second cousins once removed of the executive branch. Eleven are commissions in the regulatory and appellate fields. After the President has appointed their members, usually for overlapping fixed terms, he has little influence and less legal authority over their decisions. As a result of experience and the recommendations of Hoover I, the President has in a number of cases been authorized to designate the chairman of these bodies, who sometimes is named to act as their chief administrative officer. The presidential power of their removal, however, is circumscribed by legislation and court decisions. Four agencies in the field of banking and credit are quite autonomous and even outside budgetary control, for their administrative expenses are paid out of assessments on the member banks they regulate—the Board of Governors of the Federal Reserve System, Farm Credit Administration, Federal Home Loan Bank Board, and Federal Deposit Insurance Corporation. Although the other independent agencies are more typical executive establishments, ten of them are governed by boards or commissions, an agency structure that has always presented special problems to a president, of which not the least is whom to deal with. When asked by a congressional committee whether he needed a board to help build the Panama Canal, General G. W. Goethals, its chief engineer, is said to have replied that he did not as "it was well known that boards are long, narrow, and wooden." Many of the new agencies have boards and advisory commissions made up of persons of undoubted professional competence but representing the points of view and specializations of the interest groups that advocated their creation. These built-in centrifugal forces tend further to defeat efforts at inter-program coordination. In any event, the President deals with a single head in twelve departments and eight independent agencies.

The size and complexity of the federal executive structure have reached unprecedented dimensions. The unified federal budget, including trust funds, has increased from $92 billion in 1960 to an originally estimated amount of $195 billion for 1970. In fiscal years 1959 and 1968, the deficit alone exceeded the total of the much criticized outlays in the pre-war years of the New Deal. However, there has been a remarkably constant ratio between federal outlays and gross national product ranging from 19.6 per cent in 1959 to 20.6 per cent in 1969. Because so many of the federal programs are operated by others through grants-in-aid and contracts, the number of full-time federal civilian employees has not been markedly increased and has remained near two and one-half million for some time.

In order to depict their functions and structure, and to register my comments on the new departments and agencies that have been created since 1945, many of them from previously existing components, I have prepared Appendix II: *Federal Offices, Departments, and Independent Agencies Established Since 1945.* My classification omits most of the units of the executive office of the President which are treated subsequently, and does not attempt to describe previously existing departments and agencies, some of whose internal structures and powers have changed markedly as a result of reorganization plans and legislation.

Appendix II also omits agencies classified in the U.S. Government Manual as legislative agencies; that is, the Architect of the Capitol (known to his critics as the "non-architect"), the Comptroller General of the U.S. and his General Accounting Office (which is not the bookkeeper of the government but the respected auditor and investigator, and settler of its transactions, a function which still seems to some of us as executive in nature and incompatible with those of an independent auditor), the Government Printing Office (one of the world's largest publishers), the little United States Botanic Garden, as well as the magisterial Library of Congress.

These agency comments further illustrate the persistent centrifugal forces for autonomy in spite of the growing influence of continuing executive analysis and initiative in molding the structure and organization of the executive branch to respond to new needs of the nation since the passage of the Reorganization Act of 1939.

3. Cooperative Federalism

The profound causes for resistance to structural reorganization may be found in the institutional roadblocks we have erected, which, in turn, were influenced by our history, our laws, our way of doing things, and our general attitude toward government. The literature of political science is replete with various writings which have depicted some of the difficulties we have invented in the way we govern ourselves.[14] The tendency of congressmen to resist structural change is only the woof of the fabric. The warp consists of the threads of constitutional structure and governmental behavior patterns which Americans have fashioned over the years. The basic thread is pragmatic, the ad hoc approach resembling our attitude to mending the barn, the reaper, the motor truck, or the radar. The focus is on the part rather than the whole, the particular rather than the general, the immediate rather than the long term. Our ideologies are expressed in slogans, and we are preoccupied with gadgetry and nostrums. In spite of our increasing tendency to look to government to do things, we hesitate to give it the needed clear-cut authority and means to do them effectively. We neglect hard-core national problems for years; and then, when confronted with crises occasioned by this neglect, we over-react with crash programs, which raise impossible expectations of. immediate results. We are a nation of specialists powerfully organized by specialties, and our political decisions are often a compromise of their competing pressures. We find it hard to arrive at a consensus in the general interest, and this is demonstrated in our political behavior and reflected in the specialized aspects of our administrative structures and operating systems.

The centrifugal forces in a large, far-flung, and disparate society have served to perpetuate many of the less viable characteristics of the design of the founding fathers for a government of limited functions in a simpler age. These are particularly evident in the system of government of divided and shared powers. Professor Barry G. Karl makes this succinct comment on the origin of the system of checks and balances in the Constitutional Convention of 1787:

> Ambiguities in the location of the power to organize the executive departments were the result of what seems to have been a deliberate intent of the framers of the constitution. . . . In some ways the strength of the

new government lay in the fears it sought to allay rather than in the
positive benefits it strove to confer. These were men more experienced
in the definitions of tyranny than in the explanations of the "blessings of
liberty." Executives could become tyrants; legislatures could become
mobs. Either way protection was required.[15]

Certainly, the men of 1787 could not have been expected to foresee
the transformation that has occurred in a federation, with limited
and enumerated powers in the central government, all the other
powers being reserved to the sovereign states. The infinitely complex
kaleidoscope of federal-state-local relationships that has evolved since
the federation became a national government has been picturesquely
compared to a "marble cake" by Professor Morton Grodzins.[16] Our
political structure continues in a formal sense to rest on geography,
but it actually responds more and more to national needs and to
occupational forces. The continuing political influence of the states
can be attributed to such arrangements as the system, now under
review, of presidential elections by state electoral college votes, the
state-based structure and election of Congress, the strength of state
political parties, and the political prestige of governors and senators.
In the initiation and sponsoring of new programs to solve national
problems, the states are yielding constantly to the federal government.
Only recently a group of governors advocated the complete turnover
of the increasingly costly welfare program, as to both administration
and financing, to Uncle Sam. The theory of a federal government
of limited and enumerated powers has been forsaken. It is difficult
today to identify a field of activity in which the federal government
is unable to intervene, directly or indirectly, if only the procedural
amenities are preserved. This has come about as a result of legislative,
executive, and judicial initiatives, and these in turn have responded
to vast changes in society and technology. Instant communications
are available now not only on the continent but with every American
outpost in the world. The airplane has cut travel time from Washington
to San Francisco down to a matter of hours, whereas it was a matter
of weeks by stagecoach from Philadelphia to New York, Boston, or
Washington when the republic was founded.
Larger, as well as smaller, areas of government are required in a
highly technology-interdependent economy. The thirty-seven carto-
graphic states admitted since the thirteen charter members created
the union are in many cases unsuitable geographic units for modern
administration. To meet these problems we have improvised an over-

lay of federal administrative regions. Federal-state regional boards
are springing up. The governors tend to meet in regional conferences.
The 81,248 local authorities with taxing and borrowing powers are
even less suited to play their essential roles in modern administration.
They are generally too small to discharge effectively the services of
metropolitan areas and too large to make possible the growing demand
of the citizen for participation and a sense of belonging to a' community on a human scale. Metropolitan and neighborhood tiers of government seem to be indicated as needs of the future. As of 1967, the
local governments listed in the Official Statistical Abstract of the
United States for 1969 were:

Counties	3,049
Municipalities	18,048
Townships	17,105
Special Districts	21,264
School Districts	21,782
Total	81,248

The burden that the system of cooperative federalism has placed
on the states and localities in the past twenty years is staggering.
No consideration of structural reorganization at the federal level can
be relevant or complete today if it does not consider the state and
local dimension. A large number of the federal programs are not
direct operations at all, but are indirect and depend on loans and
grants-in-aid to enlist the operating facilities of states and localities.
The escalation of the part played by state and local agencies in
national programs is illustrated by these excerpts from the U.S. Budget
in Brief for Fiscal Year 1970:

> In keeping with our federal system, state and local governments have
> played a significant role in providing essential social programs. In recent
> years they have administered more than two-thirds of total governmental
> spending for domestic civilian purposes and financed more than half of
> these programs from their own resources. . . . Federal aid to state and
> local governments is expected to triple in the course of the current decade
> —rising from $7 billion in 1960 to $25 billion in 1970.

The Budget in Brief for Fiscal Year 1968 reported that the same
trends are evident for government employment and, while federal
civilian employment would increase 22 per cent from 1958 to 1968,
state and local governments would find it necessary to increase employment by more than 70 per cent.

The main roadblocks to cooperative federalism are found in the excessive number of discrete federal programs and agencies, the ensuing financial strains on the state and local governments, their problems of recruiting and training adequate personnel, and the need for strengthening, state and local governmental structures to meet new tasks.

Extended congressional hearings have been held and certain steps have already been taken to alleviate some of the burdens on state and local governments in the administration of "creative federalism" as President Lyndon B. Johnson called it in his Ann Arbor speech in 1964. His proposal for a Public Service Education Bill for increasing the number of students choosing government careers and his Intergovernmental Manpower Bill for training and upgrading state and local governmental employees were not enacted. The Intergovernmental Cooperation Act of 1968 (PL 90-577) sponsored by Senator Edmund S. Muskie (Maine) passed. It aimed at simplification of federal-grants-in-aid practices and at improving communications on federal programs between the federal, state, and local levels. On April 30, 1969, President Nixon urged the enactment of a Grant Consolidation Bill to give the President power to initiate consolidation of closely related federal assistance programs under the jurisdiction of a single agency. Either house of Congress would have the right to veto a proposed consolidation within sixty days, by means of the legislative veto process.

The problems of federal executive reorganization have been further complicated by the significant administrative invention of forms of delegation by contractual relationships, between government and business and between government and the world of higher education and science and research. These relationships have produced astonishing technical marvels such as the practical obliteration of malaria and poliomyelitis, the civilian uses of atomic energy, the communications satellite, and the moon landing. But the full benefits of this powerful extension of government by contract have been hampered by the extremely fractured and subdivided nature of the federal organization itself, the division of its functions in minute compartments, and the baffling problems that this presents for the government, the contracting companies, and the university and research world.

In the complex maze of the new cooperative federalism we tend to use ineffective methods of administrative "coordination" to solve problems which are actually ones of policy and legislation. Paul H.

Appleby called our attention to the fact that administrative decisions could not be delegated until general policy had been decided at the top.[17] To take his argument one step further, administrative organization cannot be devised until clear decisions have been taken on what is to be done, at what levels and areas of government, and how it is to be financed. Until these matters are more precisely defined, cooperative federalism will not give us viable programs for the solution of urgent problems of welfare and poverty, race relations, housing and urbanism, education, health, the conservation of the environment, nor even satisfactory progress in scientific research and technology. A simplification of the federal catalogue of over 400 separate programs of grants-in-aid to states and localities is an essential first step.

The long term trend is undoubtedly to look to the federal government to initiate, to finance, and to oversee large national programs to protect and extend human rights, to secure a greater measure of economic, social and political justice and opportunity, to conserve and develop the human and physical resource environment. Increasingly, the federal government is also looked to as the regulator of the excessive ups and downs of the business cycle, and of the value of the dollar, as the guarantor of a full measure of employment, as the balancer of wide discrepancies in private incomes, and as the stimulator of needed services in the private and local sectors. The states are decreasingly looked to as the centers of leadership and innovation in the solution of great national domestic problems, but their tasks of executing these programs have been increasing geometrically.

The trend toward universalizing the leadership role of the national government, with a large measure of state and local and private implementation, has greatly augmented the factors to be considered in deciding questions of federal administrative management and executive reorganization. Governmental reorganization proposals from now on will have to be more informed as to the process of implementation and the burdens to be placed on its chosen instruments.

With all the weaknesses of the federal smorgasbord of over 400 narrowly targeted programs, the conditional grant-in-aid technique has demonstrated positive values that should not be hastily discarded. It has improved the quality, competence, and integrity of state and local administration. We should think twice before we begin to shovel out large hunks of money from a phantom surplus in the federal treasury, as Professor Anderson has pointed out, by means of what is known as "revenue sharing."[18] We still have broad avenues of improvement to choose from before we open up a channel of funds to states and localities with greatly unequal tax systems of their own, which will be practically impossible to limit either in amount, in regard to the relevance of their expenditure to national goals, or to their manner of administration. We have not even begun to press for the reduction of the number of discrete programs nor for a system of more flexible grants such as the one which is already being tried in the field of public health.

Many policy questions of cooperative federalism are still undecided. The federal government has to make up its mind which grants are to go to the states, or when they should go directly to local authorities or to community organizations. It must define more clearly the conditions of minimum compliance with the purposes and conditions of a grant and under what circumstances money should be withheld. To what extent will professionals at the federal level continue to deal only with their counterparts at state and local levels, bypassing political officers such as governors and mayors and presenting them with a predetermined program and budget? These are some of the difficult and frustrating problems facing the future of cooperative federalism. Research and experimentation would seem to offer a firmer basis for their solution than by replacing the time tested method of conditional grants-in-aid with the unexplored and possibly uncontrollable device known as revenue sharing.

4. Congress and Administration

More baffling than the question of federal-state-local-private relationships is the unsolved problem of congressional intervention in the field of administration. The endless tug-of-war between the executive and legislative branches of our government is the constant factor in American politics rather than the fluctuating shadow boxing of the two loosely federated major parties. Given the weakness of the national party organizations and the lack of party discipline in both houses, the alignment on legislative policy shifts constantly, issue by issue, and measure by measure. Very few countries try to govern when the head of government and the majority of the legislature are from different parties. A skillful president may fare as well, and indeed sometimes better, on his legislative program when the opposition is in power. Even with unprecedented majorities in both houses, as Roosevelt had in 1937, he cannot automatically count on their support. No better illustrations could be given than the ones cited above on the defeat of his initial proposals for court reform and executive reorganization. The passage of the Twenty-Second Amendment, limiting the president to two terms, has brought about a progressive decline of his influence in Congress during his second term.

The practice of congressional intervention in the field of administration, even on the occasions when it has had some useful results, might be called a system of shared irresponsibility. Its historical and constitutional origins were based on a chronic distrust of government, and particularly of centralized government administered by professionals in a career system, frequently referred to as a "bureaucracy." I have paid my respects elsewhere to the imprecise and pejorative use of the term "bureaucracy."[19] Nor do I consider the term "politician" a naughty word. The derogatory charge these terms convey in common writing and parlance is indicative of this widespread mistrust.

In the nineteenth century, the devices used to guard against the dangers of an unresponsive officialdom were those of rotation in office, and the patronage system at all levels. At the state and local levels the long ballot was a device to let the citizen vote on many minor offices for fixed terms of service. It ended up by giving him so many choices that he could only vote a straight party ticket of many names nominated by the political machine. The price of these early devices was of course machine-dominated politics, boss rule, incompetence and corruption in office; but even more destructive of responsible democratic government was the loss of control of their executive establishments by mayors, governors, and president. This system led to reform movements for direct primaries, the short ballot, and civil service. Unfortunately, the long ballot still persists in many places even as we approach the twenty-first century. Fortunately, it never plagued us at the federal level.

Our contemporary way of checking on and insuring the responsiveness of the permanent career officials is to put them under the supervision of political officers. The formal way of doing it is to interpose a political undersecretary or assistant secretary between the department head and the career administrator. Most other advanced countries permit the permanent secretary of the department, a career man, to report directly to the minister. But the informal way, which tends to be both arbitrary and anonymous, is the scrutiny and control of officers of the executive branch exercised by powerful members of Congress. The effect is to erect diffused centers of irresponsible power; for, if the legislator's directive is followed and anything goes wrong, the executive official takes the rap. The directives of the powerful members of Congress may be responsive to unidentified pressures from constituents, campaign contributors, or organized lobbies. They may also spring from the fixed notions of a congressman as to how things should be run. In any event, there is no assurance to the administrator that these directives have the support of the committee, other committees, the whole house, the leaders of the party, or, least of all, the Congress as a whole.

The chairmen of congressional committees and subcommittees have well-known vantage points of power and influence to exert the most minute supervision of administration. They are elected to their posts by the seniority system. Their long tenure is achieved frequently by reelection in one-party constituencies. The unopposed congressman is not necessarily the best one. Court decisions on apportionment and the spread of the two-party system have begun to modify this system of the survival of the unfittest, but both parties still cling to the seniority rule. Congress, although it seems unable to control the age at which members continue to stand for reelection, might well bar speakers, chairmen, floor leaders, etc., from reelection to those positions after they reach the age of 65, as many universities, business enterprises, and other agencies have begun to do in regard to executive positions. These legislators will still be able to serve with dignity, and hopefully with wisdom, as members of the Congress, and of its committees.

A demoralizing ethical dilemma is faced by high officials of the executive branch when they are subjected to strong importunities of powerful committee chairmen on whose support for authorizations and for appropriations entire programs may depend. Agency heads must be specially wary of requests from freewheeling congressional staff personnel who may or may not be speaking for their senator or congressman. In my experience, all members of Congress raise questions and transmit requests but the majority of them conscientiously refrain from putting undue pressure on executive agencies, in the face of unrelenting pressures on them from their own constituents.

Congressional investigations have often played a constructive role leading to an improvement of policy formulation, organization, methods, and the uncovering of flagrant conditions of inefficiency and malfeasance. One thinks of the Teapot Dome investigations of the 1920's, the useful investigations of the Truman Committee during World War II, and the hearings in the 1950's on the Internal Revenue Service as examples of important and constructive inquiries by congressional committees. The competent studies in the 1960's, under the chairmanship of Senator Henry M. Jackson (Washington) of the Subcommittee on National Security and International Operations of the Senate Committee on Government Operations, have produced a series of distinguished state papers on problems of high importance. But congressional investigations also on occasion can do irreparable harm and cause great injustice to individuals and agencies as in the case of the communist witch hunts conducted by Senator Joseph R. McCarthy (Wisconsin) in the 1950's. Investigations are most helpful when they are conducted on a high level of fairness addressed to correcting a reform of policies, institutions, and practices rather than with a view of playing the role of the avenging angel or of the prosecuting attorney. The legislative branch can perform an essential democratic function in these reviews, but it is no more suited to discharge the judicial role than the executive one.

In his able and inclusive coverage of the many devices by which senators and congressmen impose their wills on administrative officials, Professor Joseph P. Harris treats not only the informal and personal pressures but the formal ones resulting from legislation. In many fields, including those of government printing, public works, and real property transactions, Congress has enacted legislation requiring agencies to obtain prior approval from committees and subcommittees, or "come into agreement" with them, before taking an executive decision. President after president has vetoed such measures as an unconstitutional invasion of the executive authority but some of these laws managed to get on the statute books and still remain there.[20]

5. *Minority Vetoes, Riders, and Budgetary Inaction*

Vetoes which have become parts of our unwritten constitution, by which a single senator or congressman or a small minority can prevent floor action on urgent measures, are well known. The power of an individual senator to block an appointment from his state by invoking the rule euphoniously known as "senatorial courtesy," the right of a minority to kill a measure by use of unlimited debate quaintly called a "filibuster" conducted by a few determined and durable senators, the authority of the Rules Committee of the House of Representatives to pigeon-hole a measure are all familiar techniques of this minority veto power. The power of the purse is used by the Appropriations Committees to amend substantive legislation by means of attaching "riders" to urgent appropriation bills which congress dare not defeat nor the president veto lest the government stop altogether. Friendly foreign countries have often been outraged and delicate diplomatic negotiations thwarted by non-germane riders and reservations attached to appropriation bills on which neither the Senate Committee on Foreign Relations nor the House Committee on Foreign Affairs have been consulted, and which may be anathema to them. The power of "item veto" on budget measures, which many of the states have granted their governors, has yet to be accorded to the President of the United States.

An irresponsible habit of delay in the enactment of money bills has grown up in recent years. Many appropriations do not pass until almost one-half of the fiscal year has elapsed so that there is no firm budget on the basis of which agencies can confidently go forward and the president is prevented from discharging his duty to see that the laws are faithfully executed. More recently, Congress has taken to procrastination on revenue bills as well. In 1968, it refused to pass the ten per cent income surtax, to abate inflation, recommended by President Lyndon B. Johnson until he undertook to reduce expenditures by five to eight billion dollars, thus evading the constitutional duty of Congress to review and revise appropriation requests. This tactic was supported by the "conservatives" but the "liberals" in turn delayed action in 1969 on continuing the surtax recommended by President Richard M. Nixon until they received assurances that tax reform would be enacted. In a special message to Congress in October 1969, President Nixon urgently requested action on the large backlog of eleven out of thirteen appropriation bills that had not been passed for the fiscal year 1970 which had begun July first. Further delay in these enactments would impair the President's ability to prepare the 1971 budget.

The result of procrastination on money bills is not only that executive agencies find it impossible to plan and execute their work efficiently, but that thousands of private and local decisions cannot be made; for they depend on precise and timely determination of governmental spending and revenue policies. Business enterprises, educational institutions, research centers, states, localities, international agencies, and even foreign governments are thus paralyzed in their decision-making processes. The lives and fortunes of millions of people are affected by these delays. The implementation of major programs is unconscionably impeded and their costs are increased immeasurably. Budgetary inaction by Congress has become almost as serious a threat to orderly and efficient administrative management of the government as irresponsible intervention.

In the United Kingdom, since Gladstone's time, the budget, both as to revenue and expenditure, has been regarded as a vote of confidence in the House of Commons and is voted upon as a whole. In this country serious consideration is being given to making the fiscal year coincide with the calendar year in order to give Congress more time to consider the president's budget. American industry has become aware of the critical importance of "lead time" in vast and complex operations. It is even more important that the organs of American government become aware of the decisive time factor on which not only effective administration depends but which can make or break the huge range of national and international plans and programs dependent on the resources of the world's most affluent power. We could well heed the Moslem proverb: "He gives twice who gives promptly." If Congress itself cannot find a way to remedy this situation, and in spite of its growing fears of executive encroachment, I believe there will be an increasing demand for legislation that the president's budget shall become effective, both as to revenue and expenditure, at the beginning of the fiscal year, unless Congress has amended it by that time.

The job of a congressman has long since become a full-time one, but this fact has been tardily accepted. It has just recently been acknowledged by the steep but justified increase in congressional salaries enacted early in 1969. The constitution contemplated that membership in the House or Senate would be an avocation, that the member would serve part-time during two annual sessions and that the bulk of his activity would be at home in his own business or profession. Salaries and benefits were fixed accordingly, as most of his income would be derived from his normal occupation; and salaries remained pitifully low long after this assumption had ceased to be valid. Meanwhile the costs of his election campaigns have risen greatly. The actuarial risk to his family's security of reestablishing himself at home, in the event of not being returned after separation from his previous profession, have increased greatly. In the not infrequent instances in which he continues his connection with a law firm, clients will be attracted by his influence rather than by the firm's legal acumen. His energies are thus diverted from legislative duties and statesmanship to the sordid and humiliating business of departmental shopping, and his public positions become suspect when they appear to support the interests of his clients. A code of congressional ethics might give useful guidelines in situations of this kind, but a new and sanitary method of financing political campaigns needs to be adopted and the term of a member of the House of Representatives needs to be lengthened so that he does not have to face extortionate campaign costs every two years.

In the first century of the Republic, conflicts of interest were assumed to be part of a normal way of life for legislators. They still are at the state and local levels. Madison in Federalist 10 seems to have foreseen this possibility but evidently believed that the conflicts would cancel each other out. The full-time nature of the job today has profoundly changed the situation. Congressmen often maintain only a token base in the home town to keep in touch with constituencies and from which to launch reelection campaigns, but this also costs money and obligations are incurred to support it. A full-time, well-paid legislature with generous staff assistance, handsome office space, and funding for travel and communications is another unique characteristic of the government of the United States, but these privileges call for the adoption of a code of self-denying ordinances. Congressmen have been giving thorough attention to the behavior and ethical standards of the executive and judicial branches, but still have to reassess profoundly their own behavior patterns under present conditions.

The fact that members of Congress spend most of their time in Washington is both relevant and significant to a study of administrative management. It gives them the time and staff facilities to probe deeply into the details of executive business. No study has yet been made of the powerful centralizing effect on the executive structure of this phenomenon. Nor has any cost-benefit accounting been done on the enormous sums expended by each department and agency to support the large apparatus needed to respond to congressional inquiries and requests, including such items as staff time, files, records, and communications costs. If Congress should undertake studies of this kind, the activities of the staff employees of Congress and the adoption of a code of conduct for these servants of the legislature should not be omitted. The staffs of the permanent committees are usually of high calibre, and the performance of the Legislative Reference Service of the Library of Congress has been exceptionally expert and scrupulous; but the cases of irresponsibility and venality among the increasing army of congressional janissaries present an acute problem in the management of the executive branch and a threat to the reputation and probity of their legislative masters.

What are the causes for the extent of congressional intervention in administration and has it any benefits? At least three aspects of these questions may be identified. First, is the highly specialized nature and complexity of the numerous federal programs. Individuals, states, local authorities, research institutions, interest groups, and businesses are at a loss to know their entitlements. The larger ones can afford to maintain outposts in Washington to inform them and to negotiate for them. For the many that cannot, their natural recourse is to their congressman or senator. He plays the role not only of a clearing house of government information, but of a counterweight to the overspecialized roles and missions of the executive agencies.

A second aspect results from the imprecise nature of modern legislation. This has caused an increase of rule-making powers and delegation by legislatures throughout the world. The imprecision may arise from compromises made in the process of enacting controversial measures in such fields as civil rights and school integration, or by reason of extremely technical content as in the case of the scientific programs. Great areas of discretion are left to the administration and its advisors, and every federal agency is "quasi-legislative." The modern headquarters administrator, among other attributes, must have what I have called "the statutory mind."[21] He should be skilled in the drafting of general rules and policies and procedures to define general and imprecise legislation, for otherwise he cannot delegate its application to individual cases to the members of his staff and to his regional officers. This rule-making process is a perilous business in a country which is so large and in whose localities such varied conditions and attitudes prevail. Often the administration, in order to make the laws operative, must be more precise than Congress was when it compromised and glossed over controversial questions in order to get legislation passed. The administrator's perils are increased by the fact that Congress itself is not a coordinated body. A substantive committee often has an entirely different view in such a field as foreign affairs from an appropriations committee. The application of the general rules to specific cases, particularly on large projects for urban renewal and soil conservation, enters the realm of what Professor Robert J. Morgan has identified as "negotiated administration."[22] Precise national regulations can hardly ever anticipate all the problems that will arise when applied to a specific case or locality. Two or more agencies may differ on the proper solution as in the case of running a highway through a national park or forest, the relation of a soil conservation project to a river valley program, or the location of an urban redevelopment project. In such situations communities will resort to their congressman, who will inevitably be drawn into the negotiation and the decision-making process. At times, a fair and intelligent congressman contributes to the making of sensible decisions suitable to the locality and frequently helps in obtaining local understanding and consent. The congressman thus becomes a kind of coordinator or "ombudsman" before the fact.

The third cause is the growing practice of permitting legislators, usually senators, to announce local grants. Often the senator has never heard of the project, and sometimes he voted against the law which authorized it. The late minority leader of the Senate, Everett McKinley Dirksen, had the theory that, once the law had been passed and an administrative decision made, the senators may as well get the credit from their constituents. This growing custom, which at first glance looks innocuous, has the inevitable result of enhancing the view that it is Congress where the "goodies" come from, and encouraging communities, institutions, and contractors to look to Congress for more of the same, thus fostering further legislative intervention in administration. The entire vast program of loans, grants, contracts, and public works is thus given the flavor of favoritism and the aroma of the pork barrel even when the recipient has only received an award to which he is entitled under fair laws and honest administration.

The foregoing recital of instances of congressional intervention in administrative matters is not to be construed as a plea for unlimited executive power, either to an overburdened President, the temporary appointed political heads of varying ability, or to the usually competent but overspecialized professional career officials. The present great national debate in regard to foreign policy and the dangers of becoming involved in undeclared wars of escalating magnitude have again forcefully dramatized the importance of congressional review of matters of high policy. The contemporary dilemma of our governmental system is the problem of reconciling the need for instant executive action in an atomic, space-vehicular age, with the requirements of deliberation and consultation in undertaking critical national commitments.[23] The highly technical nature of domestic as well as foreign decisions and administration is making us more and more dependent on the specialists and technicians. Another knotty problem is presented in the national security field—the reconciliation of the need for secrecy with the democratic processes of disclosure, a problem which the Administrative Procedures Act of 1966 has not yet solved.

It is evident that, even if most innovative national policies and programs continue to proceed from the President, Congress will have to be given a better opportunity to get the facts in time and must organize itself to review more effectively large issues of national policy, devote more time to such debates and less time to monitoring the details of administrative operations. Nor can the innovative influences of decisions of the judicial branch be overlooked in such fields as reapportionment of legislatures and of school desegregation, in which prickly thickets the judges have entered ahead of the other two branches.

In taking their decisions, administrative officials must be prepared today to provide increased opportunities for hearing the views of citizens and minority groups, in order to respond to the growing demand for citizen participation. But the element of timing cannot be overlooked and decisions cannot be indefinitely delayed under pressure from local activists conducting a minority citizen filibuster. The modern administrator must have not only great patience and capacity to listen, but must also have the ability to invoke executive cloture and come to a decision for action when its need and soundness have been established and before appropriations expire. The continuation of a state of things in which there is a way to block necessary and desired action and to impede the expressed will of the majority by tactics of obstruction emanating from irresponsible centers of power, wherever located, cannot be reconciled with a responsible system of representative government any more than it can provide an effective system of administrative management in our world-power service state.

To conclude this chapter on an optimistic note, it is encouraging to observe that pressure for greater coordination of federal programs has begun to emerge from the bottom up. Executive agencies and Congress are beginning to be aware that the compartmentalized federal programs determine not only what states and cities do, but gravely affect their administrative and political structure. Splinterization at the federal level has fostered splinterization at the local levels for sixty years, starting with the rural and agricultural programs and finally reaching the city slums. Direct lines have been built from specialist to specialist, up and down the federal-state-local gamut, and numerous *ad hoc* authorities, special districts, local boards, and voluntary associations have been invented to receive largesse from other levels. Politically responsible general government been by-passed and weakened and has had little to say about priorities in fields in which state and federal grants-in-aid were made. Responsible general citizen participation has been distorted by isolating it within special interest groups rather than applying it to the whole body politic. The insistence, particularly of the organized mayors and cities of the country, that the general government at the local level be strengthened, not torn apart, may turn out to be one of the most powerful forces so far to emerge in respect to coordination of federal programs. The "Model Cities Program," even if its substantive achievements are small, may prove to be a powerful lever for rationalizing the federal universe.[24]

Chapter VIII

EXECUTIVE REORGANIZATION
AND THE LEGISLATIVE VETO

1. Purposes of Executive Reorganization

THE MAGIC WORD "ECONOMY" IS NEVER OMITTED FROM THE MAJOR purposes of reorganization acts even when the possibilities of savings seem remote. It should continue to be included but not as the main goal. The economy objective has now been sensibly qualified and the legislation has added other objectives. Section 901 of the Reorganization Act now in force recites the following purposes (Appendix III):

(1) To promote the better execution of the laws, the more effective management of the executive branch, and of its agencies and functions, and the expeditious performance of the public business;
(2) to reduce expenditures and promote economy to the fullest extent consistent with the efficient operation of the government;
(3) to group, coordinate, and consolidate agencies of the government, as nearly as may be, according to major purposes;
(4) to reduce the number of agencies by consolidating those having similar functions under a single head, and to abolish such agencies, or functions thereof, as may not be necessary for the efficient conduct of the government; and
(5) to eliminate overlapping and duplication of effort.

These legislative purposes also serve as the standards established by Congress as a basis for its delegation to the President of the authority to initiate reorganization plans.

The more precise and realistic purposes of executive reorganization cannot be given statutory sanction but are implicit in the highly generalized and formal ones. In my view, they could be stated somewhat as follows:

UP- OR DOWNGRADING OF THE STATUS OF AN AGENCY

There is a close correlation of the policy orientation of a post (and of its incumbent) with its hierarchical altitude. An important element of program leadership is the ability to articulate a broad philosophy of purpose and method for an agency. Rufus E. Miles, Jr., now at Princeton University and for many years the able administrative assistant secretary of the Department of Health, Education, and Welfare, permits me to cite "Miles' Law" which asserts: "It depends on where you sit, how you stand." There are conspicuous differences in policy perspective when viewed by a regional man, a bureau chief, a head of an administration, a department head, a staff man in the Executive Office of the President, or by the President himself. There are also professional preoccupations which may slant the perspective as in the case of the lawyer, the economist, the doctor, the physicist, the engineer, or the accountant. It cannot be assumed, however, that all high level executives have the capacity to benefit by the panorama afforded by their elevation in the ladder of authority.[1]

Up- or downgrading can take place for a variety of reasons. Occasionally an agency is elevated because its head has the eminence and authority to warrant it, and sometimes it is demoted because of his limitations, but these personal causes tend to be rare. More frequently, escalation or descent results from a change in the emphasis to be given to a discrete activity in the light of crisis, pressure, or changing duties. When the Children's Bureau was transmuted from a small research and publications activity to a grant-in-aid agency dispensing great sums, its functions became inextricably intertwined with those of the general family welfare program and were subordinated to it. The creation of the Department of Defense and the growth of the authority of the secretary of Defense and of the chairman of the Joint Chiefs of Staff were essentially responsive to the change in the nature of modern warfare and the imperative need for coordinated strategy, operations, and logistics, as well as to a widespread doubt as to the wisdom of leaving major decisions to military professionals of a single service.

Agencies are also upgraded when the administration wants to symbolize at home or abroad that it considers its mission of outstanding importance. The cases of the Office of Economic Opportunity and of the United States Arms Control and Disarmament Agency illustrate the point. When an agency commands less political support, it may be subordinated for good or bad reasons. The public housing program which was begun in 1937 as an independent authority is now at the third level of the hierarchy of the Department of Housing and Urban Development and, as "public housing" seems to be a tabu word, it has been renamed "housing assistance." There were many valid reasons for placing the harassed Agency for International Development in the Department of State and there may be valid reasons for now splitting it up once more and incorporating it, but one doubts whether in either move these are the real reasons. Some agencies have a privileged status because of their vague subordination to another agency, and one wonders whether the Central Intelligence Agency actually reports to the National Security Council as required by law and by chart, or whether it reports to anybody at all.

Direct access to the President on the part of the head of an agency is the highest symbol of agency status. It may only be presumed access in view of the scores of claimants competing for presidential attention. An added immunity of direct access is the fact that a President cannot exert day-by-day supervision of an independent agency as a department head is in a position to do. Even so, freedom from departmental supervision is not quite so glamorous as it once was. Many sophisticated administrative officers perceive advantages in the political support of a powerful department head and are not eager to be in business for themselves.[2]

Upgrading glamorizes a top post and gives the President the opportunity to recruit a man of distinction to fill it. Autonomy yields certain dividends in the form of status symbols and fringe benefits. Among these are direct contacts with leaders of Congress, top officials of the Executive Office, department and agency heads, ambassadors, United Nations agencies, and the press. The autonomous agency chief enjoys a high protocol priority at official functions. His office and motor car provisions may be more elegant. He may be permitted first class air travel. Higher salaries and entitlements also accrue to members of his immediate staff. On the other hand, the importance of these perquisites can be exaggerated, and some agencies enjoy rare privileges and immunities without formal autonomy. A number of them have achieved immense prestige, popularity, immunity, and autonomy within a departmental framework. Examples of elite services of this kind, with a special professional system of rank, are the Foreign Service, the Army Corps of Engineers, and the Federal Bureau of Investigation.

COORDINATION OF PROGRAMS

Autonomous status or location in the Executive Office is considered to be a vantage point from which to exercise coordination among related programs. The Office of Economic Opportunity and the U.S. Arms Control and Disarmament Agency have coordinating missions. It is clear by now that their coordinating powers atrophy to the extent that they assume large operating functions and they begin competing for authority and funds with the outfits they are expected to coordinate. This dualism has been a factor in eroding the coordinating role of O.E.O.[3]

Coordination at the departmental level is often effected by merging a number of single-purpose bureaus having related functions under an administrator, or by giving an assistant secretary a group of related bureaus to supervise. Certainly a general tendency may be discerned in the last third of this century to spare the department heads the continuing burden of day-by-day operational coordination by delegating the supervision of a group of bureaus to an administrator. The sheer size of many of the great departments is demanding an increasing use of this device. One of the unsolved problems of its use, however, is to prevent the complete insulation of the top political echelon from major policy problems that are milling about below. Another is the introduction of one more layer in the hierarchical structure.

Various suggestions have been made by eminent authorities for more interdepartmental coordination by super cabinet officers or assistants to the President in the executive office, a topic which will be discussed later. No matter how perfect an organizational structure is contrived, there will be an increase of closely related activities which need a bridge of some kind to prevent cancelling each other out and to make more bearable the lot of the citizen, state, city, or institution that is seeking clarification and decisions in programs having an inter-agency character.

Other devices for coordination also have certain merits. Departments and agencies often work out informal, but effective, voluntary relations to this end without the need for presidential sanctions. There is a new device called the "convenor" role, in which a department head, an under secretary, or even an assistant secretary is given the right to "convene" high level counterparts in affected agencies on a given topic. In the field of foreign policy such authority was granted to officers of the State Department during the Kennedy and Johnson administrations on a formula recommended by General Maxwell D. Taylor. There is a marked tendency in President Nixon's administration to shift the "convenor" role in these matters to the National Security Council and to the assistant to the President for National Security Affairs, Dr. Henry A. Kissinger.[4]

Coordination at the field level has also been approached in a number of ways. President Kennedy's letter of May 1961 to Chiefs of Missions overseas was intended to give the ambassador coordination of all United States programs in the country to which he was assigned. The move to place the headquarters of regional offices of certain federal agencies in the same city, and if possible in one building, is intended to induce coordination by propinquity.

Coordination is too often regarded as a negative or adjudicatory function as a way of untangling inter-agency disputes and inconsistencies after they have become critical. Its preventive or positive aspects are of greater importance if they can avoid the adoption of conflicting policies and procedures before the complaints and letters to Congress come pouring in. The most extreme and authoritative coordination device is actually to place related agencies under an administrative head, but in interdepartmental affairs this is not possible unless a transfer of an activity is found to be feasible.

TRANSFER OF PROGRAMS

The placing of an activity in a more propitious home by transfer is an important purpose of reorganization action. The professional orientations of the United States Public Health Service lacked the conservation and engineering drive for attacking the increasingly urgent problems of water pollution. A better professional setting for these activities was provided in two steps: first, by the creation in the Department of Health, Education, and Welfare of the Federal Water Pollution Control Administration which received these functions from the United States Public Health Service; second, by the transfer to the Department of Interior of the Federal Water Pollution Administration from H.E.W., by Reorganization Plan 2 of February 28, 1966, following the passage of the Water Quality Act of 1965 (79 Stat. 903). The actual purposes as well as the effects of transfer are often obscure. Was the transfer of certain functions to the Civil Rights Division of the Department of Justice to improve the enforcement of court decisions or was it to abate the energetic steps in such matters as school integration that were being taken by the Department of Health, Education, and Welfare? The wholesale transfer of many units from Commerce to the new Department of Transportation reduced the scope of Commerce to small proportions and this situation calls for more profound consideration of its future than was given in President Johnson's hastily conceived project to recombine it with Labor. Professional "apartheid" can be a barrier to intradepartmental integration. Special difficulties exist in the military departments on the relations between the uniformed services and the civilian officials. The Wriston Committee Report did not entirely break down the separatism in the Department of State between members of the Foreign Service and of the Civil Service.[5]

BIRTH AND DEATH OF AGENCIES

When is the time for a new department or agency to be delivered and when has the time arrived for euthanasia of an already dormant one? When does a department become too large or too small? How many departments should there be? Cannot all the independent non-regulatory agencies be placed under major departments? When should a department be evaluated primarily from the standpoint of its operating effectiveness? When should its coordinating ability have the higher priority? I am not nearly so certain of the answers to these questions as I was three decades ago, but surely they must be asked whenever the overall departmental structure is amended or reexamined.

Rufus E. Miles, Jr., makes a good case for a separate Department of Education, while former Secretary John W. Gardner has strong arguments that education should remain in the Department of Health, Education, and Welfare.[6] When financial agencies are ready to be terminated, as in the case of the Reconstruction Finance Corporation, the Treasury Department frequently can liquidate their assets.

A program must be thoroughly accepted to win departmental status, and its components must have some plausible relationship to begin with. No matter how diverse the components, they must form a visible image when combined or related, so that a department head can be chosen who can identify with them and in turn be identified as their spokesman by the public, the press, and by Congress. "Major purpose" is today an imprecise denominator. For years, members of Congress who hoped the welfare programs were only temporary measures resisted the creation of a permanent department containing that name, and it must have surprised even President Eisenhower himself when in 1953 he won approval for his plan to create the Department of H.E.W.[7] The report of the Brownlow Committee did not foresee the necessity for combining the War and Navy Departments; if World War II had not demonstrated the overriding need for joint commands, the Department of Defense would not have been created.

The lugubrious function of "bureaucide" is not one that Congress relishes, and abolition of an activity is a special responsibility of top administrative management under the reorganization plan device. Interdepartmental committees respond to a special law of inertia and tend to carry on after the purpose of their creation has been achieved or even forgotten. With rare exceptions, they should be non-statutory, ad hoc in nature, and with a terminal date provided in their birth certificates. If still needed, they can always be given an extension of term. When abolition of an agency or function is contemplated, the prevailing doctrine of consultation or "maximum feasible participation" on the part of the intended victim is not particularly useful.[8] In a rhetoric which was unquestionably that of Luther Gulick, the Brownlow Committee opined: "There is among governmental agencies great need for a coroner to pronounce them dead, and for an undertaker to dispose of the remains." One might add that there is also the need for an obstetrician to bring new ones into the world, and for a clinic to keep the birthrate down. New autonomous agencies should not be created and, as soon as may be, most of the present ones of an executive nature should be placed in existing or future departments.

OVERCOMING CONGRESSIONAL ROADBLOCKS

This purpose is generally recognized now by members of Congress and was undoubtedly an impelling motive of Congressman Lindsay Warren when he drafted the Reorganization Act of 1939. Congressional hearings confirm the fact that there are many routine reorganizations that Congress would not identify nor ever get around to and which require executive initiative. But there are many major ones, urgently required, which a majority of Congress favors but was never given the opportunity to enact because of the built-in legislative roadblocks.

A classic example of jumping over the barricades may be found in the case of the government of the District of Columbia. Year after year, the House District Committee had blocked legislation to abolish the unrepresentative, obsolete, and sometimes venal three-man Board of Commissioners and to replace it with an elected mayor and council, although there was an increasing demand among citizens and congressmen for such a change in the direction of home rule. President Johnson's Reorganization Plan 3, effective November 3, 1967, which reads like a city charter, and which separates the executive and legislative functions of the government of the nation's capital, was, in my view, one of the most brilliant uses of the executive reorganization power so far invoked.

The three commissioners were replaced by a commissioner who is popularly called "the Mayor," an assistant to the commissioner, known as "the Deputy Mayor," and a nine-member council which is bipartisan, all appointed by the President and confirmed by the Senate. The House Committee on Government Operations (not the District Committee) had endorsed the measure by a vote of 26 to 4. The House itself struck down a resolution disapproving the reorganization plan by a vote of 244 to 116 and the Senate did not object, so it became law. There is still no elected city council, but with the popular first step taken by plan, it will not be too long before a further step, sanctioned by statute, can be taken.[9] In an ecstatic editorial headed HALLELUJAH! the *Washington Post* of August 10, 1967, bluntly identified the principal roadblock:

> Congressman McMillan (S.C.) (chairman of the House District Committee for over twenty years) understood how important yesterday's decision was. He told the House with a disarming candor that acceptance

of the President's plan would put a serious crimp in the perquisites of members, would make it much more difficult to treat the District as occupied territory. He recognized, too, that the local government, even though not elected, would become more responsive to its constituents, and less subservient to the District Committee.

2. *Effects of Reorganization by Plan and Statute*

A major effect of giving the President the authority to submit reorganization plans to Congress has been to stimulate reorganization by statutory procedure. As a result of this combination of reorganization by plan and by statute, there is today a much greater frequency of adjustment of structure to changing needs and priorities. Reorganization has become the continuing process that is needed in an era not only marked by incessant change, but in one in which the rate of change itself is accelerating.

In fact, more reorganizations are being effected by statute than by plan. A count made by the Legislative Reference Service of the Library of Congress lists 157 statutory reorganizations from 1945 to 1962 as opposed to 52 approvals of presidential plans.[10] Much of this legislation had, in fact, been recommended by presidents. This increased activity on the part of Congress is in part due to the enhanced interest in governmental structure aroused by the studies of the Brownlow Committee and of the two Hoover Commissions. In part, it can be ascribed to the desire of Congress to forestall presidential plans in a form they cannot predict, which they fear they would not like, and which they know they cannot amend. On the other hand, congressional vetos have at times caused presidents to resubmit plans in amended form which have then been approved. On at least two occasions, reorganizations of the housing agencies were disapproved until a name for the new agency could be found that Congress and the affected interests would accept.

As a result of reorganization plans and legislation, the ability of the President to initiate changes has greatly increased in spite of the ease with which either House can now veto such proposals. I am convinced that the intrenched nature of bureaus and administrations, which in the past has so often made them immune to presidential or secretarial authority or policy, has been broken through and that this has measurably enhanced the ability of the accountable political officers to manage their executive functions. An examination of reorganizations of the last ten years reveals that a great many of them were actually enacted neither by plan nor by statute, but by means of departmental orders based on authority delegated to department heads.

The greatest number of reorganization plans was presented after the passage of the Reorganization Act of 1949 (Appendix III), designed to put into effect the recommendations of Hoover I. The report of the Senate Committee of Government Operations on that measure tabulates the year-by-year frequency of presidential plans submitted and points out the sporadic and uneven use of this authority. It goes on to say:

> The adoption of the reorganization plan procedure has been a significant step toward better executive organization. It has marked acceptance of one simple fact by the administration which recommended it and by Congress which first approved the Reorganization Act procedure. The task of keeping the executive establishment in order is a continuing one, requiring constant attention to maintenance and repair. It is a task that never can be accomplished by sudden bursts of activity, sensational surveys and investigations, or blasts of publicity about some apparently insignificant governmental agency such as, for instance, the National Screw Thread Commission.[11]

To compose a total picture of reorganization progress, one must look beyond the structural dispositions to many others that have altered the system of authority and method. Authority, functions, and funds increasingly are vested in departmental and agency heads, with broad power to delegate and allocate them, thus establishing their jurisdiction over subordinate units. Changes have been adopted in programs and in managerial, budgetary, accounting, and auditing procedures. Increasing attention has been given to due process for the protection of the rights of citizens by legislative actions in the field of administrative procedure. Attempts have been made to arrest the trend to excessive secrecy by the passage of laws requiring disclosure.

The upgrading of the career services and the changes in personnel administration have also had a marked effect on executive organization and administrative management (Chapter II). The creation of the supergrade positions (General Service grades 16, 17, and 18) in the civil service and the filling of high posts by appointments of career men have begun to change the power structure of the government in ways that have not yet been entirely identified. It is my preliminary view that it has made the agencies more, rather than less, responsive to changes in policy, but this problem calls for intensive research.

Decentralization to regional and field offices has been attempted, a topic which will be treated later. Many able career officials, including military officers, believe that recentralization is taking place as a result of the excessive use of minute prescriptions and regulations caused by the increased use of automatic data processing. There is some reason to believe that the precise and detailed regulations needed to record actions taken have the effect of limiting the range of choice in actions and options otherwise available to regional officials. But in the absence of research on this matter one must be cautious about expressing a conclusion. The dangers in this field are great and administrators need to be in command of their computer specialists so that this group does not assume that "program planners" in the technical sense of the word are expected to take charge of planning programs in the policy sense of the word. I am persuaded that the modern administrator must have the capacity to program his programmers, analyze his analysts, and to evaluate his evaluators if he is to remain in command of his program and be able to defend its policies.

Another effect of reorganization legislation has been to give department heads, as well as the President, more adequate staffs with which to discharge their policy formulating and operational duties. Many departments and administrations now have trained staff aides not only for policy research but for systems analysis and operations research. A good deal of specialized competence is continuously examining operational effectiveness within the departments and recommending and helping to install improvements. Central staff in the Executive Office, however, must be used with great discretion to avoid the twin danger of undermining the vigor of departments and administrations or of tempting them to lean too heavily on higher authority. In the case of regulatory commissions, two important effects of reorganization actions may be noted. In many cases their executive duties have been transferred to a single administrator, as is most clearly illustrated by the heads of the administrations which comprise the Department of Transportation. In most of the commissions, largely as a result of the proposals of Hoover I, the President designates their chairman, who is also assigned the duties of internal administration. The President's authority to discharge members of these bodies continues to be circumscribed by law and by court decisions. He still has little influence over their policies particularly in the quasi-judicial field, and this is apparently the state of things that Congress and the Supreme Court continue to believe to be the proper one.

Although I have thought it worthwhile to describe the reorganization acts that have been passed and to recite the texts of the first one and the last one to date in Appendix III, I have resisted the temptation to describe the specific actions by reorganization plan which have been effected. An exception is made in the case of Plans 1 to 5 under the Reorganization Act of 1939 which, inter alia, created the Executive Office of the President. I refer my readers to at least three excellent printed summaries of these actions.[12] All approved reorganization plans are also to be found in Title V of the U. S. Code as they have the force of law.

Extending the Authority of the President to Submit Reorganization Plans (U.S. Senate Report No. 91–89, 91st Congress, 1st Session, Feb. 28, 1969) contains the following interesting appendices:

Appendix 1—Message of President Nixon requests the extension of reorganization authority.

Appendix 2—Table I—Statutes providing reorganization authority (1932-1965).

Appendix 2—Table II—Summary of Action on Reorganization Plans submitted between 1939 and 1968 showing that 97 plans were submitted and 75 became effective.

Appendix 3—Action taken on Reorganization Plans under authority of Reorganization Statutes, 81st–90th Congress.

3. Legality of Executive Reorganization

"We are under a Constitution, but the Constitution is what the judges say it is," remarked Charles E. Hughes while still Governor of New York. The judges do not seem to want to say very much about the legality of reorganization legislation, in which, by a complete reversal of previous procedures, a remarkable accommodation has been achieved between the other two branches of government. President Hoover's attorney general, William G. Mitchell, questioned the constitutional validity of the one-house congressional veto which, under the Economy Act of 1932, could be applied to a presidential order or a "part of same." (Appendix III.) He considered this arrangement an invasion of the President's executive power.[13] The Economy Amendments of March 3, 1933, accordingly, contained no veto provision. Subsequent legal views of the Department of Justice and of Congress seem to be based on the theory that executive reorganization is a prerogative of the Congress, which it can delegate to the President under stated standards, limitations, and conditions. Once Congress has approved a reorganization plan (or failed to veto it), and has later ratified the action by appropriations to or legislation on the new agency, the Court seems loath to question the validity of the method used to transfer the authority. It is difficult to conceive of a case that could arise and be brought to the Supreme Court before such ratifying actions had been taken. In two cases which have arisen, the plaintiff shipping companies were objecting to the substance of the orders imposed on them by the Secretary of Commerce, and the question of the legality of the transfer to him by executive order of powers formerly residing in the U.S. Shipping Board was incidental to the substantive complaint.[14] In both cases the federal courts affirmed the legality of the presidential reorganization order, pointing out that it had been ratified by the passage of the Merchant Marine Act of 1936 (49 Stat. 1985), in which Congress transferred the regulatory functions of the Secretary of Commerce to the U. S. Maritime Commission, and by appropriations.[15]

A distinction must be made, in considering the question of legality, between the legislative veto by concurrent resolution and a veto by a vote of either House. The latter method has been in force beginning with the Reorganization Act of 1949. There is a nice question here whether a legislative act is effective if it is passed by only one House even if it takes the form of a resolution of disapproval. It is not equivalent to the one-House power specifically granted by the Constitution to the Senate in the matter of confirmation of appointments and ratification of treaties. Edward S. Corwin seemed to have no doubt of the validity of certain uses of the concurrent resolution device in many fields which go far beyond the original limitation on its use to the internal affairs of the Congress. He goes so far as to say, "That Congress may qualify in this way its delegations of powers which it might withhold altogether would seem to be obvious."[16]

Certainly the reorganization laws do not deprive the President of his constitutional right to participate in the approval of legislation; for, by the very act of presenting a reorganization plan, he has, as it were, pre-audited the measure and has indicated not merely his sanction but his espousal of it. A concurrent resolution of the Senate and the House being by definition one that does not require his approval, it would be absurd to insist that he must reserve the subsequent veto power which the constitution grants him in the case of a joint resolution on a plan which he has himself introduced and which cannot be amended.

Does the inversion of procedures in reorganization acts constitute a violation of the principles of separation of powers enunciated by Montesquieu? I was startled to have this question in political theory, in which I am not an authority, hurled at me at a meeting in Brazil in 1953 where I was lecturing on the Reorganization Act just passed. My stuttered reply was that I did not believe that the separation of powers had been impaired and that I was not aware that Montesquieu himself had been so immaculate about the precise sequence of their exercise. But a number of people, myself included, have their doubts as to the validity of the one-house veto provision and particularly of the wisdom of permitting a simple majority of those present and voting in either chamber to nullify a reorganization plan.

Veto for reorganization purposes by the Congress itself is one thing and by this time an accepted thing, but legislation giving congressional committees the right to veto executive actions or requiring departments to "come into agreement with them" is quite another. Attorneys General, beginning with the administration of President Wilson, have consistently held such laws to be clearly unconstitutional. In his chapter on "The Legislative Veto," Joseph P. Harris has sharply contrasted these two devices.[17]

Additional studies are needed on the use of the executive initiative and congressional veto procedure in fields other than reorganization. With a number of variations, the device has already been applied in many fields, among which are: congressional reapportionment, alien deportation, disposal of obsolete naval vessels, disposal of wartime rubber plants, atomic energy agreements, and federal salary legislation under which pay increases in the three branches of the government were enacted early in 1969. The Grant Consolidation Bill, recommended by President Nixon on April 30, 1969, embodied the essential features of reorganization acts. An analogous but not identical device is provided by the Act of June 25, 1948 (28—U.S.C.—2072–3–4) which provides that rules of civil procedure for subordinate courts prescribed by the Supreme Court shall not take effect until the expiration of ninety days after they have been reported to the Congress.

Perhaps the most radical suggestion that has been made was to apply the executive initiative and legislative veto formula to the field of compensatory fiscal policy. Peter Schauffler, in his doctoral dissertation written in 1956 and cited in Chapter II, predicted that with the growing acceptance of the need for prompt action in the field of compensatory taxation, Congress would eventually grant to the President, within certain standards and limits, the right to initiate increases and decreases of income tax rates, subject to congressional consideration and veto. Dr. Schauffler has extended his discussion of this and related questions in his article on "The Legislative Veto Revisited."[18] President Johnson vindicated the Schauffler prophecy when he made just such a recommendation in one of his last acts, the message to Congress of January, 1969. It is unlikely that the House will readily relinquish any share of its power to initiate revenue measures. But there cannot be much doubt that the executive plan with the legislative veto within a limited period of time will more and more be applied to other fields. Matters on which parliamentary delays are too costly to the body politic, or in which the issues are too hot for Congress to touch, will be the ones on which Congress is most likely to support this type of procedure. Certainly new means will have to be found to obviate the disastrous habit of delaying the passage of appropriation bills until late in the fiscal year to which they apply.

The device of presidential initiative with congressional veto is a constitutional invention of considerable importance. It is an ingenious solution of the roadblocks that have plagued us. Its growing application will tend to give it a sanction of habitual and appropriate use in the unwritten part of our constitutional arrangements. But there are many fields in which its use would be inappropriate and inapplicable. The President should not, in my view, be given the authority to grant new powers not presently authorized by law and which have a substantive content—particularly those for which reasonable limits and standards cannot be set by Congress.

Congress has pretty well accepted the device in the case of reorganization bills and seems ready to accord this power to incoming presidents. It is averse to enacting permanent legislation or to binding future Congresses and wishes to retain its right to review the situation from time to time so that each act is given a terminal date. The acts have been strengthened over the years by suppressing the long list of excepted agencies contained in the earlier ones and have been weakened by the increasing ease with which either House can veto them. The right of the President to create a new executive department by reorganization plan has been expunged.

The Committees on Government Operations dislike "package plans," that is to say reorganization plans affecting more than one function. Nor do they like surprise packages; in 1966 the chairman of the Senate Committee extracted a promise from the Bureau of the Budget that advance notice of projected plans would be given. But to permit plans to be amended in Congress would destroy the usefulness of the device. Millett and Rogers, shortly after the passage of the Reorganization Act of 1939, pointed out that the non-amendable feature was essential:

> Nor is there any reason to open the way for legislative modification of parts of an executive plan. The proposal as a whole should be voted on: is it acceptable or unacceptable? To permit amendment would be to nullify the very purpose of the entire procedure—to remove the details of controversial subjects from the arena of legislative bickering and indecision.[19]

For the future, the form of the present legislation seems to be reasonably satisfactory, but I would hope that a bargain could be struck on three points the next time it comes up for consideration. Every president that requests such legislation should be given it for the period of his elected term of office (a duration of only one or two years is too short). The veto power should be exerted by a concurrent resolution of a simple majority of both Houses; each reorganization plan presented by the President should be limited to a single activity or function.

4. Statutory Commissions

The big statutory commissions of a mixed nature, such as the two Hoover Commissions, have one feature that the smaller presidential ones do not. They write reports for public consumption and thus help to dramatize the day-to-day operations of government and have the opportunity to educate citizen opinion on the workings of their public agencies. But the publicity cannot be any better than the product. While the recommendations of the first Hoover Commission were outstanding, those of the second one were in the main of low quality. In both cases, an extraordinary public relations effort was put forth which, with the support of the Citizens Committee for the Hoover Reports, probably helped secure congressional support for implementing legislation. Such publicity usually has to start with a parade of horribles, exaggerating the shortcomings of government, and it succeeds by raising unnecessary and unfounded citizen anxieties. The agencies praised in the second Hoover Report, and there were a few, did not make the headlines. The educational value of the publicity is mitigated by extreme castigations and by unverifiable claims of savings. At the local level, citizens' and taxpayers' associations have long since abandoned this form of shock treatment.

There are a number of other objections to the use of the large statutory mixed commission. One of them is the difficulty of finding a chairman who has the stature and prestige of a Herbert Hoover, a venerable ex-President, sophisticated on large scale organization, and an indefatigable worker. The absence of an outstanding figure as chairman would be like playing Hamlet without the prince. It is not too much to say that without a comparable chairman no mixed commission could reach important agreements. (Mr. Hoover's contributions to reorganization seem to have been more important before and after than during his term as President.)

An effort of the magnitude of the two Hoover Commissions may be justified once or twice in a century, but the expense of such undertakings greatly exceeds the reported outlays of the commissions themselves. The demands on the departments and agencies are enormous and there is no way to count the cost of the hours of regular staff time consumed, the disruptions of work, the needless anxieties raised, and the serious effect on morale. Literally hundreds of people from two dozen task forces and working groups fanned out in Washington, many of them unfamiliar with and hostile to government personnel and methods, and engaged the time of thousands in answering questions. The terms of reference need to be more precise and limited than those of Hoover II, and even Hoover I tried to cover too much territory. In fact, in the decade to come, targeted attention is needed on the content, purposes, policies, and implementation of national programs particularly in such fields as foreign affairs and national security, conservation of the environment, urbanism, race relations and other way-of-life problems, health, education, welfare, and science. The studies of substantive programs should focus more and more on the improvement of their intergovernmental or contractual performance. Reorganization prescriptions should be the by-products of such studies, not an end in themselves.

The very construction of the large statutory mixed commissions for executive organization has drawbacks. The members, whether from Congress, the executive branch, or outside, are leaders in their fields and busy men who just do not have the time to examine the voluminous and complex reports of numerous task forces. Furthermore, the governmental members are apt to have preconceived views and loyalties which color their attitudes toward various agencies and lead them to less than objective conclusions. The presence of senators and representatives on the commissions does not automatically assure congressional sanction of their findings. The cabinet members are subject to suspicions of favoritism on the part of the department heads who were not named. The "public members" of both Hoover Commissions were the most valuable members and paradoxically were charged with less "conflict of interest" than the government ones. Professor James K. Pollock of the University of Michigan, for example, was a Republican "public member" of the first Hoover Commission and entered a number of penetrating dissents. Many of its commissioners had brilliant personal assistants. Ferrel Heady, who is now president of the University of New Mexico, was assistant to Commissioner Pollock and wrote a perceptive paper on "A New Approach to Federal Executive Reorganization."[20] Don K. Price was on leave from Public Administration Clearing House as personal assistant to Chairman Hoover; and Professor Charles Aiken of the University of California at Berkeley, as assistant to Vice-Chairman Dean Acheson. The Bureau of the Budget was frequently called upon for detailing of members of its staff, among whom Alan L. Dean succeeded Professor Aiken as assistant to Mr. Acheson, William Pincus became assistant to Commissioner James H. Rowe, Jr., and Harold Seidman was coopted for a number of special studies.

The task force system had special dangers and was almost out of hand during Hoover II. Members of these task forces have told me that they had little time to examine the voluminous and technical reports of staff men which were pushed through their meetings by powerful chairmen. Dissents by task force members were not recorded. There were outstanding task forces of course, such as the task forces on personnel problems and the one on national defense in the first Hoover Commission, which took time to analyze staff reports and made notable contributions. But one gained the impression that for the most part the task forces, without the time or often the competence to examine them, acquiesced in the reports of the eager beavers who had prepared them. The members of the big commissions themselves were dismayed by the length, detail, and technical content of the task force reports and in a number of instances gave up trying to act on their contents.

It is astonishing that practically none of these questions on the efficacy of the large statutory commissions and their methods of work was raised in the prolix 622 page report, exhibits, and hearings of the

Subcommittee on Government Operations, chaired by Senator Abraham Ribicoff (D., Conn.).[21] The committee, with the enthusiastic sponsorship of 61 members of the Senate, recommended the establishment of a third "Hoover type" Commission by the Executive Reorganization and Management Act of 1968, which passed the Senate without objection but made no progress at all in the House.[22] The statements made in the hearings by Bertram M. Gross, James A. Norton, and Harvey Sherman were later reprinted under a heading: "What, Another Hoover Commission?" but were more sympathetic than the heading would lead one to believe.[23]

5. *Presidential Committees*

The contributions to the theory and practice of organization and management made by presidential commissions and committees have been notable. Beginning with Theodore Roosevelt, eight out of twelve presidents have had one. They work quietly, without much fanfare, and in close collaboration with the chief executive. They don't tear up the pavement. They report to the President, often confidentially; they disrupt the government less than the big statutory mixed commissions; and their accepted proposals are revealed in the form of executive action by means of reorganization plans or requests for legislation. They can advise the President informally about his establishment with comments that often cannot be put into written form, and can even be more critical about his own administrative shortcomings than the more formal bodies.

The problem of staffing the reorganization commissions, both statutory and presidential, has not been satisfactorily solved. In either case the work needs to be done in close cooperation with the President and with his director of the Budget, whose office of executive management under an assistant director has accumulated a vast amount of experience and data on organizational matters, and which in turn can be stimulated and refreshed by contacts with an outside group of advisers from industry and the professions. I believe that the failure in many cases of the temporary commissions to utilize to the utmost the resources of the Bureau of the Budget staff, even when they differ with its recommendations, has been a factor in undercutting the authority and prestige of the Bureau in the departments and agencies. The hastily recruited staffs of presidential committees and task forces cannot be expected to cope, without such cooperation, with the complexities of the intricate establishment they are called upon to survey.

A pithy comment by Harvey C. Mansfield has this to say on the administrative and political advantages of the presidential committee in the field of executive reorganization:

> Given the supporting staff resources now available in or to the Executive Office, and the supply of unofficial consultative talent among experienced former political executives in academic quarters and elsewhere, the advantages of confidentiality in getting advice and preparing reorganization proposals appear overwhelming from the President's viewpoint. The appointment of a mixed public commission is likely to be read as a sign of weakness or irresolution on his part.[24]

The first presidential committee was the Committee on Departmental Methods (known as the Keep Commission), 1905–1909, appointed by President Theodore Roosevelt and whose extraordinary work was referred to in Chapter II. It had no congressional sanction and its activities were resented by Congress, which enacted none of its legislative recommendations. President Taft, who was familiar with the obstacles encountered by the Keep Commission, took pains to secure congressional authority for his Commission on Economy and Efficiency, 1910–1913. President Franklin D. Roosevelt was able to obtain legislative blessing and appropriations for the appointment of his President's Committee on Administrative Management in 1936. The view prevailing in 1905 that managerial reforms in the executive branch were the exclusive prerogative of Congress has all but vanished, and Congress has come to accept as normal the appointment of presidential committees and task forces in this field.

The President's Advisory Commission on Management Improvement was established by President Truman under Executive Order 10072 of July 1949 as part of a government-wide program of management improvement, which was later given legislative support by Title X of the Classification Act of 1949. It actually was the fourth committee of the presidential type and its contribution was more original in respect to its method of work than in any new doctrine it expounded. Its final report of December 1952 is reprinted in full in the hearings of the Ribicoff subcommittee.[25] The Advisory Committee's chairman was Thomas A. Morgan, industrialist. Its members, of whom I was one, were chosen from government, business, research institutes, and universities. The Bureau of the Budget provided the staff work for the Commission; and two of its staff, Charles B. Stauffacher and William

F. Finan, acted successively as its Executive Secretary. Its life coincided with the start of a program for government-wide management improvement for which Congress had given President Truman a special appropriation. It also exerted an influence for the further implementation of the recommendations of the first Hoover Commission. Its method of work was predominantly that of inviting the heads of departments and agencies to appear before it at informal hearings and to question them on their plans for improvement of administrative management. In some cases they were thus stimulated to formulate such plans when they had not given the matter much attention before. In many instances, agency heads revealed a long-time and informed interest in such efforts. Although a few special studies were made, the method of work was managerial rather than analytical. The hearings were often penetrating, but off-the-record and friendly and understanding, and the replies were usually less defensive and franker than one finds in the hearings of congressional committees. President Truman on several occasions met with the commission and participated in its discussions. Its concluding report contained five principal recommendations:

(1) Management improvement work should continue to be centered in the Bureau of the Budget.

(2) Continuous encouragement and unrelenting executive pressure should be maintained on administrators to carry out programs of management improvement within their own areas of responsibility.

(3) Management staff facilities of the President and heads of departments and agencies should be strengthened.

(4) The President and Congress should take steps to assure an adequate supply of competent administrators in the government.

(5) The President should be given permanent reorganization authority.

The President's Advisory Committee on Government Organization (PACGO) was the most durable, and in many respects the most productive, of the presidential groups. It was appointed by President Eisenhower by Executive Order 10432 and lasted through his two terms from 1953 to 1961. It was formed just before the second Hoover Commission was organized at a time when President Eisenhower wanted immediate advice and action on reorganization during his first year in the White House. Its appointment and continuity during his two terms lend credence to many plausible but undocumentable reports circulating at that time that "Ike" and his entourage were quietly opposed to the creation of Hoover II and remained allergic to it as it got into action. The chairman of PACGO was Nelson A. Rockefeller, who left the committee in 1958 to become Governor of the State of New York, and who had had a long and varied experience in the foreign and domestic agencies of the federal government. The other two members were equally familiar with the executive branch. The able and energetic Arthur S. Flemming was a member of the U.S. Civil Service Commission and of the first and second Hoover Commissions, and became Director of the Office of Defense Mobilization and Secretary of Health, Education, and Welfare. The third member, Milton Eisenhower, was president of The Johns Hopkins University, had served as president of two other colleges, and before that had been a career man in the government for almost twenty years. In addition to his knowledge and judgment, Milton Eisenhower, in contrast to Mr. Hoover, had an unimpeded access to his brother, the President, which even Sherman Adams, the grim sentinel of the White House, could not prevent. In 1958, Don K. Price, who had just entered on his new duties as Dean of the Graduate School of Public Administration (now the John F. Kennedy School of Government) at Harvard University, was appointed to replace Governor Rockefeller. His name appears so often in this book and in the annals of public administration that I assume no introduction is necessary. This triumvirate constituted a top drawer privy council on government organization.

On the occasion of his resignation, Nelson A. Rockefeller, as chairman of PACGO, in an exchange of letters with President Eisenhower, reported on the work of the committee from January, 1953 to December 22, 1958.[26] His report revealed the method of work employed by PACGO:

> For the first three months after it was established the Committee was in almost daily session. During this time it had a major part in the development of the ten reorganization plans which were transmitted to Congress and became law in 1953.
> In November 1953 following a summer recess, the Committee appointed a full-time staff director and a small staff. Since that time there have been 65 committee meetings, or an average of once a month. In addition, the Committee members have participated in frequent informal consultations. Throughout its existence the Committee has met with the President on many occasions and also has attended cabinet meetings when government organization items were on the agenda.

Mr. Rockefeller went on to list 31 major steps taken to improve management and organization, in which his committee had participated actively, in the following categories:

Foreign Affairs Activities   6
Defense Activities   4
Aviation and Space Activities   5
Executive Office and Interdepart-
   mental Activities   5
Other Departmental and Agency
   Activities   7
Personnel Administration   4
                                      ——
                                      31

In his letter of resignation to the President, he says that the committee worked in close association with the director and staff of the Bureau of the Budget, had had the full cooperation of the members of the Cabinet, the White House staff, and the other executive branch officials with whom it consulted. The papers of the committee have been deposited in the Dwight D. Eisenhower Library at Abilene, Kansas. When the full record of PACGO becomes available to administrative analysts and historians, I predict that this small, close-knit, knowledgeable, continuous, and diligent presidential commission will prove to have made more constructive and durable contributions to federal organization and administrative management than was produced by all the massive forays of the task forces and flying squadrons of the second Hoover Commission put together.

President Kennedy, it seems, appointed no advisory committee on reorganization, but President L. B. Johnson had two of them. One was a Task Force on Government Reorganization of ten members whose chairman was the by-now seasoned reorganizer Don K. Price, but whose membership was not announced. Another one was the task force under the chairmanship of Ben W. Heineman, railroad magnate and industrialist, which had among its membership management consultants, the Director of the Budget, and the Secretary of Defense, as well as former secretary of H.E.W. John W. Gardner. Both of these task forces made confidential reports to the President, and I can find no public disclosure of their findings.

On March 12, 1970, President Nixon sent an extended message to Congress on his project for reorganizing the Executive Office of the President and transmitting, as the first step, Reorganization Plan 2 of 1970.[27] The plan proposed the creation of an Office of Management and Budget and a Domestic Council at cabinet level, which will be discussed below. The message acknowledged the advice he had received from the President's Advisory Council on Executive Organization which he had appointed in April, 1969. The membership and terms of reference of this council give promise of further constructive accomplishments.

The chairman of the council is Roy L. Ash, president, Litton Industries, and the members are: former dean George P. Baker, Graduate School of Business Administration, Harvard University; John B. Connally, lawyer, former Secretary of the Navy and Governor of Texas; Frederick R. Kappel, chairman, Executive Committee, American Telephone and Telegraph Company and of the President's (Johnson) Commission on Postal Organization; Richard M. Paget, president, Cresap, McCormick, and Paget, management consultants; and Walter N. Thayer, New York lawyer and investment banker, who had served on the Harriman mission in London in 1942–45 and then was general counsel for the Foreign Economic Administration. The mandate of the council was "to review the organization of the executive branch and its links with state and local governments." The participation of its members was reported to be one to three days per month in meetings plus individual time given by each member. It reported that study groups were working on seven organizational issues: Executive Office of the President, Social Programs, Organized Crime, Regulatory Agencies, Environmental and Natural Resources, International Trade, and Drug Abuse. The council will make no overall report but will submit memoranda to the President as they are completed and he will decide on their release. It expects to complete a major portion of its work by June 30, 1970, and to be out of business in December of that year. A considerable staff has been assembled and over $900,000 has been allocated for the council's work in fiscal year 1970. Both the executive director, Murray Comarow, and his deputy, Andrew M. Rouse, have had experience in governmental administration and surveys at high levels. Although it is understandable that the Bureau of the Budget does not appear to have participated in the first study which concerned its own reorganization, it is to be hoped that the Bureau's resources will be coopted on the balance of the agenda. Management, it appears, has emerged as a key word and as a recognized major function of the Executive Office of the President.

Chapter IX

UNFINISHED BUSINESS

1. The Long and Triangular View

IN THIS LAST CHAPTER I VENTURE AN ANALYSIS OF FACTORS TO BE TAKEN into account from now on in the redesigning of structures and systems of the federal executive branch. I shall enter the perilous field of recommendations but in very general terms, taking into account what has been learned from experience. In undertaking this task I hope my conclusions will be regarded as a general hypothesis to be applied, if at all, in the light of changing conditions. They should be read in the spirit rather than in the letter; and, although I believe in their validity, they are presented more as guidelines on how to think about organization and management than as precise prescriptions.

It may be useful to start with a number of caveats. It is not within my terms of reference to suggest basic constitutional changes. But if these are undertaken, great care should be taken not to attempt to graft on to the American presidential system bits and pieces of British parliamentary practice, lest we contrive a mixture, as certain Latin American states have done, that has inconsistent elements of both. This does not mean that we cannot profit from administrative and parliamentary experience in other countries from which we have always learned much, as they have been increasingly learning from us. I also wish to warn against panaceas, mechanistic solutions, slogans, and gadgetry as a solution to our major problems. Many of the new prescriptions have valuable applications, but the American tendency is to look for quantitative solutions to problems in which value judgments concerning ends and means demand that qualitative factors receive the highest priority. Hard thinking and painful decisions, when all possible facts and data have been marshalled, cannot be avoided. As in medicine, the new drugs of management may be powerful and useful, but they may also have unpredictable side effects. Behavioral studies have given us new insights in regard to how individuals and groups are likely to react in a variety of situations, but seem to require considerable revision in view of the increasing tendency toward group activism, demonstration, intransigence, and even violence. Systems analysis, operations research, and devices such as program-planning-budgeting are inventions of considerable importance, but they tend to be over-sold and raise expectations of universal, automatic, and standardized solutions to many problems which are highly qualitative and to which they may not be relevant. In any event, they should be regarded as providing data for decisions rather than the decisions themselves. We must also be wary of panaceas such as Mr. Peter F. Drucker's doctrine of "privatization," because the corollaries of his theory call for the use of the autonomous government corporation and the delegation to private enterprise of essentially public functions and these have not been conspicuously successful experiments. Nor is it possible to accept his premise that government is incapable of running anything.[1] None of these devices contribute very much to one of the major unsolved problems of our system of representative government, the relations of the executive and legislative branches in the field of administration. The executive branch must have the continuing advice and criticism of a legislature, but this process needs to be raised to a higher level of general interest. I am sufficiently sanguine to believe that to some extent it already has been, and am optimistic enough to believe that it increasingly will be. A high level of legislative oversight, not irresponsible intervention in executive decisions, is one of the basic ingredients of a viable democracy; and the continuing demand to defend policies and operations can be a major therapeutic instrument to counteract the ills of bureaucracy.[2]

Throughout this work I have stressed the importance of formulating purposes, objectives, and policies before assigning missions and devising systems. But I am compelled to point out that these considerations are so intimately related that the second stage must immediately follow upon the first. The high tasks of administrative management are threefold: to recommend and espouse wise and just policies, to see to it that they are translated into effective programs, and to make sure that the implementation of adopted programs is vigorously carried out. In performing these tasks, the high government official must have the statutory mind. An important element of his job consists of formulating with precision the often vague purposes expressed in authorizing legislation. The complex and technical content of modern legislation makes it almost inevitable that much sub-legislation will be delegated to the executive branch. Every executive agency is, therefore, quasi-legislative in nature. By interpretation and regulation, executive agencies devise a system in which operations can be delegated and in which an environment is created in which the staff can do its work. Subordinate staff, and in particular field staff, will then be largely engaged in applying general rules to specific cases. In fact, one criterion of the effective management of an agency is not only whether its rules make sense, but whether the great bulk of case decisions can be made without referral to top echelons. Another test is whether decisions will stick; that is to say, be accepted without appeals. The experienced administrator, usually a top flight career man, should be most useful in advising on relating programs to implementation. His advice and cooperation should be enlisted before policies are frozen, not only to evoke his motivated cooperation, but also to benefit by his experience in program execution. There will in fact be times when modifications in program will be necessary to insure more effective implementation.

A continuing task of the executive branch is to press constantly for a greater degree of unity in its policies, domestic and foreign, and for simplification of its processes as they affect the citizen, the state, the locality—its other chosen instruments and points of contact. At the very least the programs should not be so in conflict that they cancel each other, or that interagency differences unduly delay decisions, a situation which puts excessive burdens on the cooperating entities, beneficiaries, and regulatees. The specialized and fractionalized nature of our highly organized society and its political structure are constant centrifugal forces, and the executive branch is the organ most likely to introduce unity of purpose in the public services. To do this it must itself take care to use an old saw, "to keep its experts on tap not on top." It may be too much to expect the executive branch to become one completely-united government establishment in view of its diverse centers of authority, power, and pressure; but, on its agenda of unfinished business, coordination must have a high priority. The communist societies seem to encounter many obstacles to the formation of a monolithic state and in a pluralistic democratic federalist system such a state, short of an atomic war, is inconceivable. But if the executive branch, and particularly the presidency, cannot viably affect the overall view and the interrelationship of policies and processes, one wonders where such an integrating influence will come from.

The long term' view should be paramount in decisions which affect governmental structures and powers. Presidents and their advisers have increasingly taken this view when reorganization problems are under consideration. At times of transition, with a new incoming president it is most desirable that a long-term organization policy be adopted just as policies are formulated in substantive fields. The influence of the Brownlow Committee and of the first Hoover Commission has been to given presidents the basis for a long-term doctrine that has to a great extent influenced their reorganization decisions. The executive, by adopting long-term objectives in the fields of organization and management, has a stronger defense against unwise improvisations. He thereby gives himself an armor to protect against the never-ending pressures for fractionalization of programs and agencies and for prestige symbolism, which have continued to distort the executive structure.

The observation that there should be a long-term strategy as to the federal structure is an extension but not a reversal of the views expressed in Chapter I pointing to governmental organization as a continuing process. In a world that is changing at geometrical rates, executive structure must be constantly adapted to new needs and new methodologies, but this fact does not preclude adapting the parts to a general conception of the whole. In this process, as discussed above, the initiative will usually come from the President; and the important political invention of the executive reorganization plan, subject to the legislative veto, has already produced a much greater flexibility and adaptability of governmental structure to new needs, new program priorities, and new technologies. There have been more changes in executive organization in the past thirty-five years than in the previous 150 years of our administrative history. An illustration of the velocity rate of change is to be found in the specifications for the twelve major departments made in the 1937 Brownlow report which would not be suitable to the needs of today and tomorrow. Written before World War II, it did not foresee the needs for defense unification, for the administration of the now vast programs in science, invention, and technological development, nor the need for coordination in the field of foreign policy and national defense. The suggestion that there be a long-term general theory or strategy of organization does not imply a hard and fast specification for its components.

Each incoming administration tends to dramatize that it is different not only by announcing new substantive programs but by representing that even in cases in which objectives are not changed the work will be done better than under its predecessors. In fact, it might be said that "predecessor fighting" is the "New Broom Syndrome" of all incoming executives in every kind of organization and tends to divert energy and attention from more productive efforts. It often impels executives to change, for the sake of changing, satisfactory systems inherited from a phantom rival. Occasionally this compulsion results in shakeups and reforms which bring about better services to the public. But often the result proves to be merely different and no better. Reorganization should be looked at from the standpoint of its long-term effects on the presidency and on the executive structure, rather than as a series of improvisations. Each administration should be able to hand a more rational, manageable, and effective establishment to its successors.[3]

Any norms that can be posited for a more rational approach to the present and future problems of structure must, I believe, be based on a triangulation of three viewpoints: from the top down, from the bottom up, and across the board. Exclusive concentration on any one of these three elements no longer will produce sensible solutions. To be sure, their importance will not always be identical and will vary from field to field.

2. The View from the Top Down

The view from the top down will be the aspect having the highest priority in most cases. This view must be examined first and foremost from the standpoint of the President and the presidency. The situation in which the President finds himself as head of the executive branch is an intolerable one, and the charts depicting his place in the hierarchy arouse chimerical expectations. Nothing less than major surgery is required to cut away the jungle of access in which he is entwined. Unless and until he is given responsibility and authority over the independent establishments, autonomous financial boards, corporations, and regulatory commissions, at least in some degree, the problem is one of simple graphics. (Appendix II, Exhibits C and D.) When independent establishments are not, in fact, parts of the executive branch, they should not be shown as reporting to the President. Perhaps there should be two official charts of the executive establishment, one depicting the agencies responsible to and reporting regularly to the President, the other showing the autonomous agencies over which his jurisdiction is anomalous and which consult with him now and then.

But the problem transcends that of simple chartism. If indeed he has no responsibility whatever for these agencies except to appoint their members, designate the chairman, and perhaps to make a proforma review of their annual budgets, they should not have access to him as a matter of right. In special cases or those of national emergency, it is not foreclosed that he take the initiative to call in their heads for advice or requests for collaboration.

The element of access, rather than any general theory of span of control, should be the determining one in those offices, departments, and agencies that actually report to the President. Even to bring these into the realm of possible access is not a simple problem of chartism but one which calls for more drastic steps. The frequency of access is probably greatest in the White House staff, next in the institutionalized units of the Executive Office, and least in the executive departments and agencies. At present these contact points on the official chart suggest that there are 58 of them with at least 12 more on the White House staff, making no less than 70 in all. (Appendix II, Exhibit C.) Without attempting to fix a precise number of contact points, I suggest that if there were only ten members of the White House staff the President had to see regularly, seven heads of units in the Executive Office, twelve department heads and six heads of independent agencies, he still would be blessed with thirty-five points of regular access and contact. These are the cases in which access should be real and not presumed, in which officials should have a high priority on the presidential appointment calendar and sufficient time to communicate their problems and to exchange views. Eventually, one would hope, the executive list could be reduced to twenty-five but there is a considerable task ahead if it is to be limited to thirty-five, a figure which has no special magic but is one-half the present one and at least does not exceed the number of weeks in the year. It also would begin to give time for the great number of people that a President must see outside the executive branch, and for meetings of cabinet and councils.

The element of access and contact derives from the sheer amount of business that the President is now compelled to delegate. Under today's conditions, operating at his proper level, in the words of Paul H. Appleby, implies a degree of delegation previously unknown.[4] He can permit himself the luxury of dwelling on details in very few cases and these must be chosen on the exception principle. Decision on specific cases must be for the largest part assigned to members of his cabinet except in the most urgent matters such as those pertaining to relations with Congress, the media, and the people on major aspects of his program, important political appointments, problems of national security, basic changes in national policy, and national crisis situations. This amount of delegation makes it imperative that he has the time to see and confer with the people on whom he has the right to rely. Without such opportunity, members of his cabinet are rudderless, and are left in the position in which they cannot be sure that they see eye-to-eye with the President, who in turn will not be in a position to back them up and to defend their policies. When he acts on cases in their domain, their own authority is weakened and more and more of such cases will tend to gravitate to him for decision.

The President no longer can give off-the-cuff sanctions in camera to proposals made to him by heads of departments and agencies. He has to correlate these dialogues with the transactions of larger gatherings of cabinet and council. A good many of the relations of the President to the departments have been institutionalized, and he frequently must reserve final judgment until he has checked with his own immediate establishment. But as Dean Acheson expressed it so eloquently in commenting on the relations between the President and the Secretary of State, "the relationship is an intensely personal one. Insofar as this relationship is attenuated or institutionalized—or Parkinsonized— the task on which they should be jointly engaged suffers."[5] In a measure, this wisdom could also be applied to the relationships of the President with the other members of the cabinet and of his official household. The presidency can be partly institutionalized, but the President himself cannot and should not be.

A great many other advantages would accrue to the government if the structure of the government were modified so that the access points of his executive family were reduced in number to the point that presumed access would become real. On some matters, department and agency heads will accept guidance only from the President himself, not from his aides. Access will have an immediate effect in the improvement of coordination. Major "booboos" and "snafus" will often be nipped in the bud. The President will receive first-hand knowledge of what is troubling his political officers of the line if he has time to see them, and will be better oriented than if he depends exclusively on the specialized reports of his executive office staff, who often do not know. Department heads, in turn, will be kept informed of the President's own preoccupations and emphases and will be able to adjust their programs to the overall situation. Their prestige will rise with Congress and the press from the ability to command this access. Their own departmental staffs will be able to work with a clearer sense of direction. They will be aware that their views are more likely to be presented to the President. This access has a special significance for members of the Executive Office, including White House staff; for any strength they may enjoy in the management of their coordinating functions depends on a prevailing credibility that they are speaking for the President, not for themselves. At present it is impossible to be sure whom they are speaking for. The White House staff must be made aware that their role is that of a conduit to the President and not that of an insulator, which they have increasingly tended to become. The reduction of the executive contact list should contribue to their encouragement of greater access. If the top echelon of administrative access is simplified and its contacts rehumanized, the benefits will be transmitted down the line.

3. The View from the Bottom Up

The view from the bottom up calls for far greater attention that it has received heretofore, in considering changes in organization. This view in turn must be looked at from at least three aspects. The first is, of course, concerned with effectiveness of service and program to the citizen, the group, the region, or the resource, with all deliberate economy and speed. The second aspect, in view of growing demands for participation, calls for innovations in consultations with affected groups before decisions are made. This in turn calls for a clearer definition of the range of choice that can be afforded to affected and interested groups under the law. The government cannot consult, only explain, if it has no choices or options to offer. The third aspect would call for the adoption of consultative systems with those persons that will be involved in the operation of a projected program. This aspect calls for consultation not only with federal officials in the hierarchy but, in cases of grant-in-aid and contractual programs, with the potential chosen instruments: state and local governments, private firms, universities, and research institutes. Consultation with staff members, including regional and field staff, is highly desirable when new regulations are being formulated, new systems designed, or minor organization changes considered. In the case of drastic reorganization, transfers, and abolition of units, it may be completely inappropriate and self-defeating. Consultation and participation must be selective, not dogmatic. People are only embarrassed when they are consulted on matters far beyond their competence. The truck drivers of the T.V.A. would have little to contribute on the question of the height of dams or the best way to extend the Northeast electric power grid.

Considerable experience is already available with consultative methods at state and local levels. The original Economic Opportunity Act went so far as to accord a veto to governors of projected programs within their states, even though most governors were not sufficiently equipped or informed on the local programs to invoke this authority. President Johnson took this one step further. On June 11, 1966, he instructed heads of departments and agencies, in the interest of "creative federalism," to "afford to representatives of the chief executive of state and local government the opportunity to advise and consult in the development of programs which directly affect the conduct of state and local affairs." The accompanying circular of the Bureau of the Budget indicated a method of circulating proposed regulations to state and local government associations through the Advisory Commission on Intergovernmental Relations. But such consultations will be less valuable in determining overall federal structure than in simplifying and improving grant-in-aid policies and procedures.[6]

Recent studies have shown that even a larger issue is at stake in regard to state and local government when federal programs descend upon them. The organization of federal programs today not only may splinterize the federal structure but may have serious effects on the integral structure of state and local government. This is particularly true at the local level, and in the organization of the Model Cities program there seems to have been much more awareness of this point than in the earlier relations of the Office of Economic Opportunity with community action organizations which at first completely by-passed local governments. Federal reorganization and program design have the power today to make or break general government at the local levels so that the view from the bottom up has become essential in every step affecting these relationships.[7]

At the national level, many government agencies have appointed advisory committees, of which a long list could be compiled. Their use, however, is fraught with difficulties and dangers. Standing committees of advisers tend to become dissatisfied with merely offering advice and try to exert authority over agency policies. When they are appointed ex-officio as spokesmen for their professional associations, as spokesmen they are more inhibited than when they are appointed as informed individuals and are more likely to act as pressure points for their group interests rather than as objective advisers. Advisory bodies are most effective when they are ad hoc, addressed to a specific problem, with limited terms, and with instructions to report and then go back home.

Where the relationship of the federal level is a contractual one, there is already a constant interchange in the case of scientific projects with the scientific societies, individuals, and the institutes and universities. In some cases the government has abdicated to them. In spite of the danger of suspicions of conflicts of interest, and of fostering the "industrial-military complex," the contracting policies and methods of the government, particularly of the defense agencies, need a thorough-going reconsideration in which the views of the military and civilian officials as well as of the industries need to be taken into account. In development and production of highly complex defense hardware, the old cliches of governmental contracting no longer apply. Nor is the heated investigatory atmosphere of a congressional hearing, after disclosure of long delays, imperfect weaponry, and cost overruns, conducive to the wise solution of technical and economic implications of research, development, and production policies. The angry reaction of Congress to flagrant shortfalls is often to insist on an added level of supervision and second guessing in the Bureau of the Budget or in the General Accounting Office, when all facts point to the need for important modifications in structure and method in the Pentagon itself. In many cases the shortfalls and overruns originate in the Pentagon. Consideration should be given to whether technical and procurement officers should not only be exposed to training in the Industrial College of the Armed Forces but should spend a year in an industrial organization, early in their careers (rather than after their retirement), to be better informed on industrial capacities and limitations. I know first hand of at least one recent technical contract in which the principal contractor was subjected to the conflicting requirements of fourteen government agencies. In spite of my high regard for the genius of Secretary Robert S. McNamara and his brilliant attempts to reform procurement procedure, I am not convinced that the system and organization he introduced will work under other secretaries of Defense, or indeed that it worked perfectly under his aegis. Few secretaries, however, would have his capacity to analyze and articulate the intricate relations of defense policy to weapon development.[8] Much unfinished business remains in reorienting the method of obtaining military advice and indeed of fixing military responsibility on matters in which it has the most competence and restraining it in matters in which it has the least. More realistic norms for military-industrial relationships still need to be perfected, a field in which the experience of N.A.S.A. will be found invaluable. These are not areas in which solutions will be found by reorganization measures or by executive action alone. In most respects the President and the Secretary of Defense have today the necessary legal authority and staff to analyze these problems, to formulate new policies and procedures, and to modify organizational structures. There have been many reviews of governmental contracting methods and business relationships, but a broad-based review and a reassessment of the applicability of documents such as the Bell report to today's conditions seem to be called for.[9]

The gigantic size of the defense procurement effort and its effect on whole industries and on local economies make these problems relevant to the subject of federal organization and administrative management. Profound questions of strategy, technology, economics, politics, and ethics are involved. While the government's procurement policies should obviously not unduly enrich contracting corporations, perhaps the time has come when new standards should be adopted to permit the government to conserve those administratively competent and technically qualified private organizations on which it continues to depend for considerable amounts of invention and development and a vast amount of production. As in the case of public bodies, the federal government has the power to destroy its chosen instruments in the private field. If this happens its only alternative, which seems almost as remote of adoption as the probability of massive disarmament, would be to consider the radical alternative of J. Kenneth Galbraith to socialize the defense industries as President Washington did when he constructed the Springfield arsenal.

4. The View Across the Board

The third view, and in many ways the most baffling one, is to look at reorganization proposals across the board and to examine in depth the interrelationships of roles and missions in the executive structure. To avoid or to eliminate "duplication and overlapping" has always been one of the orthodox tenets of reorganization law and practice. Foreign as well as domestic programs have an extraordinary number of interlocking points, no matter how carefully designed, and they also react on each other. The intricate interrelationships of our world-power operations are even more baffling than our domestic ones.[10] In the domestic field, the executive branch, even when it has the legal authority to reorganize, cannot unilaterally change its own arrangements. Congress, as has been said before, in the organization of its own committee structure, has strong jurisdiction susceptibilities and inertias. These have to be taken into consideration and frequently must be negotiated out to make major change in the executive branch acceptable and workable. In fact, a refreshing and original theoretical defense of certain virtues of "duplication and overlapping" based on the engineering concepts of factor of safety and redundancy may be found in a recent essay by Professor Martin Landau.[11] But I do not believe that this theory needs to be reduced to absurd limits. When we consider the way in which American public programs arise, we will probably continue to get more of a factor of redundancy than we need. President Roosevelt's use of competing agencies indicates the enormous coordination efforts at top levels that this kind of a situation engenders and that it has a large element of diminishing returns.

New forms of voluntary or imposed coordination seem to be required where lateral cooperation is involved. These become imperative where the separate functions of departments and agencies impinge on the same area. Area in this case is to be construed in its two senses: geographical area such as a region, a state, or a locality; and program area such as the fields of national security and foreign affairs, the regulation of the business cycle, conservation of natural resources, scientific research, and the social way-of-life programs. There is a factor of sanity, as well as of safety, in looking at public services across the functional board from the standpoint of a geographic region. A complete analysis of the total impact of federal programs on a place or region might lead to a startling reconsideration of government structure. In a sense this would be looking across the board from the bottom up. A good example is in the field of international development. A healthy degree of balance and reality have been introduced by Paul G. Hoffman into the United Nations Development Program since it has begun to look at programs from the standpoint of the total needs, desires, and capabilities of a country, rather than from the standpoint of the pressures of specialized organizations competing for that country's attention.

A variety of patterns have been employed to solve the problem of across-the-board duplication and overlapping. At the departmental level there have been mergers and consolidations of bureaus, the grouping of bureaus in administrations of a department, the appointment of assistant secretaries at the departmental level to oversee the action and interaction of certain of its related components, and the use of special powers by the department head to regulate the agencies within his jurisdiction most likely to collide.

It seems clear by now, at least in the field of domestic civilian activities, that departmental organization is impaired when an assistant secretary is designated to oversee the activities of a single substantive field. Such an activity should be headed by an administrator or commissioner. The dissents cited above in the case of the first Hoover Commission (Chapter V) on this point and the example mentioned of Assistant Secretary James F. Allen's insistence on occupying two posts in H.E.W. are evidences of a certain awareness of the dangers of duplication and conflict inherent in this structural form. This form of organization has been carried very far in the organization of the Department of Housing and Urban Development with the deliberate purpose of placing authority over substantive programs in the hands of political executives. It may have produced some policy innovations but there is reason to believe that it has slowed down program execution. The assistant secretaries had best be regarded as extensions of the secretary himself. Their missions should be to assist him in the discharge of across-the-board and department-wide functions. Their ability to help him to direct department-wide policy and to coordinate administrations, services, and bureaus is atrophied when they become too closely identified with one of the specialized clusters of substantive activities and with its supporting pressure groups. One more level of layering is added to the departmental hierarchy which already has three line layers represented by the secretary, the administrator, and the bureau chief. An exception exists in the case of the Department of State, in which assistant secretaries act as regional and functional chiefs and are, in a sense, generalists. The continuance of secretaries as head of military departments within Defense is *sui generis* and may be justified if only on the grounds of insuring greater civilian influence over the military.

At the interdepartmental level even more intricate and varied devices have been attempted. In some cases an under or assistant secretary of a department has been made chairman of an interdepartmental committee or has been given interdepartmental "convenor" authority to adjudicate new questions of policy and application. One of the main functions of the components of the Executive Office of the President is day-by-day coordination on such matters as allocation of budget priorities, scientific and statistical activities, interdepartmental problems of emergency preparedness, intergovernmental relations, and legislative clearance on an interdepartmental basis. It has even gone to the point of prior central clearance of governmental forms that must be filled out by the private sector so that the "involuntary civil service" will not be overburdened by duplicating demands for information. A certain central influence for procedural standardization by government agencies is maintained by a number of agencies: Accounting and disbursement by the Treasury; international cables, protocol, and conferences by State; procurement and records by General Services Administration; preparation of estimates by Budget; personnel by the Civil Service Commission; and legality of expenditures by the General Accounting Office. The creation of the large new departments, such as Defense, Health, Education and Welfare, Housing and Urban Development, and Transportation, were in themselves major steps toward across the board coordination in their respective fields. The Department of Justice has a coordinating influence in the legal opinions the Attorney General issues and in his contacts with the departmental law officers, not to speak of actions of the solicitor general before the courts. Many specialized agencies exert a coordinating influence in their own fields of competence, even when their legal coordinating powers are slender. Items on today's agenda of unfinished business on interdepartmental coordination that have high priority are in the fields of national security, conservation of the environment, welfare, race relations, and urbanism. Other attempts to induce across-the-board coordination at regional levels and in the Executive Office of the President will be discussed in the concluding sections of this chapter.

5. Regionalism, Decentralization, and Layering

There has been an enormous amount of lip service in regard to the necessity for decentralization of the federal executive establishment and for getting government "closer to the people." In a brief treatment of this complex subject, only a few of its phases can be treated and they will be in the nature of questions rather than of answers. The definitive theoretical work in the study of federal field offices has been done by my friend and former colleague, Professor James W. Fesler of Yale University, starting with his pioneering essay on "Executive Management and the Federal Field Service" for the President's Committee on Administrative Management in 1937.[12] His recommendations have had a marked effect on the considerable decentralization that has already been accomplished in such fields as civil service administration, disbursement of federal funds, and procurement. The present move to establish common headquarters cities for certain federal agencies was influenced by his early recommendations, later reiterated by the first Hoover Commission. He uttered the first, but still sound, warning against overstandardization of the boundaries of federal regions in view of the great variety of federal functions. The importance of reconsidering the assumptions of regionalization and decentralization is closely related to the urgent need to consider federal structure and system from the viewpoint of the bottom up. It is also occasioned by the great growth of the departmental units and their introduction of numerous new layers in the hierarchy. It is influenced by the interrelationship of federal programs which cross departmental lines in the urban poverty and conservation programs. New elements have been introduced by the creation of regional development commissions and interstate compacts for regional development. The poverty, model cities, and grant-in-aid programs make imperative more effective federal coordination in the field. Finally, the growth of technology in regard to automatic data processing, systems analysis, and operations research, as well as the improvements in transportation and communications are changing the nature of the problem.

Field administration is a topic in which the varieties of federal activity make generalizations both difficult and hazardous. A distinction has to be made first of all between various types of federal activity. There are those which affect only limited parts of the country.

There are activities which the government operates directly, such as the collection of the internal revenue and the settlement of old-age insurance claims. There are others, as we have seen, by grants-in-aid, by loans, by insurance, and by the contractual device in which it depends on indirect administration through chosen instruments. In a number of cases, such as the Council of Economic Advisers and certain central statistical bureaus, no permanent regional or field stations are called for. In other instances, the administrative headquarters are actually outside Washington; for example, the Bureau of Reclamation has its engineering and research center in Denver. Central regulatory agencies often require no field stations. The use of electronic data processing has brought about great decentralized processing centers as in the case of disbursement, internal revenue, and social security. From time to time there are changes in the emphasis of functions which call for a reconsideration of field offices. The emphasis of the Weather Bureau, now part of the Environmental Science Services Administration, in the Department of Commerce, has over the years gone from ships at sea, to services to farmers, to services to aviation. But even within that Administration, the Coast and Geodetic Survey and its Marine Centers have, with good reason, different field offices than the Weather Bureau. Public Roads, starting with a farm-to-market mission, ended with concentration of effort on the interstate highway system, the greatest public works undertaking in history. Certain programs have seasonal, periodical, and cyclical peak workloads calling for great temporary expansion at various times, such as the Post Office at Christmas time, the Internal Revenue Service at tax time, and the Census Bureau every ten years. The location of field offices also has great permutations and combinations. Outlying installations of N.A.S.A., the National Institutes of Health, and other scientific and technical agencies are not necessarily "field offices" at all, like post offices which render identical services. Each one has a special mission and its location is based upon a variety of technical, administrative, and political factors.

The questions I wish to raise on federal field organization can be briefly stated but their answers will require a massive amount of administrative research and analysis which only the government itself is in a position to do. I have already touched lightly on the larger regional questions involving federal relations with neighborhood groups, local authorities, states, and interstate regional bodies, and omit these questions here.

THE GEOGRAPHIC VIEW AT HEADQUARTERS

In regard to the welfare, poverty, and model cities programs and in fact many related programs now in the Office of Economic Opportunity, the Department of Health, Education, and Welfare, and the Department of Housing and Urban Development, there seems to be a special need for the representation of the geographic or regional viewpoint at Washington in the headquarters of the department itself. The same factors may be present in some of the agricultural and conservation programs. The impact of these programs and their interrelationships needs the regional viewpoint at headquarters to counteract the secular pressures of the specialized bureaus and administrations and to coordinate the regulations before, not after, they are sent to the field men.

Questions: Should not the regional directors be headquartered at the national capital in Washington, and would this not serve the purposes of greater decentralization to the district and local field men than by the stationing of regional directors in regional capitals? If this is done, should not the regional director be responsible to the head of the department and not to any single bureau or administration? Is it desirable and feasible to locate district field offices of related programs in the same city in order to foster cooperation and coordination by propinquity as is being tried now in the case of regional offices?

LAYERING AT THE FIELD LEVEL

Within the social and economic services, three layers of field offices, and sometimes more, can be found: local ones, for face-to-face service to citizens; district ones, within reasonable travel distance; and regional offices covering a group of contiguous states assumed to have a certain homogeneity. Some agencies like the Federal Housing Administration have state offices, but a state director almost invariably becomes politically beholden to a single senator, and federal agencies tend to avoid their creation. At the departmental level there are at least three layers of hierarchy to clear novel or disputed cases, that of the secretary, the administrator of a service, and the chief of a bureau. This does not take into account the personnel, legal, accounting, and other functional clearances involved in modifying a procedure. If the regional level also contains three levels, regional, district, and local, one can easily visualize that numerous questions initiated at the local level may have to mount six layers before the problem, if it is important, intricate, or politically charged, can be resolved. When it involves conflicts among several departments, it may have to go through the same layering process in two or more agencies. The delays to the inquiring citizen or public authority or contractor, occasioned by this amount of layering, can frequently be unjust if not ruinous. The second grouped questions to be raised are in a sense a corollary of the first:

> Questions: In view of the availability of instant telephone and teletype facilities, is it not more effective to establish direct communications between the district office (presumably within a few hours trip of the locus of the inquirer) and the regional officer at Washington headquarters for faster, more precise, and more authoritative decisions on difficult points? Will the cost of this and the time required for settling the matter not be considerably less than if every question must be relayed through a regional director? If the problem calls for a reconsideration of basic policies and systems, will it not have to go to Washington in any event, and precisely what does the interposition of the regional director add to the process?

STRUCTURE OF A REGIONAL OR DISTRICT OFFICE

Regional offices, such as those of the Departments of H.E.W. and H.U.D., tend to be small replicas or "mini-capitols" of the departmental capitol. Each substantive program has an outposted regional officer in charge. The functional units of headquarters are also represented, such as personnel, procurement, budget and accounting, space, and sometimes even law. Each substantive and functional officer tends to seek guidance and instruction from his counterpart in Washington, and the role of the regional director is inevitably one of influence and persuasion rather than of direction.

> Questions: Has establishment of the regional office in regard to substantive and functional activities actually produced decentralization and coordination at the field level or has it in fact had a recentralizing effect by outposting the fractionalized segments of a department and their differences to the region? Does not this question lend itself admirably to an operations research project on a grand scale?

RECENTRALIZING EFFECT OF AUTOMATIC DATA PROCESSING

There is a growing amount of unassembled evidence that the precision imposed by automatic data processing systems tends to foster a rigidity of field regulations which reduces the area of discretion of outposted officials. This is a tendency which needs to be closely watched and on which research and analysis are also urgently needed. With the growing competence of digital computer technology and its increasing flexibility, there may now be possible solutions of this problem without abandonment of the many great advantages of automatic data processing and transmission. But the authority conferred on a regional or district man needs to be made more flexible and designed to increase his zones of discretion in the light of the growing insistence for more consultation and participation by consumer and producer groups of federally financed services. There is the further possibility that the amount of recording of actions that is required will be so time-consuming that it will impinge on the time needed for negotiations and operations. There is a tendency in regulations regarding data recording to prescribe not only what can be done but precisely how it is to be done. These are subtle influences and difficult to identify, but new kinds of tests are needed to diagnose them lest the use of judgment and experience by the field man be unduly restricted by the demands of mechanical data systems. The over-enthusiasm of program planners may be having the effect that the outposted officer is serving the data-hungry machine more than he is responding to the needs of the citizen or agency with which he does business. Even when the basic legislation and regulations provide certain options and present the possibility of choosing sensible alternatives in varying cases, the mechanical demands of data processing may restrict these choices and obliterate the nuances.

Basic questions of another kind are now being raised as to the effect of data gathering on the privacy of the individual and on human rights. Another phase of this problem is the danger of flooding government executives with so much data, much of it of minor relevance, that the decision-making process is impeded rather than facilitated.

> Questions: How can use of modern automatic data processing be modified so as to improve the human relations of administration in order to accord more flexible options to the field officer? What steps should be taken to safeguard private rights, and to provide only the data that are essential and relevant for the use of decision makers?

MULTIPURPOSE ONE-STOP SERVICE CENTERS

This is not a new proposal and dates back to the so-called Elberfeld plan in Germany under Bismarck in which a local office in which all the social services were available to the needy was devised long before the motor age. Denmark has recently adopted a program for conveniently located, combined social service centers. Such centers in our country seem to be an urgent need and should include all the social services whether they are city, county, state, or federal operated, and in many communities the voluntary social service organizations should be included. James L. Sundquist has reported on the growth of multi-purpose one-stop service centers under the model cities programs.[13] Many cities have no adequate public transportation and in many places the distances and the time lost from home or from work to reach numerous service centers prevent the client from receiving any service at all. One of the characteristics of poverty is to be carless, and this is a factor which motorized administrators should not overlook.

> Question: How best can the federal government encourage the provision of multipurpose one-stop local social service centers within reach of the carless?

6. The Executive Office of the President

The Executive Office of the President was the major administrative legacy of President Franklin D. Roosevelt and originated in the recommendations of the Brownlow Committee. These recommendations included the proposal for the six anonymous assistants on the White House staff. Every President has changed it and added to its scope and size and the two Hoover Commissions endorsed the strengthening of its management functions. Its existence is now taken for granted and no President would undertake to administer the presidency, given the present scope of the executive establishment, without this important institutional conning-tower. It is a fitting theme on which to conclude these administrative commentaries.

A long-term view and a philosophy of organization have been notably lacking in regard to the Executive Office and the White House establishment. It has been subject to improvisation and its structure has responded excessively to temporary pressures. These instruments are sharp and glamorous tools, and must be used with considerable restraint. When departments are baffled by new and complex problems, an easy solution seems to be to create a unit in the Executive Office to handle them. The danger is, instead of facilitating and assisting the work of the President, that it will become so loaded with miscellaneous operations that it impedes him, over-institutionalizes him, and undermines the authority and responsibility of the political department

heads. Mr. Truman said about the White House, "the buck stops here";
but much of it should be compelled to stop at a secretary's level.

A clear distinction should be made, in my view, between the character of the White House staff and the rest of the Executive Office. The
former should be kept personal, fluid, and deinstitutionalized. None of
its professionals should be assigned duties in substantive fields. It
should be greatly reduced in size. In 1939 the White House staff was
reported to have 45 people, and 250 in 1968. In the 1971 budget of
President Nixon the following statement was made:

> The 1971 estimate is a new departure, proposed in the interest of candor
> and accuracy, to give the Congress and the nation a long overdue ap-
> preciation of White House costs and needs. In fiscal year 1970 and prior
> years a considerable segment of White House staff costs has not been
> readily apparent as many White House staff personnel have been paid
> from the appropriations of other federal agencies. . . . . . . So that the
> total costs of White House Office staff operations can be clearly seen and
> accurately measured in future years, the 1971 budget requests provide
> direct funding for all regular staff assistance and administrative services
> within the "salaries and expenses, White House Office appropriation."

White House Office employment is then listed as follows:

	1970	1971
White House Office	208	548
Special Projects	95	....
Detailed from other Federal Agencies	273	....
Total	576	548

The special projects appropriation "is retained to be utilized by the
President for special requirements such as those of a non-recurring nature and those outside the normal responsibility of other funded program areas." Although this is represented as a decrease in staff from
previous years, it is apparent that, if staff is paid for out of special
projects funds, it cannot help but be an increase. Not only is the size
of this entourage appalling, but it reveals what I regard as a dangerous
tendency to overstaff and institutionalize the White House staff, bur-
dening the President with an increasing number of access points and
with the problems of administering his own establishment instead of
the government as a whole. The very office that should be an extension
of the personality of the President begins to assume the stature of an
elaborate apparatus, inevitably taking actions and positions that no
President can control. Its members, vying for position, not only must get

in each other's way but begin to assume public roles which are a far cry from the earlier concept of anonymity.

The size of the more institutionalized Executive Office seems of little importance compared to that of the White House staff, but its roles and missions must be rigorously limited. Mr. James A. Hightower of the Legislative Reference Service reports that the number of employees, excluding the 2,870 members of the Office of Economic Opportunity, but including the White House staff, rose from 570 in 1939 to 1348 in 1968.[14] The Bureau of the Budget staff represented 544 of these in 1968.

More important than numbers is the concept that should govern its components. That the President and the Ash Council are giving serious consideration to this topic is indicated by President Nixon's message referred to in the preceding chapter. The message of March 12, 1970, had among other things these encouraging comments for the future of the Executive Office:

> In 1939, President Franklin D. Roosevelt proposed and the Congress accepted a reorganization plan that laid the groundwork for providing managerial assistance for the modern presidency. The plan placed the Bureau of the Budget within the Executive Office of the President. It made available to the President direct access to important new management instruments.) . .
> Over three decades, the Executive Office of the President has mushroomed but not by conscious design. In many areas it does not provide the kind of staff assistance and support the President needs in order to deal with the problems of government in the 1970's. We confront the 1970's with a staff organization geared in large measure to tasks of the 1940's and 1950's.
> One result, over the years, has been a tendency to enlarge the immediate White House staff—that is, the President's personal staff as distinct from the institutional structure—to assist with management functions for which the President is responsible. This has blurred the distinction between personal staff and management institutions; it has left key management functions to be performed only intermittently and some not at all. It has perpetuated outdated structures.[15]

Reorganization Plan 2 of 1970 which accompanied the message distinguishes sharply, I fear too nostalgically, between policy determination and executive management. It establishes a Domestic Council of cabinet level to "coordinate policy formulation in the domestic area" and provides it with an institutional staff as a domestic counterpart of the National Security Council. The permanent institutional staff is to provide "an institutional memory" to achieve continuity.

Its executive director is to be one of the President's assistants. The Domestic Council will consolidate the work of the present Council for Urban Affairs, the Cabinet Committee on the Environment, and the Council for Rural Affairs. But various subcommittees of the new Domestic Council are contemplated to work on special topics. This cabinet-level council, with subcommittees, and a permanent professional staff, thus seems to be the Nixon pattern for policy study and formulation. How it is to be brought into relationship with outside task forces and special ad hoc study commissions, of which President Johnson created 101 in a three-year period, still remains to be seen.[16]

The creation of a cabinet level Domestic Council has a number of serious disabilities. The processing of policy is one of the most difficult tasks of the President, and almost the only principle one can be reasonably sure of is that he should leave himself the utmost flexibility in the way each policy area should be handled. By Reorganization Plan 2 of 1970, the President gives the force of law to a rigid pattern of a Domestic Council of cabinet members through which he virtually commits himself to process his requests for policy studies. In a well intentioned effort to reduce the plethora of reports and advice emanating from ad hoc commissions, task forces, and study groups such as recent Presidents have created, Plan 2 goes to the other extreme of voluntary imprisonment in a single channel.

A Domestic Council at cabinet level is not likely to prove to be boldly innovative. It may even be less so than an interdepartmental committee of career officials. Each honorable and prestigious member (or his alternate) will fight fiercely for his department's prerogatives. Agreement at this level is almost impossible to come by, and the President will find himself compelled to make the decisions, large and small. Such a council has a stupendous capacity for watering down a subject in arriving at a decision that looks like a consensus. It will be unlikely to advertise its differences by presenting a series of alternatives to the President. Subcommittees on various topics are contemplated but may find themselves inhibited by the Domestic Council as soon as they have begun to formulate proposals.

The analogy of a Domestic Council to the National Security Council which considers foreign and defense policies at first reading sounds plausible. But the actual differences are vast. The problems of the National Security Council usually arise from the pressure of external events and the action of foreign powers, and their gravity compels attention and resolution. Only two major departments are involved, State and Defense, and the difficulties of agreement even under such circumstances have been the increasing concern of Congress and the nation. With all the rest of the cabinet sitting on the Domestic Council, it is difficult to conceive how agreement could be reached even on the agenda of topics to be studied. For each topic, there will be members who will be intensely concerned and others who could not care less. Cabinet blocs will be formed and political trades will be fostered. Plan 2, furthermore, overlooks the immense areas of domestic concern of both the Secretary of State and the Secretary of Defense, who are not represented on the Domestic Council. Both the analogy and the dichotomy are invalid.

The most constructive part of the Domestic Council scheme is its provision for a permanent responsible secretariat to serve ad hoc task forces and subcommittees on policy studies. Such a secretariat in the Executive Office has long been needed. But such a unit must be more than an "institutional memory" of career officials. In spite of the growing capacity of the career services, the stimulus of outside talent in formulating innovative programs will continue to be an indispensable adjunct of a policy secretariat. The special projects appropriation to the President was intended precisely for such "nonrecurring" purposes.

The complete outline of the Executive Office reorganization has not yet been revealed. However, Plan 2 also includes a provision for creating a new Office of Management and Budget, incorporating for the most part the existing functions of the Bureau of the Budget. In addition to its units which work on budget and program evaluation, the press release identifies five other possible work units: (1) program coordination, (2) legislative reference, (3) executive development, (4) organization and management systems, and (5) management information systems. Further action is awaited as the President's Advisory Council on Executive Organization, headed by Roy Ash, continues its work, which will further clarify exactly what is intended for the Executive Office and its new component Office of Management and Budget. The high priority given to management in the title of the office has already been noted. It is not clear how the functions of "the development of executive talent" will fit in with the present duties of the Civil Service Commission and the White House staff engaged in the recruitment of political executives. But the message adds that, "The new Office of Management and Budget will place much greater emphasis on the evaluation of pro-

gram performance" on an overall basis. Nor is it yet apparent which
parts of the present Executive Office will be retained and how they
will be related to the new offices.[17]

My own summation of the kind of activities which should be
conducted in the Executive Office and the White House staff is, I
believe, not too inconsistent with the viewpoint of Robert Wood,
former Under Secretary of H.U.D., and can best be expressed in a
series of negatives:[18]

• Operating functions which serve a substantive program or the
public should be excluded from the Executive Office of the President.
The presidency should not be in a position of competing with the
substantive departments and agencies for functions, authority, funds,
or personnel.

• So far as possible the Executive Office of the President should
be kept as the across-the-board agency par excellence. Its coordinating
functions should be kept at a high general level, should not involve
day-to-day operational coordination, and should to the greatest possible extent be in the realm of overall policy, administrative management, and organization.

• No policy decision or function of coordination which can possibly
be administered at the departmental level should be undertaken by
the executive office or the presidency. The President should limit
his political and administrative exposure and share credit and blame
to the utmost with his cabinet.

• The White House aides are the President's personal assistants.
Their number should be kept small and their duties should be kept
as fluid, quiet, and personal as possible. The Executive Office is the
institutionalized part of his establishment and repetitive functions
requiring continuity and large staffs should be assigned to it under
a limited number of directors or advisers. The authority and prestige
of these directors is in direct proportion to the amount of business
they transact in the President's name and not in their own. In this
respect they differ markedly from members of the cabinet, who must
take public positions in their respective fields.

• Secretariats to staff cabinet councils and ad hoc commissions
should not be in the White House itself, but in the Executive Office
of the President, which is a more suitable environment for continuous
professional staff, some of it assigned from the career services. And
the White House should in no event be over-populated.

• On the difficult problem of overall coordination, it is no solution to furnish the President with a number of continuing top level co-ordinators, who will inevitably intervene in the functions which reside in the cabinet heads. The attempts to do this even in World War II were not too satisfactory. Ad hoc temporary coordinators may be needed at times, but the President has a number of other alternatives described above and he should not be confined to a single pattern, least of all a stable of coordinators waiting for something to co-ordinate.

• The creation of "super cabinet" officials is inadvisable. They are more of a danger to the President's control of the executive branch than the appointment of "coordinators without portfolio." From time to time, leading authorities have recommended this device particularly in the field of foreign affairs and defense. In 1955, ex-President Hoover recommended the appointment or election of two vice-presidents, one for foreign and one for domestic affairs. Governor Nelson A. Rockefeller in his testimony in 1960 before the Jackson subcommittee in the Senate called for the appointment of a first secretary of the government in the area of international affairs and national security. President Eisenhower in his last annual budget message for fiscal year 1962 took up this proposal as follows:

> I have reached the conclusion that serious attention should be given to providing in the President's Office an official ranking higher than the cabinet members, possibly with the title of First Secretary of the Government, to assist the President in consulting with the departments on the formulation of national security objectives, in coordinating international programs, and in representing the President at meetings with foreign officials above the rank of Foreign Minister and below the rank of head of State.

President "Ike" thus recommended a kind of international Sherman Adams as a counterpart to his powerful domestic one to whom he had accorded an unusual measure of authority. "Czars," "coordinators without portfolio," and "First Secretaries" have a strange resemblance to premiers and prime ministers and somehow do not sound natural in the American environment. A more flexible Executive Office and a strengthening of the department heads and their staffs seem to me more likely to succeed in the light of our customs and traditions. Such institutional arrangements will permit the President of the United States to delegate parts of his heavy load but will not compel him to abdicate any major component of his responsibility and authority.

Stephen K. Bailey, in his profound and illuminating essay on "Managing the Federal Government," perceives that there are no single and final solutions to many of the problems facing the organization of the presidency, and that each President will need to conform the structure of the Executive Office to the needs of the times and to his own style of working. He makes a strong case for having the President secure from Congress the right to structure and to manage his own office without restriction, "including the right to make in-office appointments without Senate confirmation and the right to create, shift, and abolish constituent units and personnel assignments as he deems necessary for the effective conduct of presidential business." He also advocates a large increase in the President's discretionary fund.[19]

What is a fitting ending to a book on an unending subject in which the issues are so great and the stakes so vast? In an era of chronic crises at home and abroad, the executive branch of the government of the United States has been given awesome responsibilities. The United States has emerged as the major democratic world-power service-state. It cannot relapse into a spirit of defeatism in regard to making its government more manageable. It has to be made so and the American people have the ability to make it so. The most crying international and domestic needs of our times render it imperative that it be made so. The fate of the world depends on the ability of the American government to manage its affairs: peaceful progress in this country and cooperation with other lands; the improvements of human relations and the development of the human species to its fullest capacities; the conservation of both the natural resources and of the man-made environment; and in the last analysis, the preservation of life itself on this planet.

MEETING OF THE PRESIDENT
AND HIS COMMITTEE ON
ADMINISTRATIVE MANAGEMENT
WITH THE MAJORITY LEADERS
OF THE HOUSE AND SENATE

The White House, Sunday, January 10, 1937, at 4:00 p.m.
(transcribed verbatim from the author's diary)

Present:

President Franklin D. Roosevelt
Vice-President John N. Garner
Assistant to the President James Roosevelt (the President's son)
Senators:
    Pat Harrison (Mississippi), Chairman, Finance Committee
    Joseph T. Robinson (Arkansas), Majority Leader
Representatives:
    William B. Bankhead (Alabama), Speaker of the House
    James Buchanan (Texas), Chairman, Appropriations Committee
    Robert L. Doughton (North Carolina), Chairman, Ways and Means
        Committee
    Sam Rayburn (Texas), Majority Leader
President's Committee on Administrative Management:
Members of the Committee:

Louis Brownlow, Chairman; Charles E. Merriam, Luther Gulick
Staff of the Committee:
  Herbert Emmerich, adviser (Executive Officer, Farm Credit Administration)
  Joseph P. Harris, director of research (Director of Research, Committee on Public Administration, Social Science Research Council)
  Clinton M. Hester, legal adviser (Assistant General Counsel, Treasury Department)
  William H. McReynolds, adviser (Administrative Assistant to the Secretary of the Treasury)

While waiting to see the President in the Green Room on the first floor, Congressmen Doughton and Bankhead mentioned the number of attempts that had been made with little success to reorganize the executive departments. They mentioned the terrible complexity of the executive structure and the time it took congressmen to ascertain what bureaus were handling various activities. They felt that shifting of bureaus and functions had to be done by executive action and legislation would not succeed if it named the changes to be made.

The President received us in his study on the second floor of the main house. During the entire conference he was seated on a leather couch facing the rest of the group. The committee of three were on the side of the room; senators and congressmen centered in front of the President; and the members of the staff and his son were in the back row. It was raining hard outside and the room was rather cool; unpleasantly so during the conference. A strong odor of Havana tobacco wrapper emanated from an enormous inlaid wood humidor, to which the congressional members made frequent trips. Pat Harrison sat at the other corner of the couch on which the President was seated, facing him. Although I had a full view of Harrison's face, it was impossible at any time during the two hours' conference to ascertain his reactions.

The President wore a light gray suit, soft collar, and smoked cigarettes in a little paper holder. He successfully hides his physical disability; it was only evident when he crossed his legs, which he did very quickly by lifting them with his hands. The massiveness of his head has often reminded me of a lion's and his conduct of the entire session reminded me of that animal's feline characteristics.

The presentation of the committee's recommendations was an enormous dose in one setting. At every point its iconoclasm necessarily shocked congressional habit patterns. The President presented the entire program himself, relying upon Brownlow and Gulick only occasionally for questions. He jumped around like a cat, three steps ahead of everyone. Among the numerous branches of this complicated tree he barely touched the branches which seemed to give slightly under his weight and rested securely on those which seemed to support him.

I took no notes, but the following represents to the best of my recollection, but not necessarily in the order in which the points were made, the President's presentation of the report. He read the committee's summary of the bill and enlarged upon it somewhat in the following manner:

President: I like that word "management." It is popular and this thing is going to be popular. People talk of a good housewife as a "good manager" and when the father of a big family runs things well he is called a "good manager." The problem of better administrative management is one that has troubled me for some time. In 1933 we were too busy with the problems of the emergency program to give it the consideration it deserved, but several consolidations of agencies were made at that time, and an attempt was made by the establishment of the National Emergency Council to improve the coordination of the government's program. The President's task has become impossible for me or any other man. A man in this position will not be able to survive White House service unless it is simplified. I need executive assistants with a "passion for anonymity" to be my legs.

A Senator: Try and find them.

President: I have to contact eight people alone on foreign affairs: four in the State Department; others in Commerce, Agriculture, and Tariff Commission. One of my assistants could save me many of these contacts and might help us to eliminate the necessity for the Interdepartmental Committee on Foreign Trade which has its own staff and costs money. One of the assistants would not go out. I have no legal help directly available. When I am called up about a bill from Congress, I have no one to advise me on the legal and parliamentary aspects. The Attorney General has a big department to operate, and I cannot always call on him. These are only two examples. (Several of the congressional group indicated that there would be no difficulty in getting additional assistance needed by the President through an appropriation bill.)

President: But I also need managerial agencies to help me in this job on fiscal, personnel, and planning. Greater aid should be given to me by the Bureau of the Budget, which now reports to me directly. It should be authorized to improve its staff and to perform certain services on coordination of informational activities. On the personnel side, the President needs a single administrator to operate the civil service system. He should be part of my establishment.

Congressman Doughton: The Social Security Board seems to be hiring only Republicans.

President: They are under civil service, but what can I do about the civil service now? It has old lists which are not up to date. It is the weakest agency in the government. It must be reorganized. A non-partisan board of citizens, serving without compensation, would watch the operations of the administrator and see that the merit system is upheld.

The planning board is very necessary for me and will help Buch. It may be that we will have a billion dollars' worth of public works projects submitted and Buch and I will feel, together with the Senate leaders, that we ought to spend only fifty million because of the budget and because of employment conditions. The Army Engineers, the Reclamation Service, and the Public Works Administration all think their projects should be preferred. It will be very valuable to Buch and me to have an overall agency to tell us which projects should be put on a preferred list and classify them.

Chairman Buchanan: It would be very helpful. We had such a bill for making permanent the National Resources Board last year, but it narrowly failed of passage at the end of the session.

President: Another example of lack of coordination is in this matter of crop loans. I wish some one would tell me what in hell is a crop loan or a seed loan. Farm Credit has one idea; Resettlement has another; and Harry Hopkins another.

(This remark of the President's aroused a number of very violent criticisms of the wastefulness and poor administration of the Resettlement Administration, especially by Senator Robinson; also by Congressman Buchanan and the Vice-President. The President came to the defense of the rehabilitation policy of Resettlement and stated their collection record of 75 per cent of loans made in over a hundred thousand cases and that he believed it was better to rehabilitate these small farmers than to make them permanent subjects for relief, as well as cheaper in the long run for the government.)

President: Harry Byrd was in here the other day and he said he thought we could save a lot of money by reorganization. I told him that would be fine, but how much could we save. The overhead cost of administration is, after all, a small part of the total budget of the government. Eight hundred million dollars is for interest and debt service—none of this will be saved. Over a billion dollars is for national defense—none of this will be saved. Sums for social security and for aid to states and public works cannot be saved. Out of the budget of seven billion dollars, some administrative savings might be made, but only in the item of less than two billion dollars. I asked Harry how much he thought we could save. He said 'maybe fifty million dollars.' I told him that I thought he was probably right and it is worth doing, but don't let us mislead the people that the main objective of this reorganization plan is savings. It is better organization and better management. The history of the reorganizations in the State of New York under Al Smith, where 120 bureaus were consolidated under 18 departments, made the job of governor a cinch, but they saved no money. Harry Byrd's reorganization in the State of Virginia, which Luther Gulick helped on, made negligible savings. (Here Luther Gulick cited some figures of fractional percentages of savings based on the same activities as they were before the reorganization.) Gardiner of Maine, Angus McClain of North Carolina, also improved their state governments, but the savings were not appreciable.

As Democrats we ought to be interested in the civil service provisions which the committee suggests—that is, to bring everything but the policy-forming positions under the classified civil service and to permit incumbents who have served with merit to take noncompetitive examinations.

We are also proposing to increase salaries in the top grades. We are losing good men every day now and this has always been the case when times are good. I cut the committee down somewhat. I was more hardboiled than they, but I think just a slight increase at the top will do the trick. Bringing secretaries to $20,000, career service between $12,000 and $15,000 for top positions.

Senator Robinson: Mr. President, why does this question, which seems irrelevant to the question of reorganization, have to be introduced? It is my opinion that it may defeat your main objective as there will be a great deal of opposition in both Houses. Some of the members feel that their legislative services are also of value to the government and that their present salary of $10,000 a year is adequate. I strongly urge considering making this a separate measure if you feel it is desirable and not confuse the issue in this bill.

President: You leaders of the House and Senate and chairmen of the important committees have jobs that are worth as much as any cabinet position. However, the great bulk of congressmen do not have nearly the responsibility or the work that you have.

(Several other members of Congress indicated their agreement with this view.)

President: It would be an easy matter to take this section out. Of course, the way in which legislation is introduced is up to you gentlemen, but I feel there is a real need for this if we wish to improve the executive service and make a career of it. We do not have to equal salaries paid in private life, but a few thousand dollars added at the top salaries will do the trick.

We have tried to draft a tentative outline of a bill which is just something for you gentlemen to put your teeth into.

In addition to the three managerial agencies for fiscal, personnel, and planning which I have described, there would be two additional departments. Every activity in the government would be brought under a department.

Congressman Rayburn: Would there be no exception? The Interstate Commerce Commission is the oldest agency and it is very popular. There would be a lot of objection to coordinating it.

President: There would be not one exception. Of course, I am referring to the executive and administrative functions of the independent agencies. They have grown hit or miss in the last fifty years and there are so many now I cannot keep track of them and have no control over them. I am the only one who is responsible under the constitution. I am not referring to their judicial functions. These should be independent as though they were part of the district court.

Vice-President: All the bureaus will be up on the Hill saying they should be left out of this plan. The President will not object, I am sure, if I relate that at a recent cabinet meeting I stated to the department heads that the bureau chiefs could object all they wanted to, but if they did they should have their heads chopped off.

President: This bill gives the President broad powers to reorganize all the agencies within these departments. The question arises as to whether or not he has the right to dismiss employees after consolidations. That is always the hardest thing to do. This bill gives him the right, doesn't it, Mr. Brownlow?

Mr. Hester: Yes, that is in the bill.

President: The bill creates two new departments. One of Public Works and one of Social Welfare.

Senator Robinson: I hope you will consider that question of the Department of Social Welfare very seriously. It seems to me that if we create such a department we will never be able to get rid of a lot of the welfare activity and it will cost a great deal of money. Special groups will insist that the government extend their welfare activities indefinitely. Our experience with departments and bureaus has been that they are always trying to extend their work. I had hoped that we could now liquidate some of the activities of the emergency rather than make them permanent.

(Mr. Brownlow explained the functions that were intended to be exercised by the Department of Social Welfare and the functions that might properly be exercised by the Department of Public Works as proposed in the report and in the draft of the bill.)

Senator Robinson: I would prefer the word "public" to "social" in the name of the new department.

President: The Department of Public Works would not necessarily build all the public works. Buch and I are having a problem right now with the Army Engineers. We are being criticized because of the large army appropriation for defense, but almost one-fourth of a billion dollars is for the Army Engineers' river and harbors public work. That should not be in the War Department appropriation. The Army Engineers should be a standby organization for times of war. That is what it is for. Who can tell me whether Reclamation, Public Works, or Army Engineers should build a new dam or irrigation project? We have problems of river control, power, navigation, and irrigation on these big projects. There is competitive bidding among the various contracting agencies of the government building public works and unsatisfactory timing. I have to deal with too many of them. So does Buch. This bill would give us one public works program where we can see it. It does not necessarily mean that this department would do all the construction. The building of federal buildings is in the Treasury Department. It should come out. Public Health Service has no place in the Treasury and should be in Welfare. Then we are proposing that Interior's name be changed to "Conservation."

I am saying in my message transmitting this report, which I am sending up to you Tuesday, that this committee has not spared me, has not spared government corporations, and has not spared the Comptroller General. They don't like the way we have set up government corporations without control. (Congressman Buchanan showed great glee over this remark.) They think the Comptroller General ought to be the Auditor General and that Congress should have a committee to receive his reports and that he should be independent of the executive. The executive should have the right to settle claims and provision is made for reference to the Attorney General who has to defend these cases. He is the proper law officer and that is where it should be. The Auditor General should be like Haskins & Sells, C.P.A.s, making an independent audit of the General Motors Corporation for the board and stockholders, and should not have any jurisdiction over current operations and expenditures.

Vice-President: There was considerable talk in the debates on this question when they abolished the six auditors in the Treasury. Have you read those debates?

Mr. Brownlow: We have and former Governor Lowden of Illinois and Senator Glass, then secretary of the Treasury, both testified in those hearings that this would not work and that audit should be separate from accounting and control of expenditures. I recently spoke to ex-Governor Lowden and he still has that view.

President: The first Comptroller General extended his jurisdiction constantly and he was licked in the courts practically every time there was a case. He did not give reports to Congress that the law contemplated and that you were entitled to. This subject is very important.

Speaker Bankhead: When this bill is introduced, it will have to be referred to an appropriate committee.

President: That is right—it will have to be referred somewhere.

Speaker Bankhead: It cannot be referred just anyplace that we think is desirable. Chairman Cochran of the House Committee on Expenditures in the Executive Departments may move to have it referred to his committee and the House may sustain him. I don't see how the civil service provisions would belong there.

Vice-President: May I suggest, Mr. President, that we arrange for a conference with the legislative counsel of the House and Senate and the committee. We would like it if you did not send up the bill with your report, but let us give it consideration for a few days as to the best way of handling it. Maybe a special committee in each House should be appointed and maybe it could be referred to the committee under Mr. Doughton and Senator Harrison.

President: That is all right, and we can do that very well. It would be very easy, if necessary, to take some of the personnel clauses out of this bill.

As you all know, this is not a program that can be carried out quickly. I estimate that it will take at least three years to accomplish the reorganization once the necessary authority is granted.

❖ ❖ ❖ ❖

After some further discussion of the parliamentary problems, the congressional delegation left about six o'clock.

Mr. Brownlow presented the rest of us to the President.

President: I hope you gentlemen of the committee and you who have been assisting with this report are not in a mood after this conference to disclaim having any paternity over this report and bill. It is going to be a fight.

(It was agreed that Mr. Hester, legislative counsel of the Treasury, would see the legislative counsel of the House and Senate the first thing Monday morning. He knows them very well and thought that matters could be satisfactorily arranged.)

President: You see, Louis, what I am up against. This was quite a little to give them this afternoon. Every time they recovered from one blow, I socked them under the chin with another. I will see you at four o'clock Monday afternoon at the press conference.

The committee and the staff then departed.

❖ ❖ ❖ ❖

General Observations:

McReynolds was right when he predicted that the increased salary clauses were the greatest obstacles.

The Comptroller General thing went over like I never thought it could. Buchanan was the big obstacle and he was so pleased with the cracking down on the corporations that he was on the band wagon when the General Accounting Office was taken for a ride.

The President *told* them—he did not ask them, except on ways and means of getting it through. They knew it and they knew who was the boss. I have never seen these gentlemen humble before. Their only objections were on the parliamentary and political strategy.

Senator Robinson reminds me of an obstreperous old draft horse who has reluctantly consented to harness and who continues to carry the big load effectively and persistently, but one always feels, with many mental reservations.

Speaker Bankhead seemed very nervous and was helped considerably by the Vice-President's fatherly advice on parliamentary strategy.

The Vice-President showed himself again to be not only loyal, but extraordinarily able as the President's adviser on congressional technic. *

I have never anticipated a bed of roses, but I am more convinced than before that this program, if it goes across, could only be put across now, immediately after the President's extraordinary majorities and at the height of his prestige.

I was interested by the fact that every member of the House and Senate delegation was a southerner—three from Texas, one from Alabama, one from Arkansas, and one from North Carolina. Most of them are from agricultural communities and small cities. The weight of seniority in a party that was for a long time largely southern has brought about this result.

The committee report rightly extols the wisdom of a strong executive in the American system. What a spectacle this was, though, of the situation caused by the division of power between the legislative and the executive. Even with unprecedented majorities and at the crest of his popularity, the President has to wrangle and plead with the leaders of the legislative arm and go through contortions to avoid sidetracking of a program of the administration by a single member of Congress, protected by his parliamentary privileges.

---

*Vice-President Garner's opposition to President Roosevelt became apparent in the last part of the second term. He opposed the third term nomination of the 1940 Democratic Convention and was succeeded by Henry A. Wallace.

FEDERAL OFFICES, DEPARTMENTS, AND INDEPENDENT AGENCIES ESTABLISHED SINCE 1945

(with classification and comment by the author)

A. *The Four New Departments*

1. DEPARTMENT OF DEFENSE (1947)

This is probably the largest government department in the world and has the unique feature of having four secretaries: a Secretary of Defense of cabinet rank at the summit, and a secretary for each of the three military departments: Army, Navy, and Air. World War II had so forcefully demonstrated the need for joint operations in modern warfare that the unification of the historic War and Navy Departments was inevitable in an era of chronic crisis and military readiness. The creation of a third military department for Air was a recognition of the strategic importance of the Air Force which had already achieved a separate status in World War II as well as a sentimental bow to the crusader for Air Force independence, the late Colonel "Billy" Mitchell (1879–1936). The Unification Act assured the separate identities of the three armed services and "triplification" became "quadruplification" when the commandant of the United States Marine Corps landed at the meetings of the Joint Chiefs of Staff. Unification was expected to produce under civilian control, combined with joint military staff work, a coordinated administration of strategic war plans and operations, and united effort in the fields of logistics and procurement, research and development, and policies and services.

My close contact with the War and Navy Departments as executive secretary of the War Production Board had convinced me of the dysfunctional and wasteful results of separatism in military logistics and procurement. I later acted as consultant to Director of the Budget James E. Webb during the inter-service debate on unification in 1946 and 1947. When Chairman Hoover consulted me in 1947 on the proposed agenda of work for his first commission, I strongly urged the inclusion of a study on defense organization, a topic which had been omitted. (See Chapter IV, p. 98.) The item was added and the ensuing report of the task force under the able chairmanship of Ferdinand Eberstadt influenced both the 1949 legislation and executive action that greatly strengthened the national security organization.

Largely as a result of early Navy opposition to unification, the Department of Defense (D.O.D.) started as a loose federation of the three services, known as the National Military Establishment, created by The National Security Act of 1947 (61 Stat. 578). It was established as an executive department by The National Security Act of 1949 (63 Stat. 578). Subsequent amendments, executive actions, and internal changes have gradually enlarged the authority of the Secretary of Defense and of the Chairman of the Joint Chiefs of Staff, particularly under the dynamic administration of Secretary Robert S. McNamara. In spite of some conspicuous errors and delinquencies, the unification has achieved many of the original objectives although the strong separatist traditions of the uniformed services have made this one of the most difficult mergers to achieve. Even if the military results of the strange wars in Korea and Vietnam were inconclusive, the management of their logistical aspects has been extraordinary.

The unification process was aided on the congressional flank by the replacement of the former separate committees on War and Navy by unified committees on the Armed Services in the House and Senate. There is some evidence that these committees are too uncritical of military requests and that in the matter of military contracts they show a greater interest as to *where* they are let rather than as to the *how* or *why*.

Among the dread decisions that a Secretary of Defense must make are the determination of our total security needs in respect to our foreign policy and world commitments; the selection of weapon systems for research and development in the light of these needs; the procurement of weapon systems in relation to total cost-effectiveness; the extent of review and control to be exercised over the military in regard to logistics and operations; and management judgments on the day-to-day work of a vast establishment. A thoughtful and analytical appraisal of his approach to these problems is to be found in Robert S. McNamara, *The Essence of Security; Reflections in Office* (New York, Harper & Row, 1968).

The gigantic size of the Department of Defense, which spends 42

Exhibit A—Department of Defense: Counterpart Diagram (Officials Reporting to Civilian Secretaries)*

Roles & Missions	Defense	Army	Navy	Air Force
Policy	Secretary Deputy Sec.	Secretary Under Sec.	Secretary Under Sec.	Secretary Under Sec.
Advice & Command	Armed Forces Pol. Council	- - -	- - -	- - -
	Chairman, Jt. Chiefs of Staff	Chief of Staff	Chief of Naval Operations Commandant, Marine Corps	Chief of Staff
Administration	Asst. Sec.	Admin. Sec.	Exec. Asst.	Admin. Asst.
Atomic Energy	Asst. to the Secretary	- - -	- - -	- - -
Civil Defense	- - -	Director	- - -	- - -
Financial Management	Asst. Sec. (Comptroller)	Asst. Sec.	Asst. Sec.	Asst. Sec.
Information & Public Affairs	Asst. Sec. Public Aff.	Chief, Pub. Information	Director, Off. of Inf.	Director, Off. of Inf.
International Security Affairs	Asst. Sec.	- - -	- - -	- - -
Installations & Logistics	Asst. Sec.	Asst. Sec. R. & D.	Asst. Sec. R. & D.	Asst. Sec. R. & D.
Legal	General Counsel	General Counsel	Gen. Coun. Judge Adv. General	General Counsel
Legislative	Asst. to the Secretary	Chief, Leg. Liaison	Chief, Leg. Affairs	Director, Leg. Liaison
Manpower & Reserve	Asst. Sec.	Asst. Sec.	Asst. Sec.	Asst. Sec.
Program Appraisal	- - -	- - -	Director, Office of	- - -
Research, Development & Engr.	Director, R. & E.	Asst. Sec.	Asst. Sec.	Asst. Sec.
Systems Analysis	Asst. Sec.	- - -	- - -	- - -

* Diagram does not show military, logistical, and service commands and other units reporting to Joint Chiefs of Staff, its chairman, Chief of Staff of the Army, Chief of Staff of the Air Force, Chief of Naval Operations, or Commandant, Marine Corps.

per cent of the federal budget, with over 2.8 million men in uniform, with its large bases and missions throughout the world, its privileged cover of secrecy, its powerful effect on the economy, and its strong voice on foreign policy in the National Security Council has justifiably aroused national anxieties concerning excessive military influence on foreign and domestic policies. In my view, civilian and democratic control of its activities will remain one of the most serious continuing problems of our armed democracy, but would be even harder to achieve if the unification had not taken place. Certain counterpart and joint agency features of the Department of Defense organization are depicted in Exhibits A and B.

Exhibit B—Department of Defense:
List of Joint Agencies and Joint S rvice Schools
(Serving D.O.D. and Military Departments)

Defense Atomic Support Agency (DASA): Defense Communications Agency (DCA):	Directors (military) responsible to Secretary of Defense through the Joint Chiefs of Staff.
Defense Contract Audit Agency (DCAA):	Director (civilian) responsible to Secretary of Defense.
Defense Intelligence Agency (DIA):	Director (military) responsible to Secretary of Defense.
Defense Supply Agency (DSA):	Director (military) responsible to Secretary of Defense.
National Security Agency (NSA):	Director (military) responsible to Secretary of Defense.
The National War College:	Commandant (military) under the direction of the Joint Chiefs of Staff.
Industrial College of the Armed Forces:	Commandant (military) under the direction of the Joint Chiefs of Staff.
Armed Forces Staff College:	Commandant (military) under the direction of the Joint Chiefs of Staff.
Armed Services Board of Contract Appeals:	Civilian chairman and two vice-chairmen designated by assistant secretaries of Military Departments.

2. DEPARTMENT OF HEALTH, EDUCATION, AND WELFARE (1953)

At the time of the report of the Brownlow Committee, the respected United States Public Health Service was still in its historic location in the Treasury Department; the tiny Office of Education was in the Department of the Interior; and the Social Security Board was a new and growing independent agency whose functions were the direct administration of the old age and survivors insurance system and indirectly, through grants-in-aid, of the public assistance program. The Brownlow Report advocated the grouping of these and other functions in a new Department of Welfare. Although the Reorganization Act of 1939 pro- hibited the creation of new departments, it was found possible to place this group of activities in a Federal Security Agency under an adminis- trator (Reorganization Plan 1 of 1939).

President Eisenhower created the Department of Health, Education, and Welfare (H.E.W.) by Reorganization Plan 1 of 1953. It is the only major department created by presidential plan under the only Re- organization Act (1949) which authorized such creations. The new department received its functions and powers primarily from the Fed- eral Security Agency, which it superseded.

This huge departmental conglomerate, with expenditures greatly exceeding those of any other civilian department, administers social security, including medicare, and a complex array of programs, mostly of the grant-in-aid variety, in the fields of health, education, and wel- fare, including public assistance. It bears the brunt of executing the most controversial human and social way-of-life programs of our service state. The distinguished former secretary, John W. Gardner, made a strong case for keeping these functions in one department. Professor Rufus E. Miles, Jr., its former assistant secretary for administration, has cogently argued "The Case for a Department of Education" (in *Public Administration Review*, March 1967—Vol. 27, No. 1.).

Other authorities have proposed a separate Department of Educa- tion and Scientific Research to combine all functions having to do with relationships with educational systems, universities, and other scientific research and training institutions. Until the programs and policies of these activities, particularly in regard to public assistance, which are presently undergoing national review are more firmly determined, I do not see the possibility of making structural changes of a sweeping nature. As stated before, the definition of policy and purpose must precede the reallocation of missions and functions in the governmental structure.

In view of the wide variety of its numerous highly specialized and professionalized services and of the sheer size of the department, which, including trust funds, spends over $50 billion annually (one quarter of the federal budget) a reconsideration of its structure should eventually be undertaken. Such a reexamination must give major con- sideration to the impact of its programs on state and local governments and of its relations to activities of the Department of Housing and Urban Development and the poverty programs.

3. DEPARTMENT OF HOUSING AND URBAN DEVELOPMENT (1965)

The creation of the Department of Housing and Urban Development (H.U.D.) culminated a series of actions taken on presidential initiative, each one fraught with heated controversy not only because of the hostility of the private builders and realtors to public housing, but because of highly charged disputes among the various private interests themselves. Its establishment was a symbol of recognition of the concentration of people in the urban places of the country and the continuing problems of housing shortages and urban decay. First recommended by President John F. Kennedy by means of a reorganization plan which the House rejected in February 1962, the department was authorized by Act of Congress in the Johnson administration on September 9, 1965 (79 Stat. 667).

Its earliest predecessor was the National Housing Agency (N.H.A.) established by President F. D. Roosevelt, February 24, 1942, by Executive Order 9070 under authority of the First War Powers Act of December 18, 1941 (55 Stat. 838). It was created after Pearl Harbor to focus and coordinate the efforts of ten competing housing and home finance agencies on the preeminent need of housing for war workers. The National Housing Agency also superseded and was accorded more adequate coordinating powers than had been granted to the Office of Defense Housing Coordination beginning in July 1940. I left the War Production Board to serve as Federal Public Housing Commissioner (1942–4) in the N.H.A. under the astute leadership of its first administrator, John B. Blandford, Jr. With the aid of direct government funding and mortgage insurance, practically all housing built during World War II was directed to the needs of war workers. The number of units built in 1943 and 1944 for this purpose was twice as many *per month* as had been built during the entire period of World War I. Over one-half million of the World War II family housing units were temporaries, and provide one of the few examples of government-built temporary structures that were eliminated before they became substandard.

A peacetime orientation was given to housing activities when President Harry S. Truman established the Housing and Home Finance

Agency (Reorganization Plan 3 of 1947), which succeeded to the functions of N.H.A. with Wilson W. Wyatt, former mayor of Louisville, as its first administrator. The Federal Home Loan Bank Board seceded under the Housing Amendments of 1955 (69 Stat. 640) from a loose union it had never relished. The Federal National Mortgage Association, affectionately known in Wall Street as "Fannie May," departed from the government, pursuant to the provisions of the Urban Development Act of 1968 (82 Stat. 536), and became a "government sponsored private corporation," leaving a limited collection of functions and mortgages in the newly created Government National Mortgage Association, which may become known as "Fannie May Not."

H.U.D. has a complex range of legislative authorizations aimed at increasing the national housing supply for low and middle income families and for reconstructing obsolescent urban areas. Its method is that of loans, grants, and guarantees to local public authorities and financial incentives including F.H.A. mortgage insurance to private enterprise or combinations of these two. It does not build nor operate projects directly, as some of the New Deal and World War II agencies did. Nor do I see a need for the federal government to become a large scale peacetime landlord. The department's impact on urban slums requires close liaison with programs in the fields of health, education, welfare, poverty, race relations, air and water pollution and supply, and transportation.

Since its inception in 1965, the department has been severely handicapped in carrying out its already difficult mandates. Many of its authorizations are only partially funded. The drastic inflation that has been taking place in land and construction costs, in interest rates on mortgages, in maintenance expenses, and the critical shortage of mortgage money have increased the difficulties of building for low and middle income ranges. Under conditions of growing urban and racial unrest, many of its sponsored projects are subject to further delay by reason of local controversies. This unrest may reach crisis proportions unless some way is found for overcoming the ever-increasing deficit in the national housing supply and the rapid deterioration of the urban environment.

4. DEPARTMENT OF TRANSPORTATION (1966)

The collection of agencies from other departments which were pieced together to form this one had experienced frequent previous transfers. The Department of Transportation (D.O.T.) was created to develop and to coordinate national transportation systems, everyone of which got started on direct or indirect government subsidies. Many important transportation powers however remained in the respective independent regulatory commissions, a situation which opens the way to endless jurisdictional disputes for many years to come.

Created by the Department of Transportation Act of October 15, 1966 (80 Stat. 931), it describes its internal structure with refreshing candor in the Government Organization Manual:

> The organization plan reflects a concept of an executive team comprising the Secretary, the Under Secretary, and the heads of the operating agencies which include the Administrations, the Coast Guard, and the Saint Lawrence Seaway Development Corporation.

The administrations referred to are the Federal Aviation Administration, Federal Highway Administration, Federal Railroad Administration, Urban Mass Transportation Administration, and National Transportation Safety Board. The Maritime Administration, with a large assist from shipbuilders, operators, and trade unions, refused to be budged from its comfortable home in the Department of Commerce. The new department still has to achieve a personality, to establish a modus vivendi with the regulatory commissions, to vindicate its functions, and to make its mark in the federal constellation.

B. New Agency for Government Wide Housekeeping Services

1. GENERAL SERVICES ADMINISTRATION (1949)

This useful but unspectacular basket of internal government-wide activities both serves and coordinates other government agencies within the spheres of its competence. This gives it a hybrid character of "line and staff" that defies the classical dichotomy which, in any event, is rarely found in its pure form. The administration's functions are not so unrelated to each other as they might seem and certainly are more closely related than they were to the functions of their historic overlords, the Departments of State, Treasury, Defense, and Commerce. Coordination, whatever meaning one gives to that vague and overworked term, seems to be less unacceptable in the government as a whole when it emanates from agencies that are not within a regular department, except possibly at the level of the secretary's office, and which are considered to be government-wide.

General Services Administration (G.S.A.) was established by Section 101 of the Federal Property and Administrative Services Act of 1949 (63 Stat. 379) and is the government's central agency for housekeeping, buying and selling, storage and issue of supplies and equipment, construction and maintenance of government office buildings, and custodian of governmental records. The creation of G.S.A. was recommended by the first Hoover Commission. It has charge of real estate outside the public domain, purchased or leased for civilian official use. It administers the transportation and communications services for civilian government personnel. One of its duties is the management of the government's stockpile of critical material, in close cooperation with Defense and other departments. It embraces for these operations: The Federal Supply Service, Property and Management Service, Transportation and Communications Service, and the National Archives and Records Service which, among other things, publishes the Federal Register and administers the presidential libraries. It has advanced the standardization and control of government purchasing and the orderly management of real and personal government property as well as the expert custody of the permanent archives and records of the government, not to speak of the regulated disposal of tons of ephemeral paper in the departments and agencies.

C. New Agencies in Science, Technology, Research, and Culture

1. ATOMIC ENERGY COMMISSION (1946)

This is the only large postwar operating agency which has the commission form of organization. It is administered by a chairman designated by the President and confirmed by the Senate, and four other members so appointed. Established by the Atomic Energy Act of 1946 (60 Stat. 755), it was given broad powers to place under civilian control the awesome tasks of management of the uses of atomic energy and nuclear materials. It took over the plants and activities begun so brilliantly and secretly under presidential initiative by the Manhattan Engineer District of the War Department during World War II. The Atomic Energy Commission (A.E.C.) cooperates with the Defense

Atomic Support Agency in the Department of Defense on the military uses of nuclear energy and with the National Aeronautics and Space Administration on nuclear propulsion for space vehicles. It has accelerated research and development in the peaceful uses of nuclear energy for electric power generation, for medicine, and for other purposes. It contracts with public and private organizations. It has important regulatory and licensing powers in connection with the distribution and use of nuclear energy and the dissemination of scientific information in the interests of national security and defense and for the protection of the health and safety of the public. It maintains constant relations with the International Atomic Energy Commission, headquartered in Vienna.

The organization and procedures of A.E.C. were influenced by those of the Tennessee Valley Authority and its first chairman was David E. Lilienthal of T.V.A. fame. It has its own personnel system. Its administrative functions are exercised by two officers, both of whom report to the commission: a general manager and a director of regulations. Congress created a Joint Committee on Atomic Energy to oversee its operations and to process its legislation.

Some observers assert that A.E.C. is too subservient to congressional pressures. Although I was one of its consultants at the time that A.E.C. was being organized, I have not had a recent firsthand opportunity to observe its operations, but inevitably there would be such a tendency in an agency headed by five full-time commissioners. The commission form was adopted not only on account of A.E.C.'s regulatory duties but because of a widely-held view at the time that the administration of nuclear energy was fraught with such unpredictable perils that the authority should not be vested in a single administrator.

2. NATIONAL SCIENCE FOUNDATION (1950)

In the urge to establish many of the new scientific agencies of the government, there was a high degree of stimulus from the element of competition with the Soviet Union. The National Science Foundation (N.S.F.) was one of the agencies that resulted from this rivalry, supported by a clamor from American scientists that, given our huge commitments in technology and applied engineering, we should not fall behind in the basic sciences. Established by legislation in 1950 (64 Stat. 149), the National Science Foundation has a significant record of accomplishment in furthering research and education in science theory. In fact, basic research in American universities and institutes on anything like the present scale has become dependent on its support.

N.S.F. disseminates scientific information, awards scientific grants and contracts, maintains a current register of scientific and technical personnel and a central clearing house for scientific data and resources, awards graduate fellowships in the mathematical, medical, biological, physical engineering, and social sciences, and conducts certain programs in the methodology of research and education. Among its fields of growing national and international interest are oceanography and exploration of the marine environment.

In arriving at decisions in regard to the intricate problem of priorities, its director, who is the chief executive officer and chairman of the Executive Committee, has the advice of a distinguished National Science Board of 24 members, of which he is a member, all appointed by the President and confirmed by the Senate.

Because of the scientific nature of the subject matter, the government has felt it necessary to delegate, by such devices, large decision-making powers to scientific bodies and their leaders. This has raised baffling problems concerning the relationship of these decisions to the normal political processes to which we are accustomed in a democracy. Don K. Price has identified these complex problems in his profound book on *The Scientific Estate* (Cambridge, The Belknap Press of Harvard University, 1965).

3. NATIONAL AERONAUTICS AND SPACE ADMINISTRATION (1958)

N.A.S.A. was established by the National Aeronautics and Space Act of 1958 (72 Stat. 426) as amended, to create a civilian agency for the solution of problems of flight within and without the earth's atmosphere and to accelerate the work on space, rockets, and satellites previously administered by the military. Its creation and the subsequent scale of its operations may also be attributed to the stimulation of early achievements of the Soviet Union in the space field. N.A.S.A.'s spectacular technological successes with the manned space vehicle programs, such as Mercury, Gemini, and finally the Apollo moon landing projects, were televised and are well known to the public. Its work, which produced these marvels, with universities, research centers, and industry is less well known. A host of civilian industries and products as well as new avenues of research and development have been opened up by its vast operations. They include such fields as astronomy, communications, computers, electronics, geology, medicine, miniaturization, optics, propulsion, and telemetry. Its contributions to administrative management have been signal and an illuminating account of these is contained in the book, *Space Age Management; The Large Scale Approach,* by its dynamic second administrator, James E. Webb (New York, McGraw-Hill Book Co., 1969).

A good deal of N.A.S.A.'s scientific and technical background was influenced by the long term creativity of the National Advisory Committee for Aeronautics, founded in 1915, whose more than advisory functions it inherited; by the activity of the military departments; and by the work of such pioneers in rockets and space as Goddard in the U.S.A. and Von Braun in Germany and the U.S.A. Its future support on so large a scale by the American people will depend on to what extent there is an increasing awareness of its many contributions to science and to the civilian economy and, quite literally, on how far we want to go, how soon.

4. NATIONAL FOUNDATION ON THE ARTS AND HUMANITIES (1965)

Established so recently (79 Stat. 845) this unit is too new to evaluate. Its elaborate structure practically prevents it from having the benefit of executive leadership, and it lacks both the competitive appeal and the other elements of dynamic growth of its scientific counterpart. It has a tripartite structure: a National Endowment for the Arts, a National Endowment for the Humanities, and a Federal Council for the Arts and Humanities, each with its own large board. Thus atomized, the foundation seems better endowed with internal protection from its diverse components than with a central driving force to push forward a general program. I say this with regret, because it has the possibility of enriching the cultural life of the country in fields which will increasingly require public support.

5. NATIONAL INSTITUTES OF HEALTH (1940 AND 1968)

Although not an independent agency, but actually a cluster of institutes and units within the Public Health Service, Department of H.E.W., its importance in the medical and biological sciences and its relative autonomy seem to call for its special identification. Its subordinate position on the chart does not diminish its actual high prestige and independence. It consists of ten major research institutes in the field of various diseases and health problems as well as of six major components dealing with various aspects of health research and education. The foundation of some of the institutes dates back to the 1940's. It was reconstituted in its present form as an agency by the Reorganization Order of the secretary of H.E.W. dated April 1, 1968, under which it took over the health manpower programs and the National Library of Medicine. It works by contract in close collaboration with universities, research centers, and the laboratories of the aggressive and affluent American pharmaceutical industry. Its close relations with the Public Health Service place it in a position for prompt implementation of new discoveries in the field of prevention and cure. Under its distinguished director, Dr. James A. Shannon, who served 1955 to 1968, it won cooperation and respect in health and biological circles throughout the world. It has undoubtedly made major contributions to the preeminence of American medicine and epidemiology.

Like the National Science Foundation, the National Institutes of Health has some of the collegial aspects of organization of a university or research institute which deviate in many respects from the conventional bureaucratic hierarchical structure. Its various advisory committees of outside scientists have the controlling voice in approving its large projects and contracts. This raises some of the problems concerning the relationship between government and science pointed out by Don K. Price in *The Scientific Estate* mentioned above. The unconventional administrative methods of N.I.H., which have produced some remarkable results, have also been the subject of investigations and of legislative amendments on the part of Congress, which have somewhat abridged its operating freedom. The autonomy and specialization of its several institutes, while giving them a sharp cutting edge, may also tend to diminish administrative flexibility and transfer, as the need for one program expands while that for another abates.

The N.I.H. may be considered the research arms of the U.S. Public Health Services. Their ten laboratories conduct and foster research in the causes, control, and prevention of disease. The investigations cover cancer, heart, arthritic and metabolic diseases, dental research, mental health, neurological diseases and blindness, allergy and infectious diseases, and human development and general medical services.

6. GROWTH OF RESEARCH AND DEVELOPMENT PROGRAMS SINCE 1945

The growth of scientific and technological programs of research and development throughout the government has been so rapid and pervasive that a full account would go far beyond the scope of this recital. Federal expenditures for research and development (estimated for 1969, excluding R. & D. plant) were reported by the *Statistical Abstract of the United States—1969* (Table 774) as amounting to almost $17 billion. Nearly half of this sum was expended by units of the Department of Defense, which has become one of the great supporters of science and technology that, while weapon oriented, has also important civilian applications. The figure of $17 billion is further broken down into $11 billion for development and $6 billion for basic and applied research. Some of the work is done in government laboratories and institutes, but the great bulk of the research and development activity is performed under contract with research centers and with industry.

D. Foreign Affairs and Security Agencies

1. CENTRAL INTELLIGENCE AGENCY (1947)

Although technically under the National Security Council in the Executive Office of the President, the C.I.A. enjoys a degree of autonomy which entitles it to treatment in the independent agency category. This house of mystery, occupying its own fortress in the Virginia countryside, rocked in the cradle of secrecy and generally misunderstood, was established under the National Security Act of 1947 (61 Stat. 497). Its operations are a by-product of "the cold war" and were greatly influenced at its inception by methods and personnel inherited from the Office of Strategic Services headed by Major General William J. Donovan during World War II. Allen Dulles, the best known of its directors, who served in that capacity from 1953 to 1961, had been one of General Donovan's able associates. C.I.A.'s "cloak and dagger" exploits have become a legend of "whodonit" literature and television, but its main activities are not widely known.

Its principal mission is to supplement and coordinate the intelligence activities of numerous government agencies acting in the interest of national security. It does fact gathering, research, analysis, and evaluation of political, social, economic, and military data concerning countries and regions. Most of its headquarters' staff are highly trained intellectuals, not spies nor thugs. It correlates and evaluates intelligence data and distributes its findings to the appropriate agencies.

Officially, it is supposed to receive its directives from the National Security Council and the President, and to work in close conjunction with the Departments of State and Defense, but in these areas it exercises a large degree of initiative and wields a powerful influence. The public hears little of its work until there is a failure or disclosure of one of its secret projects as in the case in May 1960 of the Soviet capture of its U-2 reconnaissance plane, of the ill-fated Bay of Pigs landing by Cuban exiles in April 1961, or of the revelations in 1967 of its clandestine funding of certain university and small foundation projects. It has unique freedoms from the usual government controls in respect to expenditures, personnel, contracting, and reporting. Persuaded as I am, on the basis of the little information available, of the value of C.I.A.'s "intelligence arm," I am also convinced that its "operations arm" can cause such mischief in our foreign relations that, if continued at all, it needs to be brought under the rigorous control of the Secretary of State.

2. AGENCY FOR INTERNATIONAL DEVELOPMENT (1948)

This agency carries out the United States bilateral programs of foreign aid of economic and technical assistance to less developed countries, and is now part of the Department of State, under orders issued pursuant to Section 621 of the Foreign Assistance Act of 1961 (75 Stat. 445). Its country AID missions work under the general aegis of the American ambassador. On the ostrich-like assumption that foreign aid, which in one form or another has been going on for thirty years, should not be considered a permanent program, its administration suffers from the insecurity of having to seek annually not only appropriations but authority for another twelve months of life. At the end of 1969 Congress, after making severe cuts in its appropriations, did grant it, for the first time, a twenty-four month reprieve.

During World War II there had been a beginning of aid to occupied countries both of a civil and military character by the civil affairs division of the Army. This had been closely connected with military operations and was in the nature of relief and rehabilitation. The Foreign Economic Administration also performed foreign aid functions which it took over from the Offices of Lend-Lease Administration, Foreign Relief and Rehabilitation Operations, Economic Warfare, and the Export-Import Bank of Washington, and from certain operations designed to encourage the production of scarce military materials. An early successful technical assistance program was conducted in Latin America by an Office and Institute of Inter-American Affairs going back to 1940 under the able administration of Nelson A. Rockefeller.

The main impetus which led to the establishment of A.I.D.'s postwar predecessors was the Marshall Plan of 1947 for European recovery and the famous "Point Four" of President Harry S. Truman's message to Congress of January 1949. He himself later said that Point Four had been inspired both by the Marshall Plan and the "Truman Doctrine" in 1947 which induced Congress to vote $400 million for aid to Greece and Turkey to combat communism. From the beginning the American foreign aid programs have been compelled to carry out mixed objectives: the prevention of the spread of communism, both by development and military aid, the altruistic one of helping the stricken and backward countries, and the serving of American interests by relating the aid program to the disposal of American surplus commodities and the extension of American investment, trade, and commerce.

This hardy annual, on which tomes have been printed, has had a remarkable number of successful programs by any reasonable criterion, operating as it does under handicaps as severe as any known in American politics and administration. It has been subject to many changes of identity, personnel, policies, and methods which have deprived it of continuity, an element so much needed in the essentially long-term task of working with developing countries. A large reform occurred in President Kennedy's administration in strengthening its country and regional divisions and relating them to the regional and country desks of the State Department. This structural change should have the advantage of enabling a donor agency to look at the total needs of a country and not be too much infleunced by the competing pressures of the specialized units in various professional fields. The various previous incarnations of the AID program have been as follows:

1948–1951: Economic Cooperation Administration (E.C.A.)

E.C.A. administered the Marshall Plan for European recovery under the exceptionally creative leadership of Paul G. Hoffman, who at 78 still administers the United Nations Development Program.

1951–1953: Mutual Security Agency (M.S.A.)

As Europe recovered, M.S.A. was formed in President Truman's time to assume world-wide functions in foreign aid and technical cooperation.

1953–1955: Foreign Operations Administration (F.O.A.)

Foreign countries do not like to be "operated" by Uncle Sam so this name was the most unfortunate of all and translated badly. F.O.A. inherited the functions of M.S.A., Technical Cooperation Administration from the State Department, and the Institute of Inter-American Affairs early in the Eisenhower administration. Under its administrator, Harold E. Stassen, it initiated the system of training and advice by means of contracts with American universities, institutes, and private firms.

1955–1961: International Cooperation Administration (I.C.A.)

I.C.A. was established in the State Department with responsibility for the F.O.A. mutual security programs except those for refugees and for military assistance.

1961 to present: Agency for International Development (A.I.D.)

A.I.D. administers civilian programs of overseas development and technical assistance, commodity assistance, Food for Peace (in conjunction with the Department of Agriculture under Public Law 480), encouragement to private investment and non-profit groups working abroad, development loans and grants; all as an agency within the Department of State.

The agency has suffered from a succession of administrators, some of whom were lukewarm about the program. It has been subject to a parade of hobbies, to a series of abrupt changes in policy and priorities, and to periodic attacks, quixotic amendments, and detailed supervision by committees of Congress. In recent years its appropriations have declined. It has a dual relationship with the United Nations' development program and regional multilateral development agencies, for it cooperates as well as competes with them. Its fluctuations cause unusual difficulties in recruiting and retaining high calibre personnel. The many able people who have loyally stuck by a program beset with so many vicissitudes deserve an award of the civilian equivalent of the purple heart. Its indispensable demonstrated value to the United States and to the world entitles it to recognition as a permanent function of our government.

3. U.S. INFORMATION AGENCY (1953)

The ancestry of U.S.I.A. can be traced from the Office of Facts and Figures established in October 1941 with Archibald MacLeish as its director, then through the Office of War Information from June 1942 until 1945 when its foreign information activities were transferred to the Department of State. During World War II it had partial domestic orientation, but its present mission is confined to the communicating of American information and viewpoints abroad. It is, in a good sense of the word, the first peace-time "propaganda" agency the United States has maintained. Like the aid program, the information program has gone through many changes and transfers. It also has a number of objectives which are difficult to reconcile. It aims to give a true picture of American life, culture, and institutions while at the same time it acts as the official support agency overseas for American foreign policies. Its continuation in peace time was partly motivated by the felt need to correct the flood of hostile and distorted emissions regarding America from Moscow and Peking.

U.S.I.A. received its present legal authority from the U.S. Information and Educational Act of 1948, as amended (62 Stat. 6). Its establishment as an independent agency was effected by Reorganization Plan 8 of 1953 and by Executive Order 10477 of the same year. It has informational, educational, and cultural programs. It advises the President and government agencies on the state of foreign opinion. It uses the various techniques and media of communication—personal contact, radio broadcasting (The Voice of America), libraries, book publication and distribution, press, motion pictures, television, exhibits, English language instruction, etc. The United States Information Service, as it is known abroad, has public affairs officers under the chiefs of mission. Its work is closely related to that of the Bureau of Educational and Cultural Affairs headed by an Assistant Secretary of State. The former Assistant Secretary, Charles Frankel, has a lucid and original treatment of these activities under the title "Culture, Information, and Foreign Policy," *Public Administration Review* (Vol. 29, Nov.–Dec. 1969).

4. U.S. ARMS CONTROL AND DISARMAMENT AGENCY (1961)

The creation of this agency as an independent establishment in 1961 (75 Stat. 631) provides an excellent case study of the complex of reasons which leads to placing agencies outside a regular department. In this case the symbolic necessity to dramatize the high priority given by the United States to disarmament was a major cause. By this device it also was given the prestige of an agency reporting to the President and not trammeled by supposedly encrusted positions of State and Defense whose confidence it nevertheless must command. The fact that the elevated status of such an agency can attract a director of the wide experience and high calibre of William C. Foster, who served from 1961 to 1968, is another justification for its independence. Finally, it must relate its policies to those of the Departments of State and Defense and to the programs of atomic energy and of outer space, and thus play an interagency coordinating role, which is harder to do for a subordinate unit of a large department.

The agency has wide terms of reference. Established by the Act approved September 26, 1961 (75 Stat. 631), it performs research on arms control and disarmament policy formulation and negotiates and administers arm control treaties. It advises the President and Secretary of State and "under the direction of the Secretary of State has primary responsibility within the government for such matters." At the United Nations and in Geneva, its director played a major role in negotiating treaties on the banning of nuclear weapons tests and on the nonproliferation of nuclear weapons. The agency has initiated studies of more general disarmament proposals such as strategic arms limitation and the control of the international traffic in conventional arms. Eventually, the agency should find its home in the Department of State and in many respects already functions as if it lived there.

5. PEACE CORPS (1961)

President John F. Kennedy created this agency by Executive Order 10924 on March 1, 1961, soon after his inauguration to fulfill a campaign promise he made in a speech to University of Michigan students. He appointed as its first director his dynamic brother-in-law, R. Sargent Shriver, Jr., who later became the founder of the Office of Economic Opportunity. The President regarded the Peace Corps as an opportunity for voluntary service overseas which would appeal particularly to the idealism of young university people. He also believed it would fill a need for a highly motivated face-to-face operation in rural villages and remote regions in developing countries for the transmission of basic skills, which would compensate for the rigidities and highly impersonal types of technical assistance rendered by mature A.I.D. experts usually in capital cities. Congress sanctified the program by the passage of the Peace Corps Act, as amended, in September 1961 (75 Stat. 612). The Peace Corps is now a unit of the Department of State.

The Peace Corps, a highly imaginative and innovative concept, has learned a lot by doing and by early errors. It still commands the high idealism and motivation of volunteers, but is no longer confined in its appointments to young college people. It is placing a greater emphasis on choosing people who have transmittable skills needed in the remote areas to which they will be assigned at the request of a foreign government. The United Nations agencies which scoffed at the inception of a plan that seemed to them to smack of American romanticism, if not hypocrisy, have remained to praise and are beginning to emulate some elements of its voluntarism and face-to-face service in their own programs of technical cooperation. The Peace Corps may also fairly be credited with inspiring the O.E.O. domestic volunteer service program known as VISTA.

6. OTHER PROGRAMS IN FOREIGN AFFAIRS AND NATIONAL SECURITY

As practically every domestic program in an interconnected world has overseas implications (and vice versa), there has been a proliferation of international units and agencies throughout the government. I have described some of the difficulties of administrative management caused by this universal enthusiasm for participation in overseas matters in my article on "Complexities of Administered Diplomacy." (Introduction to a symposium on "Administrative Problems of Multipurpose Diplomacy" which appeared in *Public Administration Review*, Oct.–Nov. 1969, Vol. 29, No. 6.) I reported that I had identified sixteen departments and agencies which had assistant secretaries or directors of divisions for international affairs, and I am certain that there are more. The symposium also has essays treating the problems of economic and cultural coordination, personnel administration overseas, and the high administrative policy questions raised by the activities of the National Security Council and the office of the assistant to the President for National Security Affairs which will be referred to in the section on the Executive Office of the President.

E. Agencies Addressed to Special Problems

1. SMALL BUSINESS ADMINISTRATION (1953)

This agency was established by Congress in 1953 (67 Stat. 232) by the Small Business Act with additional authority from subsequent enactments. It was designed to protect and preserve small private enterprise, by direct aid rather than by legal protection of the anti-trust variety, from the growing predominance of the chains, trusts, conglomerates, and other large corporate undertakings. It aids, counsels, assists, and protects the interests of small business. It has authority to review government contracting policies and practices, to make loans, to improve management skills by training programs, and to make economic studies. It has a special interest in fostering the ownership of small businesses among the black race. It was left out of the Department of Commerce (which since losing the transportation functions is underassigned), largely because of a fear of the predominance of big business influence in its councils, but probably belongs there if a sympathetic Secretary of Commerce is found who can reassure its clientele.

2. OFFICE OF ECONOMIC OPPORTUNITY (1964)

This is the highly controversial agency directing its attention to "eliminate the paradox of poverty in the midst of plenty in this nation by opening to everyone the opportunity for education and training, the opportunity to work, and the opportunity to live in decency and dignity." This ambitious program was initiated in the administration of President John F. Kennedy, but only took effect after his assassination on the passage of the Equal Economic Opportunity Act of 1964 (78 Stat. 508), as amended. Because its program called for a government-wide attack on poverty and impinged on the programs of the Departments of H.E.W. and H.U.D., and because its mandate was to invent and experiment with untried approaches, it was not placed in an existing department or agency which it was thought might be too greatly addicted to traditional and inadequate policies and practices.

Accordingly, it was located in the Executive Office of the President.

Its functions have the character both of an initiating and coordinating body as well as those of an operating agency. The Act provides for a Job Corps program, Work and Training programs, Special Impact programs, Urban and Rural Community Action programs, Special programs to combat poverty in Rural Areas, Employment and Investment Incentives, Work Experience and Day Care programs, and Domestic Volunteer Service programs (VISTA), and others such as the well-known Headstart program for young children. Its direct relations with and financing of hastily organized urban community action organizations has been its most controversial area, but it has been creative and boldly experimental. The Act also provides for a cabinet level Economic Opportunity Council and a National Advisory Council on Economic Opportunity.

This type of organization raises almost every vexing problem of administrative management. Can a research and planning agency also perform operating responsibilities? Even if in its nascent stage, when it must combine action and initiation with thought, it is placed in the executive office of the President, should continuing operating functions remain there or should they be transferred to existing agencies? This process has begun and several O.E.O. programs have already been transferred to regular departments. In its community action programs should O.E.O. act with the advice and consent of the existing organs of state or local government? The insistence of mayors has gradually brought about their greater participation in these matters.

In implanting new policies, programs, and practices in the federal establishment, is it desirable to involve the interest and invoke the experience of permanent agencies rather than to build temporary, insecure, and inexperienced staffs which duplicate and circumvent their activities? There is a wealth of experience and wisdom in the high personnel of existing agencies and a considerable willingness to innovate and experiment if only they are informed on the program objectives. Incoming administrations invariably fail to exploit this asset and their chronic underestimation of existing institutions often is a cause of over-organization.

The greatest indirect contribution of the ambitious and still hopeful poverty program has been the reassessment of the basic welfare policies of the country, their administration and financing. The hard-core way-of-life problems to which the poverty program has addressed itself has, in view of the persistence of dependency, become one of the highest priority needs of the nation, as illustrated by the contents of the valuable symposium *Agenda for the Nation* (Washington, Brookings Institution, 1968). The program itself has stimulated research into new approaches to poverty problems in universities and institutes as well as in government agencies at all levels. Whatever its future structure and functions within the executive branch, the alleviation and overcoming of poverty in an affluent society have been dramatized by the creation of O.E.O. and have become a major long-term goal of the American people.

F. Agencies of an Intergovernmental and Regional Character

The Tennessee Valley Authority, established in 1933, was a three-man federal board which early decided to contract with other government agencies, state and local authorities, and cooperative organizations. Its functions were multipurpose, cutting across monopurpose agencies at all levels, and its success has been largely due to its administrative diplomacy and to its policy of identifying itself with regional institutions. The late Senator George W. Norris of Nebraska, the sponsor of the T.V.A. legislation, prepared a bill in 1937 which was designed to create similar federal authorities in other great river valleys, in which he had the strong backing of President F. D. Roosevelt. But the resistances at federal, state, and local levels and in the electric power lobbies were too great to command support for the measure.

Mainly as a result of the massive report of the Commission on Intergovernmental Relations (mentioned in Chapter V), created by Public Law 109, 83rd Congress, First Session, 1953, and chaired by the late Myer L. Kestnbaum of Chicago, a number of new arrangements to deal with regional problems are being employed. By executive action the federal government is moving toward establishing identical regional headquarters cities for the agencies dealing with human and physical urban problems. Federal executive boards have been created in the ten metropolitan areas having the greatest concentration of federal regional directors. Some of these are encountering the same difficulties that beset the regional Federal Business Councils which were the pride and joy of salty General Charles G. Dawes, the first director of the budget, who organized them in the early years of the Harding Administration. After he left, they became increasingly preoccupied with trifling matters, but Dawes could never forgive FDR for abolishing them. Those interested in such history should read Don K. Price, "General Dawes and Executive Staff Work," *Public Administration Review* (Summer 1951, Vol. 11, No. 3).

Another interesting product of the Kestnbaum Commission report is the growing trend to create federal-interstate regional commissions by the use of federal-interstate compacts, approved by acts of Congress. By giving a seat on these commissions to the governors and to a high ranking federal officer, they will probably be more effective than the earlier Commissions on Interstate Cooperation, which were advisory, consisted mainly of state legislators, and were fostered in the 1930's by the Council of State Governments. Important new agencies of this kind are:

1. ADVISORY COMMISSION ON INTERGOVERNMENTAL RELATIONS (1959)

Established by the Act of September 24, 1959 (73 Stat. 703), as amended, the creation of this body was recognition of the fact that the complex problems of federal-state-local relationships are matters requiring continuous studies and consideration. It has a broad mandate to consider common problems of cooperative federalism, grant programs, allocation of governmental functions to the various levels, proposed legislation, and the financing of such programs by taxation and otherwise. It has a unique structure of twenty-six members: three private citizens, three representatives of the federal executive branch, four governors, three United States senators, three United States representatives, four mayors, three members of state legislative bodies, and three elected county officers. Its first uniquely suitable chairman was Frank Bane, formerly executive director of the Council of State Governments, after a distinguished career at all three levels of government. The commission has already produced an impressive collection of study documents on emerging problems in the field of intergovernmental relations. Their contents reveal a desire to improve the effectiveness of cooperative federalism rather than to reassert the ancient dogmas of states' rights and local autonomy.

2. DELAWARE RIVER BASIN COMMISSION (1961)

Established by federal-interstate compact with Pennsylvania, New Jersey, New York, and Delaware by Act of Congress approved September 27, 1961 (75 Stat. 688), this commission is responsible for the development and approval of a comprehensive plan for the programming, scheduling, and controlling of projects and activities within the Delaware River basin. Its federal member is the Secretary of the Interior; its state members are the four governors. It is a multiple-purpose agency with executive offices located in Trenton, N.J. Its functions and structure were markedly influenced by the thorough study and recommendations of a research group headed by Professor Roscoe C. Martin of Syracuse University.

3. APPALACHIAN REGIONAL COMMISSION (1965)

Created by Congress in 1965 (79 Stat. 5), its duties are to develop plans and to coordinate comprehensive programs for regional and economic development in a large underdeveloped region of the country. Its membership consists of the governors of the thirteen Appalachian States who alternate semi-annually as co-chairman and a federal co-chairman appointed by the President, by and with the advice and consent of the Senate. All recommendations of the commission must be approved by a majority of the governors and by the federal co-chairman. It has thus a number of built-in vetoes. Because of the state-federal nature of the commission its staff members are not federal employees. The commission expenses since 1967 have been shared equally by the federal government and the Appalachian States. Although it cannot point to sensational results, it has made steady progress in enlisting the cooperation of the numerous federal, state, and local agencies which have long-time vested beachheads, wherever it wishes to land.

4. ECONOMIC DEVELOPMENT REGIONAL COMMISSIONS (1965)

Title V of the Public Works and Economic Development Act of 1965 (79 Stat. 552) authorizes the Secretary of Commerce to designate economic development regions, and then to invite the states concerned to establish a regional commission. Members of the commissions are the federal co-chairman and the governors who elect a state co-chairman. There is a Federal Advisory Council on Regional Economic Development to provide coordination and guidance to the regional commissions, including the Appalachian one, and to the Federal Field Committees in Alaska. The regional commissions so far established are:

Coastal Plains: 159 counties in North Carolina, South Carolina, and Georgia.
Four Corners: 92 counties in Arizona, Colorado, New Mexico, and Utah.
New England: States of Connecticut, Massachusetts, New Hampshire, Rhode Island, Vermont, and Maine.
Ozarks: 134 counties in Arkansas, Kansas, Missouri, and Oklahoma.
Upper Great Lakes: 119 counties in Michigan, Minnesota, and Wisconsin.

G. Quasi-judicial and Appellate Agencies

This group of agencies is in the field of what James M. Landis called "the administrative process," exercising regulatory or so-called "quasi-legislative" and "quasi-judicial" functions, such as the Civil Aeronautics Board, Federal Communications Commission, Federal Maritime Commission, Federal Trade Commission, Interstate Commerce Commission (the first one, founded in 1887), National Labor Relations Board, Securities and Exchange Commission, and U.S. Tariff Commission. There is a good deal of controversy as to whether they are executive agencies at all. Many of them have chairmen so designated by the President, and in many of them the chairman is authorized to act as chief administrative officer, but the President's influence and authority over their activities are remote and tenuous. Founded to regulate rates and services of private corporations in the public interest and to correct discriminatory practices, their secular trend is to become increasingly protective of the organizations they regulate. Congress has not hesitated to delegate "quasi-legislative" functions in other fields to agencies in regular departments throughout the government, such as the Food and Drug Administration, nor to provide citizens with a special body like the Tax Court for appeals from Internal Revenue Service rulings. In the fields of transportation and communications, the independent commissions have tended to concentrate on their regulatory duties and to neglect both the development of their special wards and the coordination of their programs with the wards of the other commissions. The Department of Transportation was created in part to satisfy this developmental and coordinative need. The executive structure, in my view, would have been less confused and Montesquieu would have rested more quietly in his grave if this "headless fourth branch" of independent commissions had never been invented. There is a large literature on the complex problems of these agencies, which are less familiar to me than the strictly executive ones, and I list the principal new ones with little comment:

1950   Subversive Activities Control Board (64 Stat. 987)
1951   Renegotiation Board (65 Stat. 7)
1953   Federal Coal Mine Board of Review (66 Stat. 697)
1954   Foreign Claims Settlement Commission of the U.S. (Reorganization Plan 1 of 1954—68 Stat. 1279)
1961   Federal Maritime Commission (Reorganization Plan 7, August 12, 1961), to administer functions going back to the Shipping Act of 1916.
1961   Administrative Conference of the United States (5 USC 571—6), a study group to study and recommend improvements in legal procedures, without regulatory powers.
1964   Equal Opportunity Employment Commission—Title VII of the Civil Rights Act of 1964 (78 Stat. 241)—deals with discriminatory employment practices outside the federal government.

H. Agencies Omitted

In concluding these profiles at this point I am aware of numerous and serious omissions. I have arbitrarily omitted those that are neither new departments nor new independent establishments. The omitted ones usually are not new but in many cases have experienced major modifications and changes in name and function of organizations already at work in 1945. The most glaring omissions are, first, those units in the agricultural and conservation areas, with particular reference to pollution of air and pollution and supply of water. The second area of omissions is the large cluster of agencies in the field of economic matters, statistics, banking, credit, and finance. The third is in the area of labor relations, mediation and conciliation, and standards. The fourth is in the consumer protection area. I regret that time and space did not permit giving them all the treatment their importance deserves. For a more complete overview of the scope of modern government, a well organized and lucid book is J. W. Peltason and James M. Burns, *Functions and Policies of American Government*, Second Edition (Englewood Cliffs, N.J., Prentice-Hall, Inc., 1962). But to give a more complete picture of the contemporary subdivisions of the executive branch, I append the list that follows, taken from the *U.S. Government Organization Manual, 1969–1970*, with a classification of my own.

Exhibit C—*Offices, Departments, and Agencies of the Executive Branch (Based on the* United States Government Organization Manual 1969–1970, *chart p. 590—classified by the author)*

Executive Office of the President   (13)
    Overall Policy and Administration   (6)
        The White House Office,*Bureau of the Budget, Council of Economic Advisors, Office of Science and Technology, Office of Emergency Preparedness, Office of Intergovernmental Relations
    Specialized Missions   (3)
        Central Intelligence Agency, Office of Economic Opportunity, Office of Special Representative for Trade Negotiations
    Cabinet Level Councils   (4)
        National Security Council, National Aeronautics and Space Council, National Council on Marine Resources and Engineering Development, Council for Urban Affairs (N.B.: A council on the environment is to be appointed.)
Departments   (12)
    State, Treasury, Defense, Justice, Post Office, Interior, Agriculture, Commerce, Labor, Health Education and Welfare, Housing and Urban Development, Transportation.
Quasi-judicial and Appellate Agencies   (11)
    Administrative Conference of the United States, Civil Aero-

---

*The White House Office, with about 100 professionals in 1969, has tended to become divided roughly into the following groups: Cabinet Secretariat, Congressional Relations, Executive Branch Communications, Legal Counsel, Military Affairs, National Security Affairs, Press and other Media, Personal Aides, Political Appointments, Special Advisers, Urban Affairs, and Office of the Vice-President. These increase by at least a dozen (12) the groups whose heads have access to the President, to which should be added an unknown number of *ad hoc* task forces and advisory commissions.

nautics Board, Federal Communications Commission, Federal Maritime Commission, Federal Power Commission, Federal Trade Commission, Interstate Commerce Commission (the first one, founded 1887), National Labor Relations Board, Securities and Exchange Commission, United States Tariff Commission, Tax Court of the United States.

Independent Banking and Lending Agencies (4)
Farm Credit Administration, Federal Deposit Insurance Corporation, Federal Home Loan Bank Board, Board of Governors of the Federal Reserve System.

Independent Offices (Administrator form) (8)
Federal Mediation and Conciliation Service, General Services Administration, National Aeronautics and Space Administration, Selective Service System, Small Business Administration, United States Arms Control and Disarmament Agency, United States Information Agency, Veterans Administration.

Independent Offices (Board or Commission form) (10)
Atomic Energy Commission, District of Columbia, Export-Import Bank of the United States, National Foundation on the Arts and Humanities, National Mediation Board, National Science Foundation, Railroad Retirement Board, Smithsonian Institution, Tennesee Valley Authority, United States Civil Service Commission.

Other Boards and Commissions (Not listed on official chart) (10)
American Battle Monuments Commission, Canal Zone Government, Commission of Fine Arts, Equal Employment Opportunity Commission, Federal Coal Mine Safety Board of Review, Foreign Claims Settlement Commission of the United States, Indian Claims Commission, Panama Canal Company, Renegotiation Board, Subversive Activities Control Board. (The U.S. Government Organization Manual lists an additional fifty (50) selected boards, committees, and commissions not included on the chart.)

Exhibit D—Number of Offices, Departments, and Agencies of the Executive Branch

Executive Office of the President		13
Departments		12
Independent Agencies and Establishments:		
Quasi-judicial and Appellate	11	
Banking and Lending	4	
Administrator Form	8	
Board or Commission Form	10	33
Charted sub-total		58
Other Boards and Commissions (not listed on the official chart)		10
Total		68

REORGANIZATION LEGISLATION

A. War Powers Legislation: Reorganization by Executive Order

1. THE OVERMAN ACT OF 1918 (P.L. 65-152, 40 STAT. 556) (CHAPTER 78)*

President Woodrow Wilson
Approved: May 20, 1918   Terminated: September 3, 1921

(Text of Statute)

An Act authorizing the President to coordinate or consolidate executive bureaus, agencies, and offices, and for other purposes, in the interest of economy and the more efficient concentration of the government.

Be it enacted by the Senate and House of Representatives of the United States of America in Congress assembled, that for the national security and defense, for the successful prosecution of the war, for the support and maintenance of the Army and Navy, for the better utilization of resources and industries, and for the more effective exercise and more efficient administration by the President of his powers as Commander in Chief of the land and naval forces the President is hereby authorized to make such redistribution of functions among

*Introduced by Honorable Lee Slater Overman (1854–1930), senator from North Carolina from 1903–1921 and chairman from 1913 of the Senate Rules Committee as well as the ranking member of the Judiciary and Appropriations Committees.

245

executive agencies as he may deem necessary, including any functions, duties, and powers hitherto by law conferred upon any executive department, commission, bureau, agency, office, or officer, in such manner as in his judgment shall seem best fitted to carry out the purposes of this Act, and to this end is authorized to make such regulations and to issue such orders as he may deem necessary, which regulations and orders shall be in writing and shall be filed with the head of the department affected and constitute a public record: provided, that this Act shall remain in force during the continuance of the present war and for six months after the termination of the war by the proclamation of the treaty of peace, or at such earlier time as the President may designate: provided further, that the termination of this Act shall not affect any act done or any right or obligation accruing or accrued pursuant to this Act and during the time that this Act is in force: provided further, that the authority by this Act granted shall be exercised only in matters relating to the conduct of the present war.

SEC. 2. That in carrying out the purposes of this Act the President is authorized to utilize, coordinate, or consolidate any executive or administrative commissions, bureaus, agencies, offices, or officers now existing by law, to transfer any duties or powers from one existing department, commission, bureau, agency, office, or officer to another, to transfer the personnel thereof or any part of it either by detail or assignment, together with the whole or any part of the records and public property belonging thereto.

SEC. 3. That the President is further authorized to establish an executive agency which may exercise such jurisdiction and control over the production of aeroplanes, aeroplane engines, and aircraft equipment as in his judgment may be advantageous; and, further, to transfer to such agency, for its use, all or any moneys heretofore appropriated for the production of aeroplanes, aeroplane engines, and aircraft equipment.

SEC. 4. That for the purpose of carrying out the provisions of this Act, any moneys heretofore and hereafter appropriated for the use of any executive department, commission, bureau, agency, office, or officer shall be expended only for the purpose for which it was appropriated under the direction of such other agency as may be directed by the President hereunder to perform and execute said function.

SEC. 5. That should the President, in redistributing the functions among the executive agencies as provided in this Act, conclude that any bureau should be abolished and it or their duties and functions conferred upon some other department or bureau or eliminated entirely, he shall report his conclusions to Congress with such recommendations as he may deem proper.

SEC. 6. That all laws or parts of laws conflicting with the provisions of this Act are to the extent of such conflict suspended while this Act is in force.

Upon termination of this Act all executive or administrative agencies, departments, commissions, bureaus, offices, or officers shall exercise the same functions, duties, and powers as heretofore or as hereafter by law may be provided, any authorization of the President under this Act to the contrary notwithstanding.

○ ○ ○ ○

Reorganization Orders: Twenty-four or more executive orders were issued by President Wilson pursuant to the Overman Act. After the expiration of the Act in September 1921 the only changes retained were those given permanent status by the National Defense Act of 1920.

2. FIRST WAR POWERS ACT, 1941 (55 STAT. 838) (TITLE I)

President F. D. Roosevelt
Approved: December 18, 1941   Terminated: June 30, 1947

The First War Powers Act, 1941, was approved December 18, 1941, just eleven days after Japan catapulted the United States into World War II by the attack on our fleet at Pearl Harbor. Title I of the 1941 Act resembles the Overman Act of 1918, which was not enacted for President Wilson until the United States had been at war with Germany for over one year. The 1941 Act authorized the President to make transfers and consolidations of government agencies by executive order without submission to Congress and without the delay of a sixty-day period within which Congress could veto the action. It authorized the coordination of executive bureaus and agencies "in the interest of the more efficient concentration of the government." The powers granted to the President were to be exercised only "in matters relating to the conduct of the present war." He could "make such distribution of functions of agencies as he may deem necessary." Abolition of statutory functions of agencies were, however, to be submitted to Congress for its approval by ordinary legislative processes. Whenever new wartime powers were needed which affected the economy, Congress still had to enact special legislation in the regular way, which it did, inter alia, in such matters as priorities, price control, war mobilization, and reconversion.

The combination of authority granted to President F. D. Roosevelt by the creation of the Office of Emergency Management in the Executive Office of the President [See Reorganization Act of 1939.] and the provisions of Title I of the 1941 Act, gave him a very great grant of flexibility in the administrative management of World War II. The only major wartime agency created by statute was the Office of War Mobilization and Reconversion, approved October 3, 1944 (58 Stat. 785), to which Congress gave unprecedented powers to coordinate the war agencies. But the President had led the way even in this case by having established an Office of War Mobilization by Executive Order 9347 on May 27, 1943. He had been unwilling to vest such great powers in an industrialist or a general but appointed as director of the powerful office James Byrnes, who had been a senator for many years, and who relinquished his position as associate justice of the Supreme Court to accept the post.

The authority granted under Title I of the 1941 Act was to cease six months after termination of the war; and, as in the case of the Overman Act, all agencies were to resume the exercise of duties, powers, and functions "as heretofore or hereafter by law provided." American participation in hostilities of World War II lasted almost forty-five months whereas in World War I it had lasted but nineteen. One hundred and thirty-five executive orders had been issued by President Roosevelt in regard to war organizations as contrasted with some twenty-four issued by President Wilson. The complexity of unravelling such a vast war organization and mobilization of manpower and resources was enormous. Some of the legislative powers had to be modified or discontinued by Acts of Congress. President Truman by proclamation determined the date of the cessation of hostilities as December 31, 1946 and the powers of the Title I, First War Powers Act of 1941, terminated six months later. Most of the war agencies had been already liquidated by the end of 1945.

The liquidation of the vast and complex war machinery was greatly assisted by the Reorganization Act of 1945, one of its stated purposes having been "to facilitate orderly transition from war to peace." President Truman's Reorganization Plan No. 1 issued in 1946 (House Doc. 594) was rejected by Congress, which objected to the way in which it was proposed to continue the National Housing Agency. His reorganization Plan 3 of 1946 (House Doc. 596) and Plan 1 of 1947

(House Doc. 230) were sustained, however, making possible the continuation of a number of war transfers of lasting value. The grouping of the housing agencies under a new name of Housing and Home Finance Agency was accomplished in that plan and was accepted by Congress. Otherwise the components of the housing agency would have reverted to thirteen agencies in seven departments. This grouping, with a few defections, became the basis for the creation of the Department of Housing and Urban Development in 1965.

President Truman in his message to Congress of May 1, 1947 (House Doc. 230, 80th Congress, 1st Session) pointed out the vital role played by Title I in the successful prosecution of the war, particularly the drastic overhauling of the War and Navy Departments.

As to wartime legislation for regulation of the economy, twenty wartime economic measures terminated December 31, 1946 and an additional thirty-three terminated six months later, including the authority for the government to seize strike-bound plants. Congress reluctantly continued a few controls for short periods, but sixty other emergency war powers were repealed by an omnibus bill of July 25, 1947 (P. L. 80-239).

3. DEFENSE PRODUCTION ACT OF 1950 (69 STAT. 298)

President Harry S. Truman
Approved: September 8, 1950   Terminated: June 30, 1952

During the Korean War, Congress passed the Defense Production Act of 1950 (64 Stat. 798). It had the aspects of war powers acts although the Korean War was legally a United Nations action. Agencies could be created under this Act by executive order without submission to Congress. They were similar, on a smaller scale, to the World War II agencies. Among these were the Office of Defense Mobilization established by Executive Order 10193 of December 16, 1950 in the Executive Office of the President, to direct, control, and coordinate all mobilization activities including production, procurement, manpower, stabilization, and transport activities. The Defense Production Administration was established by Executive Order 10200 (Section 1) of January 3, 1951. Its functions were transferred to the Office of Defense Mobilization by Executive Order 10433 of February 4, 1953.

The war in Korea was only one aspect of the increasing threat to national security believed in 1950 to be implicit in actions of the Soviet Union and of Communist China. The Act authorized the President to allocate defense materials, requisition property, make loans to expand defense production, and set up price-wage controls if necessary. The military budget and manpower and construction estimates were increased, accelerated stockpiling of critical materials was authorized, and selective service was extended.

Some of the powers of these agencies have never been revoked and some have been invoked during the Vietnam War. From time to time they have been exercised by agencies also charged with the duties of civil defense, such as the National Civil Defense Administration, and the function of stockpiling of critical materials in the National Security Resources Board. The Act of August 26, 1958 (72 Stat. 861) combined these functions in an Office of Civil and Defense Mobilization. The administration of civil defense operations was transferred to the Department of Defense in 1961. The Office of Emergency Planning in the Executive Office of the President succeeded to the functions of the Office of Civil and Defense Mobilization by Act of September 22, 1961 (75 Stat. 630) and its name was changed to its present designation of Office of Emergency Preparedness in the Executive Office of the President by Act of October 21, 1968 (82 Stat. 1194).

B. *Reorganization Legislation: Reorganization by Executive Plan Subject to Legislative Veto*

1. THE ECONOMY ACT OF 1932 (TITLE IV OF THE LEGISLATIVE APPROPRIATION ACT FOR FISCAL YEAR 1933, 47 STAT. 413–15)

President Herbert Hoover
Approved: June 30, 1932, 72nd Congress, 1st Session.

Declaration of Policy: SEC. 401. In order to further reduce expenditures and increase efficiency in government, it is declared to be the policy of Congress

(a) To group, coordinate, and consolidate executive and administrative agencies of the government, as nearly as may be, according to purpose;

(b) To reduce the number of such agencies by consolidating those having similar functions under a single head;

(c) To eliminate overlapping and duplication of effort; and

(d) To segregate regulatory agencies and functions from those of an administrative and executive character.

Power of President and Exemptions: The President was given power to transfer, coordinate, and consolidate all executive and independent agencies (the latter being defined as agencies not under the control or jurisdiction of any executive department) by executive order. However, the President could not abolish any executive department or agency created by statute.

Veto Procedure: Executive order was to be transmitted to Congress while in session and would become effective after the expiration of sixty calendar days during a continuous session. The Congress, however, could approve sooner by concurrent resolution, or either House could disapprove the order or any part of same by simple resolution, in which case the order would be null and void to the extent of the disapproval. In effect, this gave either House not only a general veto power but an item veto power as well.

Expiration Date: This was permanent legislation.

Action Taken: President Hoover submitted eleven orders, all of which were disapproved by a Democratic House on the grounds that the incoming President's views should be considered.

2. THE ECONOMY AMENDMENTS OF MARCH 3, 1933 (AMENDMENT TO THE ECONOMY ACT OF JUNE 30, 1932 CONTAINED IN THE TREASURY POST OFFICE APPROPRIATION ACT, 47 STAT. 1515, CHAPTER 212, SEC. 16)

President Herbert Hoover   73rd Congress, 1st Session

Declaration of Purpose: The amendment of 1933 declared that "serious emergency exists by reason of general economic depression" and that it was "imperative to reduce drastically governmental expenditures." For this purpose, the restriction on the abolition of statutory agencies contained in the 1932 legislation was removed. In other respects, the declaration of purpose remained essentially the same.

Power of President and Exemptions: The President thus had the power to transfer, consolidate, coordinate, and abolish all executive and independent agencies. The President, however, could not abolish entire executive departments.

Veto Procedure: The Presidential order had to lay before the Congress for sixty days of continuous session. Unlike the 1932 Act, there was no provision for veto; therefore, the legislative veto could only be exercised by ordinary legislation, which was in turn subject to presidential veto (cf. 37 Att. Gen. 63-64). The effect of this Act, therefore, was that the order of the President could only be overridden by a two-thirds vote of both Houses.

Expiration Date: The Act was of two-year duration.

Actions Taken: A number of executive orders were issued by President Franklin D. Roosevelt under this Act, of which No. 6166 dated June 10, 1933, contained eighteen sections. Major actions under these orders, not including many transfers, consolidations, and abolition of numerous agencies and commissions, were as follows:

> Procurement Division established in Treasury Department. Enlarged National Park Service established in the Interior Department and various public reservations transferred to it.
>
> Division of Disbursement established in Treasury Department embracing all functions of non-military disbursements of money.
>
> Division of Territories and Insular Possessions created in Interior Department, taking over functions relating to Puerto Rico from War Department. Solicitors of the Departments of Treasury, Commerce, and Labor decentralized from Department of Justice by transfer to their respective departments.
>
> Farm Credit Administration established as an independent agency under Executive Order 6084, effective March 27, 1933, superseding the Federal Farm Board and the Federal Farm Loan Board.

3. REORGANIZATION ACT OF APRIL 3, 1939 (53 STAT. 561)

President F. D. Roosevelt   76th Congress, 1st Session

Title I—Reorganization

Declaration of Policy: This was similar to the statement in the 1933 legislation except that the words "by reason of continued national deficits" replaced the statement "by reason of the general economic depression" in stating Congress' belief that the Act was necessary.

Power of President and Exemptions: The President could not, under this Act, abolish an executive department or create a new one. Moreover, some twenty-one agencies were exempted from the provisions of the Act. Further, it was specifically stated in the Act that the President could not use the reorganization power to authorize any agency to perform a function which was not specifically authorized by law. The Act further required that the President, in his transmittal messages, state the reduction of expenditures which would probably be brought about by the specific reorganization proposed.

Veto Procedure: The reorganization plan had to lay before the Congress for sixty days of a continuous session, during which time it could be disapproved (not amended) only by a concurrent resolution of both Houses, for which extraordinary rules of procedure with debate and delays severely limited are precisely prescribed. These rules contravened all existing procedures, proscribed unlimited debate and delays in reaching the floor of both Houses in order not to nullify the congressional veto right within the sixty-day period.

Expiration Date: The Act was to expire on January 21, 1941.

Title II—Budgetary Control

Amended paragraph 2 of the Budget and Accounting Act of 1921 to include any regulatory commission or board in the definition of "department and establishment."

Title III—Administrative Assistants

Authorized the President to appoint six administrative assistants at $10,000 per annum.

Origin and Significance: The Act was the first of the contemporary series of reorganization measures providing for reorganization by presidential plan subject to congressional veto within sixty day from submission. The Act was the compromise measure passed after the defeat of the Reorganization Act of April, 1938, which had been drafted on the basis of the Report of the President's Committee on Administrative Management (Brownlow Committee).

Principal Actions Taken: Plans under this Act effected an astonishing number of the reforms recommended in the Brownlow report. Because of their long-term influence on the structure of the government, they are cited here in some detail.

Reorganization Plan 1 of April 25, 1939, House Document 262, Part I created the Executive Office of the President and transferred to it the Bureau of the Budget (from Treasury) and the National Resources Planning Board (from Interior). Merged with the latter were the functions of the Federal Employment Stabilization Board (from Commerce) which were forerunners of the functions later assigned to the Council of Economic Advisors. Farm Credit Administration and Commodity Credit Corporation went to Agriculture.

Part II of Plan 1 established the Federal Security Agency under an administrator, and transferred to it the Social Security Board, the

United States Public Health Service (from Treasury) and the Office of Education (from Interior) in addition to various functions allied to these fields. This complex became the nucleus for the eventual creation of the Department of Health, Education, and Welfare in 1953.

Part III of Plan 1 established the Federal Works Agency under an administrator, and received selected general works functions, not part of the regular programs of a permanent agency, and construction loans and grants to state and local governments.

Part IV of Plan 1 established the Federal Loan Agency under an administrator, to which were transferred the Reconstruction Finance Corporation (and nine related government corporations), the Home Owners Loan Corporation, the Federal Home Loan Bank Board, the Federal Savings and Loan Insurance Corporation, the Federal Housing Administration, the Electric Home and Farm Authority, and the Export-Import Bank of Washington.

Reorganization Plans 2 (May 1939), 3 (April 1940), 4 (April 1940), and 5 (May 1940) were based on a consistent theory of departmental functions. A fiscal assistant secretary was authorized in the Treasury to head a new service grouping a number of fiscal offices and bureaus. Conservation functions affecting biological survey, migratory birds, fish, and wild life went to Interior, rural electrification to Agriculture, and inland waterways and other transportation functions to Commerce, including the Civil Aeronautics Administration. Immigration and Naturalization went to Justice from Labor. Food and Drug Administration went to the Federal Security Agency. A number of useful intradepartmental consolidations were effected.

4. REORGANIZATION ACT OF DECEMBER 20, 1945, (59 STAT. 613)

President Truman   79th Congress, 1st Session

Declaration of Policy: The preambles to the 1933 and 1939 Acts—those referring to depression and to continued deficits—were dropped; an additional purpose of the 1945 Act was "to facilitate orderly transition from war to peace." Congress also stated that it expected "that the transfers, consolidations, coordinations, and abolitions under this Act shall accomplish an overall reduction of at least twenty-five per centum in the administrative costs of the agency or agencies affected." In other respects, this part of the Act resembled its predecessors.

Power of President and Exemptions: The President could not abolish or create an executive department. Only eleven agencies were partially or wholly exempted from the provisions of the Act. Moreover, the Act precluded the imposition, in connection with the exercise of any quasi-judicial and quasi-legislative function possessed by an independent agency, any increased limitation upon the exercise of independent judgment and discretion.

Veto Procedure: The veto procedure was the same as in 1939; the bill had to lay before Congress for sixty days, during which time it could be disapproved by a concurrent resolution of both Houses.

Expiration Date: The Act was to expire on April 1, 1948.

5. REORGANIZATION ACT OF JUNE 20, 1949 (63 STAT. 203)

President Truman   81st Congress, 1st Session

This is the statute which, although amended and re-enacted (5 U.S.C. 101 et seq.), has been the basis of the President's reorganization power since 1949. The notable new feature of this Act was that the President was not precluded from the creation of a new executive department.

Declaration of Policy: SEC. 2 (a) The President shall examine and from time to time reexamine the organization of all agencies of the government and shall determine what changes therein are necessary to accomplish the following purposes:

(1) to promote the better execution of the laws, the more effective management of the executive branch of the government and its agencies and functions, and the expeditious administration of the public business;

(2) to reduce expenditures and promote economy to the fullest extent consistent with the efficient operation of the government;

(3) to increase the efficiency of the operations of the government to the fullest extent practicable;

(4) to group, coordinate, and consolidate agencies and functions of the government, as nearly as may be, according to purpose;

(5) to eliminate overlapping and duplication of effort.

Power of President and Exemptions: The Act specifically authorizes five basic types of action. These are (1) the transfer, (2) consolidation, (3) coordination, (4) abolition of the whole or any part of any "agency" or of the functions of any "agency," and (5) the authorization of any officer to delegate any of his functions. Agency is defined very broadly to include the departments, the independent commissions, and the executive agencies. The provisions of previous Acts for exemption of enumerated agencies are eliminated. The President could not, however, abolish or transfer an executive department or all its functions nor consolidate any two or more executive departments or their functions. "Agency" does not include the General Accounting Office nor the Comptroller General of the United States.

Veto Procedure: Congress could veto a plan if, by a majority of its authorized membership, either House passed a resolution of disapproval. As in the previous Acts, this action had to be taken within the first sixty days of continuous session.

Expiration Date: The Act was to expire on April 1, 1953.

6. FEBRUARY 11, 1953 (67 STAT. 4)

President Eisenhower   83rd Congress, 1st Session

The Reorganization Act of 1949 was extended to April 1, 1955, with no changes made.

7. MARCH 25, 1955 (69 STAT. 14)

President Eisenhower   84th Congress, 1st Session

The Reorganization Act of 1949 was extended to June 1, 1957.
No changes were made in the Act.

8. SEPTEMBER 4, 1957 (71 STAT. 611)

President Eisenhower   85th Congress, 1st Session

The Reorganization Act was extended to June 1, 1959. The Act was amended so that a reorganization plan could be vetoed on passage of a disapproval resolution by a simple majority of the members of either House present and voting rather than by a majority of the authorized membership of that House.

9. APRIL 7, 1961 (75 STAT. 41)

President Kennedy   87th Congress, 1st Session

After a lapse of two years, from 1959–1961, the Reorganization Act, as amended, was extended to June 1, 1963. No changes were made.

In June 1963, the reorganization power was allowed to lapse and was not re-enacted until July 1964, after Lyndon B. Johnson's succession. Congress had resented the fact that President Kennedy had sent up Reorganization Plan No. 1 on January 20, 1962, to create a Department of Urban Affairs and Housing while a bill to the same effect (S. 1633) had been reported to the Senate in 1961 and had been introduced in the House and was languishing in its Rules Committee. So the House rejected his plan by Resolution No. 530, on February 21, 1962.

10. JULY 2, 1964 (78 STAT. 240)

President L. B. Johnson   88th Congress, 1st Session

After a lapse of one year, the Reorganization Act of 1949, as amended, was extended to June 1, 1965. The Act was amended to prohibit the use of the reorganization power to create a new executive department.

11. JUNE 18, 1965, (79 STAT. 135)

President L. B. Johnson   89th Congress, 1st Session

The Reorganization Act, as amended, was extended to December 31, 1968. No further changes were made in the Act.

In 1965, President L. B. Johnson had requested Congress to enact a permanent extension of the 1949 Act, pointing out the lapses of the reorganization power from 1959 to 1961 and from 1963 to 1964. Congress, as before, was unwilling to approve permanent reorganization legislation, but it did grant an extension in the Act of 1965 of three and one-half years, virtually for the balance of Johnson's unexpired term and the longest duration of any Act since the one passed in 1949.

12. MARCH 27, 1969 (83 STAT. 6)

President Nixon   91st Congress, 1st Session

The Reorganization Act, as amended, was extended, without change, to April 1, 1971.

Text of Reorganization Act, latest model

Precise legalists should note that the Reorganization Act of 1949, as amended, was actually repealed (80 Stat. 655). It was re-enacted, with a few drafting revisions, as part of the continuing congressional codification process, as Chapter 9 of Title 5 of the United States Code by Public Law 89–554, approved September 6, 1966 (80 Stat. 393 et seq.).

It has been extended to April 1, 1971 (see item 12 above). Because it illustrates the unique features of the legislative veto and since it is the Act now in effect, I am reproducing its full text in the pages that follow. I am also citing the text of Chapter 1—Organization, which is part of Title 5 and contains certain definitions governing Chapter 9, for a complete view of contemporary authority for federal reorganization by executive plan subject to legislative veto:

13. REORGANIZATION PLAN FOR 1966—EXCERPTS FROM THE STATUTE

AN ACT

To enact title 5, United States Code, "Government Organization and Employees," codifying the general and permanent laws relating to the organization of the Government of the United States and to its civilian officers and employees.

Be it enacted by the Senate and House of Representatives of the United States of America in Congress assembled, That the laws relating to the organization of the Government of the United States and to its civilian officers and employees, generally, are revised, codified, and enacted as title 5 of the United States Code, entitled "Government Organization and Employees," and may be cited as "5 U.S.C., §," as follows:

TITLE 5—GOVERNMENT ORGANIZATION AND EMPLOYEES

PART I—THE AGENCIES GENERALLY

CHAPTER 1—ORGANIZATION

§ 101. Executive departments

The Executive departments are:

    The Department of State.
    The Department of the Treasury.
    The Department of Defense.
    The Department of Justice.
    The Post Office Department.
    The Department of the Interior.
    The Department of Agriculture.
    The Department of Commerce.
    The Department of Labor.
    The Department of Health, Education, and Welfare.

§ 102. Military departments

The military departments are:

    The Department of the Army.
    The Department of the Navy.
    The Department of the Air Force.

§ 103. Government corporation

For the purpose of this title—

    (1) "Government corporation" means a corporation owned or controlled by the Government of the United States; and

    (2) "Government controlled corporation" does not include a corporation owned by the Government of the United States.

§ 104. Independent establishment

For the purpose of this title, "independent establishment" means—

    (1) an establishment in the executive branch which is not an Executive department, military department, Government corporation, or part thereof, or part of an independent establishment; and

    (2) the General Accounting Office.

§ 105. Executive agency

For the purpose of this title, "Executive agency" means an Executive department, a Government corporation, and an independent establishment.

CHAPTER 9—EXECUTIVE REORGANIZATION

Sec.
901. Purpose.
902. Definitions.
903. Reorganization plans.
904. Additional contents of reorganization plans.

§ 901. Purpose

(a) The President shall from time to time examine the organization of all agencies and shall determine what changes therein are necessary to accomplish the following purposes:

(1) to promote the better execution of the laws, the more effective management of the executive branch and of its agencies and functions, and the expeditious administration of the public business;

(2) to reduce expenditures and promote economy to the fullest extent consistent with the efficient operation of the Government;

(3) to increase the efficiency of the operations of the Government to the fullest extent practicable.

(4) to group, coordinate, and consolidate agencies and functions of the Government, as nearly as may be, according to major purposes;

(5) to reduce the number of agencies by consolidating those having similar functions under a single head, and to abolish such agencies or functions thereof as may not be necessary for the efficient conduct of the Government; and

(6) to eliminate overlapping and duplication of effort.

(b) Congress declares that the public interest demands the carry-out of the purposes of subsection (a) of this section and that the purposes may be accomplished in great measure by proceeding under this chapter, and can be accomplished more speedily thereby than by the enactment of specific legislation.

§ 902. Definitions

For the purpose of this chapter—

(1) "agency" means—

(A) an Executive agency or part thereof;

(B) an office or officer in the civil service or uniformed services in or under an Executive agency; and

(C) the government of the District of Columbia or part thereof, except the courts;

but does not include the General Accounting Office or the Comptroller General of the United States; and

(2) "reorganization" means a transfer, consolidation, coordination, authorization, or abolition, referred to in section 903 of this title.

§ 903. Reorganization plans

(a) When the President, after investigation, finds that—

(1) the transfer of the whole or a part of an agency, or of the whole or a part of the functions thereof, to the jurisdiction and control of another agency;

(2) the abolition of all or a part of the functions of an agency;

(3) the consolidation or coordination of the whole or a part of an agency, or of the whole or a part of the functions thereof, with the whole or a part of another agency or the functions thereof;

(4) the consolidation or coordination of a part of an agency or the functions thereof with another part of the same agency or the functions thereof;

(5) the authorization of an officer in the civil service or uniformed services to delegate any of his functions; or

(6) the abolition of the whole or a part of an agency which agency or part does not have, or on the taking effect of the reorganization plan will not have, any functions;

is necessary to accomplish one or more of the purposes of section 901(a) of this title, he shall prepare a reorganization plan for the making of the reorganizations as to which he has made findings and which he includes in the plan, and transmit the plan (bearing an identification number) to Congress, together with a declaration that, with respect to each reorganization included in the plan, he has found that the reorganization is necessary to accomplish one or more of the purposes of section 901(a) of this title.

(b) The President shall have a reorganization plan delivered to both Houses on the same day and to each House while it is in session. In his message transmitting a reorganization plan, the President shall specify with respect to each abolition of a function included in the plan the statutory authority for the exercise of the function and the reduction of expenditures (itemized so far as practicable) that it is probable will be brought about by the taking effect of the reorganizations included in the plan.

§ 904. Additional contents of reorganization plans

A reorganization plan transmitted by the President under section 903 of this title—

(1) may change, in such cases as the President considers necessary, the name of an agency affected by a reorganization and the title of its head; and shall designate the name of an agency resulting from a reorganization and the title of its head;

(2) may provide for the appointment and pay of the head and one or more officers of an agency (including an agency resulting from a consolidation or other type of reorganization) if the President finds, and in his message transmitting the plan declares, that by reason of a reorganization made by the plan the provisions are necessary. The head so provided may be an individual or may be a commission or board with more than one member. In case of such an appointment, the term of office may not be fixed at more than 4 years, the pay may not be at a rate in excess of that found by the President to be applicable to comparable officers in the executive branch, and, if the appointment is not to a position in the competitive service, it shall be by the President, by and with the advice and consent of the Senate, except that, in the case of an officer of the government of the District of Columbia, it may be by the Board of Commissioners or other body or officer of that government designated in the plan;

(3) shall provide for the transfer or other disposition of the records, property, and personnel affected by a reorganization;

(4) shall provide for the transfer of such unexpended balances of appropriations, and of other funds, available for use in connection with a function or agency affected by a reorganization, as the President considers necessary by reason of the reorganization for use in connection with the functions affected by the reorganization, or for the use of the agency which shall have the functions after the reorganization plan is effective. However, the unexpended balances so transferred may be used only for the purposes for which the appropriation was originally made; and

(5) shall provide for terminating the affairs of an agency abolished.

§ 905. Limitations on powers

(a) A reorganization plan may not provide for, and a reorganization under this chapter may not have the effect of—

(1) creating a new Executive department, abolishing or transferring an Executive department or all the functions thereof, or consolidating two or more Executive departments or all the functions thereof;

(2) continuing an agency beyond the period authorized by law for its existence or beyond the time when it would have terminated if the reorganization had not been made;

(3) continuing a function beyond the period authorized by law for its exercise or beyond the time when it would have terminated if the reorganization had not been made;

(4) authorizing an agency to exercise a function which is not expressly authorized by law at the time the plan is transmitted to Congress;

(5) increasing the term of an office beyond that provided by law for the office; or

(6) transferring to or consolidating with another agency the government of the District of Columbia or all the functions thereof which are subject to this chapter, or abolishing that government or all those functions.

(b) A provision contained in a reorganization plan may take effect only if the plan is transmitted to Congress before December 31, 1968.

§ 906. Effective date and publication of reorganization plans

(a) Except as otherwise provided under subsection (c) of this section, a reorganization plan is effective at the end of the first period of 60 calendar days of continuous session of Congress after the date on which the plan is transmitted to it unless, between the date of transmittal and the end of the 60-day period, either House passes a resolution stating in substance that that House does not favor the reorganization plan.

(b) For the purpose of subsection (a) of this section—

(1) continuity of session is broken only by an adjournment of Congress sine die; and

(2) the days on which either House is not in session because of an adjournment of more than 3 days to a day certain are excluded in the computation of the 60-day period.

(c) Under provisions contained in a reorganization plan, a provision of the plan may be effective at a time later than the date on which the plan otherwise is effective.

(d) A reorganization plan which is effective shall be printed (1) in the Statutes at Large in the same volume as the public laws and (2) in the Federal Register.

§ 907. Effect on other laws, pending legal proceedings, and unexpended appropriations

(a) A statute enacted, and a regulation or other action made, prescribed, issued, granted, or performed in respect of or by an agency or function affected by a reorganization under this chapter, before the effective date of the reorganization, has, except to the extent rescinded, modified, superseded, or made inapplicable by or under authority of law or by the abolition of a function, the same effect as if the reorganization had not been made. However, if the statute, regulation, or other action has vested the functions in the agency from which it is removed under the reorganization plan, the function, insofar as it is to be exercised after the plan becomes effective, shall be deemed as vested in the agency under which the function is placed by the plan.

(b) For the purpose of subsection (a) of this section, "regulation or other action" means a regulation, rule, order, policy, determination, directive, authorization, permit, privilege, requirement, designation, or other action.

(c) A suit, action, or other proceeding lawfully commenced by or against the head of an agency or other officer of the United States, in his official capacity or in relation to the discharge of his official duties, does not abate by reason of the taking effect of a reorganization plan under this chapter. On motion or supplemental petition filed at any time within 12 months after the reorganization plan takes effect, showing a necessity for a survival of the suit, action, or other proceeding to obtain a settlement of the questions involved, the court may allow the suit, action, or other proceeding to be maintained by or against the successor of the head or officer under the reorganization effected by the plan or, if there is no successor, against such agency or officer as the President designates.

(d) The appropriations or portions of appropriations unexpended by reason of the operation of this chapter may not be used for any purpose, but shall revert to the Treasury.

§ 908. Rules of Senate and House of Representatives on reorganization plans

Section 909–913 of this title are enacted by Congress—

(1) as an exercise of the rule-making power of the Senate and the House of Representatives, respectively, and as such they are deemed a part of the rules of each House, respectively, but applicable only with respect to the procedure to be followed in that House in the case of resolutions described by section 909 of this title; and they supersede other rules only to the extent that they are inconsistent therewith; and

(2) with full recognition of the constitutional right of either House to change the rules (so far as relating to the procedure of that House) at any time, in the same manner and to the same extent as in the case of any other rule of that House.

§ 909. Terms of resolution

For the purpose of sections 908–913 of this title, "resolution" means only a resolution of either House of Congress, the matter after the resolving clause of which is as follows: "That the _____ does not favor the reorganization plan numbered _____ transmitted to Congress by the President on _____, 19_____.", the first blank space therein being filled with the name of the resolving House and the other blank spaces therein being appropriately filled; but does not include a resolution which specifies more than one reorganization plan.

§ 910. Reference of resolution to committee

A resolution with respect to a reorganization plan shall be referred to a committee (and all resolutions with respect to the same plan shall be referred to the same committee) by the President of the Senate or the Speaker of the House of Representatives, as the case may be.

§ 911. Discharge of committee considering resolution

(a) If the committee to which a resolution with respect to a reorganization plan has been referred has not reported it at the end of 10 calendar days after its introduction, it is in order to move either to discharge the committee from further consideration of the resolution or to discharge the committee from further consideration of any other resolution with respect to the reorganization plan which has been referred to the committee.

(b) A motion to discharge may be made only by an individual favoring the resolution, is highly privileged (except that it may not be made after the committee has reported a resolution with respect to the same reorganization plan), and debate thereon shall be limited to not more than 1 hour, to be divided equally between those favoring and those opposing the resolution. An amendment to the motion is not in order, and it is not in order to move to reconsider the vote by which the motion is agreed to or disagreed to.

(c) If the motion to discharge is agreed to or disagreed to, the motion may not be renewed, nor may another motion to discharge the committee be made with respect to any other resolution with respect to the same reorganization plan.

§ 912. Procedure after report or discharge of committee; debate

(a) When the committee has reported, or has been discharged from further consideration of, a resolution with respect to a reorganization plan, it is at any time thereafter in order (even though a previous motion to the same effect has been disagreed to) to move to proceed to the consideration of the resolution. The motion is highly privileged and is not debatable. An amendment to the motion is not in order, and it is not in order to move to reconsider the vote by which the motion is agreed to or disagreed to.

(b) Debate on the resolution shall be limited to not more than 10 hours, which shall be divided equally between those favoring and those opposing the resolution. A motion further to limit debate is not debatable. An amendment to, or motion to recommit, the resolution is not in order, and it is not in order to move to reconsider the vote by which the resolution is agreed to or disagreed to.

§ 913. Decisions without debate on motion to postpone or proceed

(a) Motions to postpone, made with respect to the discharge from committee, or the consideration of, a resolution with respect to a reorganization plan, and motions to proceed to the consideration of other business, shall be decided without debate.

(b) Appeals from the decisions of the Chair relating to the application of the rules of the Senate or the House of Representatives, as the case may be, to the procedure relating to a resolution with respect to a reorganization plan shall be decided without debate.

NOTES

CHAPTER I

1. James Hart, *The American Presidency in Action, 1789* (New York, The MacMillan Co., 1948), p. 135.
2. Louis Brownlow, *The President and the Presidency* (Chicago, Public Administration Service, 1949), p. 62.
3. Hart. See note 1, p. 136.
4. A. Merriman Smith, *A President is Many Men* (New York, 1948), p. 9. Mr. Smith was for years dean of the White House correspondents corps, one of whose duties is to say when the time is up, "thank you Mr. President," at presidential press conferences.
5. Leonard D. White, *The Federalists* (New York, The MacMillan Co., 1948), p. 27.
6. Burton J. Hendrick, *Lincoln's War Cabinet* (Boston, Little, Brown, and Co., 1946).
7. Brownlow. See note 2, p. 64.
8. *Myers vs. United States*, 272 U.S. 52 (1926).
9. Edward S. Corwin, *The President, Office and Powers*, 3rd ed., rev. (New York, New York University Press, 1948), p. 89.
10. *Humphrey's Executor vs. United States*, 295 U.S. 602 (1935).
11. °*Task Force Report on Regulatory Commissions*, p. 14.
12. *Wiener vs. United States*, 357 U.S. 349 (1958).
13. *United States vs. Lovett*, 328 U.S. 303 (1946).
14. *Morgan vs. T.V.A.*, 28 *Federal Supplement*, 732 (1941).
15. C. Herman Pritchett, "The Government Corporation Control Act of 1945," *American Political Science Review* (June 1946), p. 509.
16. Paul H. Appleby, *Policy and Administration* (University of Alabama Press, 1949), pp. 35 ff.
17. S. 140, 80th Congress, 1st session (1947). Under pressure from labor, welfare, and consumer groups, the Senate committee amended the bill to drop the requirement of representation, but retained the separatist

structural scheme for the candid purpose of encouraging support of medical groups. (S. Rept. 242, 80th Congress, 1st session).

18. *Social Security and Education*, p. 43.

19. *Ibid*.

20. Harold Stein, *Public Administration and Policy Development, A Case Book*, "The Foreign Service Act of 1946" (New York, Harcourt Brace & Co., 1952), p. 661 *et seq*. (Also available separately as CPAC No. 9, in reprints of Interuniversity Case Program, Indianapolis, Bobbs-Merrill Co., Inc.)

21. H.R. 4102, 80th Congress, 1st session (1947).

22. *New York Times* (Aug. 7, 1947).

23. *Social Security and Education*, p. 45.

24. Harvey C. Mansfield, *The Comptroller General* (New Haven, Yale University Press, 1939).

25. *Report of the President's Committee on Administrative Management*, p. 23.

26. *Budgeting and Accounting*, pp. 35 ff.

27. Lucius Wilmerding, Jr., *The Spending Power* (New Haven, Yale University Press, 1943), p. 307.

*Reports are documents of the Commission on Organization of the Executive Branch of the Government (Hoover I) Washington, Superintendent of Documents.

Chapter II

1. Bertram M. Gross, *The Managing of Organizations—The Administrative Struggle*, The Free Press of Glencoe (New York, The Crowell-Collier Publishing Company, 1964), two volumes. See Chapter 6, "The Pioneers, the Gospel of Efficiency," and Chapter 7, "The Pioneers, New Beginnings."

2. Leonard D. White, *A Study in Administrative History* (New York, The MacMillan Company)—also in paperback—four volumes:

2-A. *The Federalists*, 1789–1801 (1948)

2-B. *The Jeffersonians*, 1801–1829 (1951)

2-C. *The Jacksonians*, 1829–1861 (1954)

2-D. *The Republican Era*, 1869–1901 (1958)

3. Paul Van Riper, *History of the United States Civil Service* (New York, Harper & Row, 1958).

4. Bureau of Executive Manpower, United States Civil Service Commission, *The Characteristics of the Federal Executive* (Washington, November 1969), paperbound in-house document.

5. Frederick C. Mosher, "Some Observations About Foreign Service Reform," *Public Administration Review*, Vol. XXIX, No. 6 (Nov.-Dec. 1969), p. 600.

6. James B. Richardson, ed., *Messages and Papers of the Presidents* (New York, Bureau of National Literature, 1918), Vol. XVII, 1897 to 1914,

p. 7485. (A compilation prepared under the direction of the Joint Committee on Printing of the House and Senate.)

7. Oscar Kraines, "The President Versus Congress: The Keep Commission, 1905–1909, First Comprehensive Presidential Inquiry Into Administration," *The Western Political Quarterly*, Vol. XXIII, No. 1, March 1970, pp. 5–54.

8. Professor Charles E. Merriam, who in 1936 became a member of the President's Committee on Administrative Management, was invited to serve on the Taft Commission but declined as he was a member of the city council of Chicago and ran unsuccessfully for mayor in 1912.

9. Harold D. Smith, *The Management of Your Government* (New York, McGraw-Hill Book Company, Inc., 1945).

10. 61 *Congressional Record* 1921.

11. Woodrow Wilson, *Congressional Government, A Study in American Politics* (Boston, Houghton, Mifflin & Company, 1885). (Also, New York, Meridian Books, 1956—paperbound, with an introduction by Walter Lippman.)

12. Woodrow Wilson, "Cabinet Government in the United States," *International Review*, (August 1879).

13. Woodrow Wilson, "The Study of Public Administration," New York, *Political Science Quarterly* (June 1887). Reprinted separately as a monograph (Washington, Public Affairs Press, 1955), in the series "Annals of American Government."

14. Peter P. Schauffler, *Study of the Legislative Veto*, Widener Library, Harvard University (unpublished typescript of doctoral dissertation), December 1956.

15. Louis Brownlow, "Reconversion of the Federal Administrative Machinery from War to Peace," *Public Administration Review*, Vol. IV, 1944, p. 322.

16. House Document 254, 72nd Congress, 1st session, *Special Message of President Herbert Hoover of February 17, 1932*. The month before, Senator Walter F. George (D./Georgia) had introduced a reorganization bill which failed of passage and which provided for the legislative veto device, S. J. Resolution 76, January 6, 1932.

CHAPTER III

1. S. Doc. 8, 75th Cong., 1st sess., p. 2. Jan. 1937—Special Message of President Franklin D. Roosevelt Transmitting the *Report* of the President's Committee on Administrative Management.

2. Louis Brownlow, *A Passion for Anonymity, Autobiography, Second Half* (Chicago, University of Chicago Press, 1958), Chapters XXVIII to XXXI, incl.

3. A provision in the First Deficiency Appropriation Act for the fiscal year 1936 authorized the President to allocate not more than $100,000 from appropriations under the 1935 Emergency Relief Appropriation Act for a committee to "make a study of the emergency and regular agencies

of the executive branch of the government for the purpose of making recommendations to secure the most efficient organization and management of that branch of the public service." (49 U.S. Stat. 1600.)

4. Barry Dean Karl, *Executive Reorganization and Reform in the New Deal* (Cambridge, Harvard University Press, 1963). A history of government reform movements since 1900 with interesting profiles of Brownlow, Merriam, and Gulick.

5. Harvey C. Mansfield, "Federal Executive Reorganization, Thirty Years of Experience," *Public Administration Review*, Vol. XXIX, No. 4, (July/Aug. 1969).

5-A. See Brownlow, *Autobiography, Second Half*, p. 457.

6. Senator Byrd took the lead in the confusion of aims. Before the *Report* was completed he took issue with the President's disparagement of possibilities of economy resulting from reorganization. In a radio address made the evening before the President submitted the *Report* to the Congress he indicated that its recommendations would not meet with his support. (*Washington Post*, Jan. 12, 1937.)

7. *Time*, Jan. 25, 1937. Even before the *Report* had been made public, the "jobjitters" of officeholders had been reported. According to a *New York Times* article, "Day after day dismal rumors chill the food at bureaucratic luncheon tables, muddy the afterwork libations at cocktail bars, rear their baleful heads in hundreds of cafeteria lines and in thousands of muttered corridor conferences." (*New York Times*, Nov. 15, 1936.)

8. There was some scoffing, also, at the language of the proposal for administrative assistants. The qualification of a "passion for anonymity" innocently borrowed by Mr. Brownlow from a characterization of the head of the British Cabinet Secretariat, evoked derisive comment from some journalists. "The six selfless synthesists," one remarked, "would be mystery men. . . . if they cease being mysterious, they will no longer be the Brownlow-Gulick-Merriam boys from the administrative laboratory of the University of Chicago." (Arthur Krock, *New York Times*, Jan. 13, 1937.)

9. *Washington Post*, Jan. 13, 1937.

10. *New York World-Telegram*, Jan. 13, 1937.

11. *St. Louis Post-Dispatch, Philadelphia Inquirer, Boston Traveler*, Jan. 13, 1937.

12. *Baltimore Sun*, Jan. 13, 1937.

13. *Chicago Tribune*, Jan. 14, 1937.

14. *New York Herald-Tribune*, Jan. 13, 1937.

15. *New York Times*, Oct. 16, 1937.

16. *Chicago Herald-Examiner*, Mar. 14, 1938.

17. Richard Pollenberg, *Reorganizing Roosevelt's Government, The Controversy over Executive Reorganization* (Cambridge, Harvard University Press, 1966).

18. H.R. 7730, 8202, 8276, and 8277, 75th Cong., 1st sess. (1937).

19. S. 2970, 75th Cong., 1st sess. (1937).

20. H.R. 7730. See Note 18.

21. H.R. 8202. See Note 18.

22. S. 3331, 75th Cong., 3rd sess. (1938).

23. Technically, thus, the provisions of the House bills included in the Byrnes bill actually received the endorsement of a majority of both Houses.

24. The vote on the motion to recommit was 204–196 with 29 not voting. (83 *Congressional Record* 5123, Sept. 2, 1938).

25. In the Overman Act in World War I the Congress delegated general reorganization powers for the war years. The Economy Act of 1932 authorized the President to reorganize by Executive order subject to veto by either House of Congress in 60 days (47 U.S. Stat. 413). A rider to the Treasury-Post Office Appropriation Act of March 3, 1933, granted the President a two-year authority to reorganize by Executive order with no provision for congressional veto (47 U.S. Stat. 1517) (Appendix III).

26. *Report of the President's Committee on Administrative Management,* pp. 36, 37.

27. 84 *Congressional Record* 2493.

28. Louis Brownlow, "Reconversion of the Federal Administrative Machinery from War to Peace," *Public Administration Review,* Vol. IV (Autumn 1944), p. 322.

29. It provided a "nicer balance" between the President and the Congress —an approach to the "philosopher's stone" sought by students of administration. John D. Millett and Lindsay Rogers, "The Legislative Veto and the Reorganization Act of 1939," *Public Administration Review,* Vol. I, No. 2 (Winter 1941), p. 189.

30. Joint Congressional Committee on Government Organization, *Hearings,* 75th Cong., 1st sess., p. 8.

31. *Report of the President's Committee on Administrative Management,* p. 37.

32. John D. Millett and Lindsay Rogers, "The Legislative Veto and the Reorganization Act of 1939," *Public Administration Review,* Vol. 1, No. 2 (Winter 1941), p. 176.

CHAPTER IV

1. Arthur M. Schlesinger, Jr., *The Coming of the New Deal, The Age of Roosevelt,* Vol. II (Boston, Houghton, Mifflin and Company, 1958) p. 3.

2. Henry Steele Commager, Introduction to *The T.V.A. Years, 1939–1945,* from the *Journals of David E. Lilienthal,* Vol. I (New York, Harper & Row, 1964).

3. *United States Government Organization Manual,* 1969–70, Office of the Federal Register, National Archives and Records Service, General Services Administration, Appendix A, "Executive Agencies and Functions of the Federal Government, Abolished, Transferred, or Terminated Subsequent to March 4, 1933" (Washington, Superintendent of Documents, 1969), p. 635.

4. Harold Stein, ed., *American Civil-Military Decisions, A Book of Case Studies,* A Twentieth Century Fund Study, published in cooperation with the Inter-University Case Program (University of Alabama Press, 1963).

5. Louis Brownlow, *A Passion for Anonymity, Autobiography, Second*

Half (Chicago, The University of Chicago Press, 1958), Chapter XXXIV, "Preparation for War."

6. James W. Fesler, George W. Auxier, et al, *Industrial Mobilization for War, History of the War Production Board and Predecessor Agencies, 1945– 1950,* Volume I, Program and Administration, Bureau of Demobilization, Civilian Production Administration (Washington, Superintendent of Documents, 1947).

7. Clinton Rossiter, *The American Presidency* (New York: Harcourt, Brace, and World, Inc., revised edition 1960), p. 134.

8. Louis Brownlow. See Note 5, p. 428.

9. Pendleton Herring, chairman, Committee on Records of War Administration, "The War Agencies of the Executive Branch of the Government," *The United States at War,* Appendix I (Washington, Superintendent of Documents, 1946). This volume was No. 1 of Historical Reports on War Administration of the Bureau of the Budget.

10. Luther Gulick, *Administrative Reflections from World War II* (University of Alabama Press, 1948).

11. Louis Brownlow, "Reconversion of the Federal Administrative Machinery from War to Peace," *Public Administration Review* (Autumn, 1944), Vol. IV, No. 4, p. 309.

12. Louis Brownlow. See Note 5, "Stimson and Knox, "Chapter XXXV.

13. Clinton Rossiter. *The American Presidency.* See Note 7, p. 130.

CHAPTER V

1. Public Law 162, 80th Cong., 1st sess.

2. The contrary result, in fact, is suggested by the recent commentary attributing the weakness of the 1949 Reorganization Act to the opposition of the Senate committee chairman to any bill failing to exempt the Army Engineers. Ferrell Heady, "The Reorganization Act of 1949," *Public Administration Review,* Vol. IX (Summer 1949), p. 174.

3. Paul H. Appleby, "The Significance of the Hoover Commission Report," *Yale Review,* (Autumn 1949), pp. 12 ff.

4. He found himself in the minority, however, in opposing the designation of the service secretaries as under secretaries and in opposing the limitation of the Advisory Board to the United Medical Administration to advisory functions.

5. 84 *Congressional Record* 2493.

6. *Report of the President's Committee on Administrative Management,* p. 38.

7. *New York Herald-Tribune,* Feb. 9, 1949.

8. *Chicago Daily News,* Feb. 10, 1949.

9. *Chicago Tribune,* Feb. 11, 1949.

10. *General Management of the Executive Branch,* p. viii.

11. Herman Finer, "The Hoover Commission Reports," *Political Science Quarterly,* (September 1949), p. 412.

12. *General Management of the Executive Branch,* p. 2.

13. Paul H. Appleby, "The Significance of the Hoover Commission Report." See Note 3, p. 9.

14. *Personnel Management,* p. 49.

15. James R. Watson, "The Hoover Commission Report on Personnel Management," *Public Personnel Review,* July 1949, p. 137.

16. *Department of Commerce,* pp. 11 ff.

17. *Task Force Report on Public Welfare,* pp. 465 ff.

18. *Task Force Report on Agriculture Activities,* pp. 59 ff.

19. The Public Affairs Institute, *Half a Loaf,* p. 7.

20. C. Herman Pritchett, *The Roosevelt Court* (New York, 1948).

21. Senate Committee on Expenditures in the Executive Departments, *Hearings on the 1949 Reorganization Bill,* S. 526, p. 72.

22. *General Management of the Executive Branch,* p. 45.

23. *Department of Agriculture,* errata sheet to p. 29.

24. *United States News and World Report,* June 3, 1949, p. 22.

25. Senate Committee on Expenditures in the Executive Departments, *Hearings on 1949 Reorganization Plan I,* p. 8.

26. *Ibid.,* p. 10.

27. Public Law 152, 81st Cong., 1st sess.

28. Public Law 216, 81st Cong., 1st sess.

29. Public Law 73, 81st Cong., 1st sess.

30. Public Law 109, 81st Cong., 1st sess.

31. Reorganization Plans II to VII, 1949.

32. Public Law 359, 81st Cong., 1st sess.

33. Reference works on Hoover I—The Commission on Organization of the Executive Branch of the Government:
A. *The Reports:* In addition to the official reports which were issued separately as they appeared and were printed by the Superintendent of Documents, Washington, D.C., they may be found in a bound volume: *The Hoover Commission Report on Organization of the Executive Branch of the Government* (New York, McGraw-Hill Book Company, Inc., unsigned, undated, and uncopyrighted, sponsored by the publishers, circa 1950).
B. "Summary of the Reports of the Hoover Commission," *Public Administration Review,* Vol. IX, No. 2 (Spring 1949), pp. 73–99. An unsigned summary by the editors.
C. "The Hoover Commission: A Symposium," *American Political Science Review,* Vol. LXIII (October 1949), pp. 933–1000. The authors were all political scientists who had participated in the work of the first Hoover Commission:
(1) *Introduction*
    Charles Aiken (assistant to vice chairman and Commissioner Dean Acheson) and Louis W. Koenig (member of Task Force on Foreign Affairs).
(2) *The Operation of a Mixed Commission*
    Ferrel Heady (assistant to Commissioner James K. Pollock).
(3) *The Presidency*
    John M. Gaus (member of the Task Force on the Department of Agriculture).

(4) *Departmental Management*
     John D. Millett (member of the research group on the Executive
     Office of the President).
(5) *Foreign Affairs*
     Daniel S. Cheever and H. Field Haviland, Jr. (staff members of the
     Task Force on Foreign Affairs).
(6) *The Regulatory Commissions Revisited*
     C. Herman Pritchett (staff member of the Task Force on the Regula-
     tory Commissions and the Department of Commerce).
(7) *Improving Federal Management Services*
     Lewis B. Sims (member of the Task Force on Personnel).

CHAPTER VI

1. Public Law 108—Chapter 184, 83rd Congress, 1st sess. (S. 106) approved July 10, 1953.
2. Public Law 162—Chapter 207, 80th Congress, 1st sess. (H.R. 775) approved July 7, 1947.
3. For an exposition of this thesis, see James W. Fesler, "Administrative Literature and the Second Hoover Commission Reports," *American Political Science Review*, LI (March 1957), p. 148. This essay is one of the most acute and perceptive commentaries on the unevenness and imbalances of the second Hoover Commission report.
4. Ferrel Heady, "The Operation of a Mixed Commission," *American Political Science Review*, LXIII (October 1949), p. 942.
5. This statement was delivered at a press conference called by Mr. Hoover.
6. U.S. Congress, Senate Committee on Government Operations, *Senate Report no. 216,* 83rd Congress, 1st session, 1953, p. 1.
7. U.S. Congress, House Committee on Government Operations, *House of Representatives Report no. 505,* 83rd Congress, 1st session, 1953, p. 2.
8. Quoted in Commission on Organization of the Executive Branch's *Final Report to the Congress,* June 1955, p. 6.
9. Public Law 109—83rd Congress, 1st session. Approved July 10, 1955.
10. *Senate Report 216,* 83rd Congress, 1st session, p. 4.
11. *Senate Report 216,* 83rd Congress, 1st session, p. 4.
12. William R. Divine, "The Second Hoover Commission Reports: An Analysis," *Public Administration Review,* XV (Fall 1955), p. 263.
13. *Christian Science Monitor,* July 29, 1953.
14. At Mr. Hoover's suggestion, members of the second commission and of its staff and the task forces were exempted from the conflict of interest statutes. Public Law 108, Section 2 (b).
15. James W. Fesler, "Administrative Literature and the Second Hoover Commission Reports," *American Political Science Review,* LI (March 1957), p. 151. (See, for example, the reports on Legal Services and Procedures and Overseas Economic Operations.)
16. *Ibid.*

17. *Report of the President's Committee on Administrative Management* (Washington, 1937), p. 4.

18. Commission on Organization . . . , *Final Report to the Congress* (Washington, 1955), p. 19.

19. *Ibid.*

20. "Summary of the Objectives, Operations and Results of the Commissions on Organization of the Executive Branch of the Government" (committee print), Committee on Government Operations, House of Representatives, 88th Congress, 1st session, 1963—Appendix G, p. 35. *Memorandum to the President,* dated February 10, 1958.

21. For a concentrated report of the recommendations of Hoover I and II see *Congress and the Nation; 1945 to 1964: A Review of Government and Politics in the Post War Years;* Washington, D.C., Congressional Quarterly Service, 1965, Chapter 11, Part IV, pp. 1458–1464. (This chapter also summarizes the several Reorganization Acts and the Reorganization Plans pursuant to those acts submitted by the President.)

22. Commission on Organization . . . , *Federal Medical Services,* a Report to the Congress. February 1955, p. 21.

23. Commission on Organization . . . , *Water Resources and Power,* Vol. 1, a Report to the Congress. June 1955, p. 38.

24. *Ibid. Water Resources and Power,* Vol. 2.

25. *The New York Times,* June 30, 1955.

26. Albert T. Stone, "The Hoover Reports on Water Resources and Power—A Commentary," *California Law Review,* 43 (December 1955), p. 750.

27. *Ibid.*

28. *The New York Times,* March 3, 1955.

29. Herbert Emmerich and G. Lyle Belsley, "The Federal Career Service —What Next?" *Public Administration Review,* XIV (Winter 1954), pp. 3–4.

30. *Congressional Quarterly Weekly Report,* Vol. 13 (June 17, 1955), pp. 691–697.

31. Neil MacNeil and Harold W. Metz, *The Hoover Report—1953–1955 —What it Means to You as Citizen and Taxpayer.* Introduction by Herbert Hoover (New York, The MacMillan Company, 1956).
(N.B. Although obviously a semiofficial polemic for the work of Hoover II by two true believers, it is a skillful summation of the work of Hoover II. Both men had professional backgrounds of education and experience and both participated actively in the work of the second Hoover Commission.)

CHAPTER VII

1. Luther Gulick, *Administrative Reflections from World War II* (The University of Alabama Press, 1948), p. 20.

2. Corinne Silverman, "The Office of Education Library," in Harold Stein (ed.), *Public Administration and Policy Development: A Case Book* (New York, Harcourt, Brace and Company, 1952). Also available separately as

CPAC No. 16 in the reprint series sponsored by the Inter-University Case Program, Inc. (Indianapolis, Bobbs-Merrill & Co., 1950).

3. The 82nd Congress, 2nd session changed the names of the Committees on Expenditures in the Executive Establishments to the Committees on Government Operations, by Senate Resolution 280, March 3, 1952 and by House Resolution 647, July 1952. See also: *Evaluation of the Effect of the Legislative Reorganization Act of 1946*, Senate Report 1175, 80th Congress 2nd session, 1948, pp. 2–3, and also: *Activities of the Senate Committee on Government Operations*, Senate Report 5, 83rd Congress, 1st session, 1953, page 4.

4. *Reorganization Plan I*, pursuant to Reorganization Act of 1949, transmitted with message by President Truman, March 13, 1950. This was the first of 21 plans sent to Congress, of which Plans 1 to 13 were to implement the recommendations of the first Hoover Commission. See also House Documents 503 and 504, 81st Congress, second session.

5. *Reorganization Bill of 1938:* S. 3331, 75th Congress, third session. See 83 *Congressional Record* 5123, April 8, 1938.

6. The President's Committee on Administrative Management, *Report of the Committee with Studies of Administrative Management in the Federal Government*, contains special message to Congress of President Franklin D. Roosevelt of January 12, 1937 (Washington, U.S. Government Printing Office, 1937).

7. Barry Dean Karl, *Executive Reorganization and Reform in the New Deal: The Genesis of Administrative Management; 1900–1939* (Cambridge, Harvard University Press, 1963). An interesting account of the movement for governmental reform with profiles of Louis Brownlow, Luther Gulick, and Charles E. Merriam.

8. Louis Brownlow, *A Passion for Anonymity: The Autobiography of Louis Brownlow—Second Half* (Chicago, University of Chicago Press, 1958).

9. Reorganization Bill of 1938: See Note 5.

10. Court Reorganization Bill: President Roosevelt's message of February 5, 1937, recommended that Congress authorize the appointment of one new justice of the Supreme Court for each sitting justice who remained on the court after reaching the age of seventy, to a maximum limit of fifteen justices instead of nine. This measure was rejected, but Congress later passed a compromise bill permitting federal justices to retire after seventy on full pay.

11. Richard Pollenberg, *Reorganizing Roosevelt's Government: The Controversy over Executive Reorganization, 1936–1939* (Cambridge, Harvard University Press, 1966).

12. *Reorganization Act of 1939*, (53 Stat. 561).

13. Mary Parker Follett, "The Illusion of Final Authority," paper given at Oxford University in 1926 and printed in L. Urwick (ed.), *Freedom and Coordination* (London, Pitman, 1949).

14. See, for example, Woodrow Wilson, *Congressional Government: A Study in American Politics* (Boston, Houghton Mifflin & Company, 1885). Also in New York, Meridian Books, 1956, with an introduction by Walter

Lippman; and James MacGregor Burns, *The Deadlock of Democracy: Four Party Politics in America* (Englewood Cliffs, N.J., Prentice-Hall, Inc., 1963).

15. Barry Dean Karl, p. 176. See Note 7.

16. Morton Grodzins, *The American System: A New View of Government in the United States,* edited by Daniel J. Elazar (Chicago, Rand McNally & Company, 1966).

17. Paul H. Appleby, *Politics and Administration* (The University of Alabama Press, 1949).

18. William Anderson, "The Myths of Tax Sharing," *Public Administration Review,* XXVIII (Jan.–Feb. 1968) p. 10.

19. Herbert Emmerich, *Bureaucracy* (Chicago, Encyclopaedia Britannica, 1968).

20. Joseph P. Harris, *Congressional Control of Administration* (Washington, D.C., The Brookings Institutions, 1964.) (Also, Anchor Edition, Garden City, N.Y., Doubleday & Company, Inc., 1965.)

—————, *The Advice and Consent of the Senate* (Berkeley, University of California Press, 1953).

21. Herbert Emmerich, "The Scope of the Practice of Public Administration," in James C. Charlesworth (ed.), *Theory and Practice of Public Administration; Scope, Objectives, and Methods; Monograph 8* (Philadelphia, the American Academy of Political and Social Science, 1968). Co-sponsored by the American Society for Public Administration.

22. Robert J. Morgan, *Governing Soil Conservation: Thirty Years of the New Decentralization,* published for Resources of the Future, Inc. (Baltimore, The Johns Hopkins Press, 1965). This book is a political study of decentralization and participation in the rural field and has many insights which would be useful to those now concerned with urban problems.

23. Roscoe C. Martin, (ed.) *Public Administration and Democracy; Essays in Honor of Paul H. Appleby* (Syracuse, N.Y., Syracuse University Press, 1965).

24. James L. Sundquist (with the collaboration of David W. Davis), *Making Federalism Work* (Washington, The Brookings Institution, 1969).

CHAPTER VIII

1. Herbert Emmerich, "The Specific Gravity of Decisionism," *Public Administration Review,* Vol. XXIV, No. 4 (December 1964), p. 250.

2. Anthony M. Solomon, "Administration of a Multipurpose Economic Diplomacy," *Public Administration Review,* Vol. XXIX, No. 6 (Nov.–Dec. 1969), p. 585.

3. James L. Sundquist (with the collaboration of David W. Davis), *Making Federalism Work* (Washington, The Brookings Institution, 1969), Chapter 2.

4. Edward J. Kolodziej, "The National Security Council: Innovations and Implications," *Public Administration Review,* Vol. XXIX, No. 6 (Nov.–Dec. 1969), p. 573.

5. Henry M. Wriston, *Toward a Stronger Foreign Service,* Report of the

Secretary of State's Public Committee on Personnel, Department of State Publication 5458 (Washington, U.S. Government Printing Office, June 1954).

6. Rufus E. Miles, Jr., "The Case for a Federal Department of Education," *Public Administration Review*, Vol. XXVII, No. 1 (March 1967), p. 1.

7. *Reorganization Plan No. 1*. Effective April 11, 1953.

8. Frederick C. Mosher, "Participation and Reorganization," in *Governmental Reorganizations, Cases and Commentary*, published for the Inter-University Case Program, Inc. (Indianapolis, the Bobbs-Merrill Company, Inc., 1967), p. 513.

9. *Reorganization Plan No. 3 of 1967 (Government of the District of Columbia)*. *Hearings* before a Subcommittee of the House Committee on Government Operations, Ninetieth Congress, 1st session, June 1967 (Washington, U. S. Government Printing Office, 1967).

10. *Reorganization by Plan and Statute, 1945–1962*. Subcommittee of the House Committee on Government Operations—Committee Print, 88th Congress, 1st session (Washington, U. S. Government Printing Office, 1963), p. 1.

11. *Extending the Reorganization Act of 1949*. Senate Committee on Government Operations, 88th Congress, 2nd session, Report No. 1057 (Washington, U.S. Government Printing Office, 1964), p. 104.

12. Reorganization plan summaries:

(A) "Reorganization of Federal Government," in *Congress and the Nation, 1945–1964* (Washington, Congressional Quarterly, Inc., 1965), Chapter 11, Part IV, pp. 1455–1470. (A second volume of *Congress and the Nation, 1964–1968* is now available.)

(B) "Executive Reorganization Since 1929 by Reorganization Plan Procedure," Appendix B in *Extending the Reorganization Act of 1949*. Report of the Committee on Government Operations, U.S. Senate, 88th Congress, 2nd session, Report No. 1057 (Washington, U.S. Government Printing Office, 1964), pp. 57–114. This section of the report prepared by W. Brooke Graves, specialist in American government and public administration, and Mark H. Freeman, research assistant of the Legislative Reference Service, Library of Congress.

(C) "Executive Agencies of the Federal Government, Abolished, Transferred, or Terminated Subsequent to March 4, 1933." Appendix A in *The U. S. Government Organization Manual, 1969–70*, prepared by the Office of the Federal Register, National Archives and Records Service, General Services Administration (Washington, U.S. Government Printing Office, 1969), pp. 635–689.

13. *Opinions of the Attorney General*, Vol. 37, (Jan. 24, 1933) pp. 63–64. See also Memorandum of Department of Justice, after hearings on Reorganization Act of 1949, in Senate Report 232, 81st Congress, pp. 18–20, affirming the right of Congress to disapprove reorganization plans by concurrent resolution.

14. *Isbrandsten-Moller Company, Inc., vs United States*, 300 U.S. Reports 139 (1937), and *Swayne and Hoyt, Ltd. vs United States*, 300 U.S. Reports 297 (1937).

15. Eli E. Nobleman, professional staff member, "Constitutional and Legal Aspects of Reorganization Act Procedures to Amend the Reorganization Act of 1949," U.S. Senate Committee on Government Operations. See *Hearings*, 89th Congress, 1st session, on S. 1134 and S. 1135—March 29, 1965.

16. Edward S. Corwin, *The Constitution and What it Means Today*, edition XII (New York, Atheneum [paperback] 1963), p. 25. For a constrained and detailed discussion of presidential authority, see Professor Corwin's *The President: Office and Powers, 1787–1957* (New York University Press, 4th rev. ed., 1957).

17. Joseph P. Harris, *Congressional Control of Administration* (Washington, The Brookings Institution, 1964), Chapter 8. Also in paperback, Garden City, New York, Doubleday–Anchor Books, 1965.

18. Peter P. Schauffler, "The Legislative Veto Revisited," in *Public Policy —1958* (Cambridge, The Graduate School of Public Administration, Harvard University, 1958).

19. John D. Millett and Lindsay Rogers, "The Legislative Veto and the Reorganization Act of 1939," *Public Administration Review*, Vol. I, No. 2 (Winter 1941), p. 189.

20. Ferrel Heady, "A New Approach to Federal Executive Reorganization," *American Political Science Review* (1947), p. 1125. Also see his article on "The Reorganization Act of 1949," *Public Administration Review* (Summer 1949), p. 174.

21. *Modernizing the Federal Government, Establish a Commission on the Organization and Management of the Executive Branch.* Hearings before the Subcommittee on Executive Reorganization of the U.S. Senate Committee on Government Operations, January, February, April, and May 1968 (Washington, U.S. Government Printing Office, 1968), 90th Congress, 2nd session.

22. U.S. Senate Bill S. 3640, Executive Reorganization and Management Act of 1968, 90th Congress, 2nd session, passed in the Senate July 27, 1968 and referred to House Committee on Government Operations, which did not act on it. See also Senate Report No. 1451, calendar No. 1433, July 24, 1968.

23. "What, Another Hoover Commission?" *Public Administration Review*, Vol. XXVIII, No. 2 (March–April 1968), p. 168.

24. Harvey C. Mansfield, "Federal Executive Reorganization: Thirty Years of Experience," in *Public Administration Review*, Vol. XXIX, No. 4 (July–Aug 1969), p. 335. Also available as a monograph from The Brookings Institution, Washington, D.C.

25. See Note 21, p. 596.

26. White House Press Release, December 29, 1958.

27. White House Press Releases of March 12, 1970: (1) President Richard M. Nixon's Message to the Congress of the United States; (2) Reorganization Plan 2 of 1970; (3) Summary of Executive Office Reorganization Plan.

Chapter IX

1. Peter F. Drucker, *The Age of Discontinuity* (New York, Harper & Row, 1968–69).

2. Herbert Emmerich, "Bureaucracy" in *Encyclopaedia Britannica* (Chicago, 1968), in which bureaucracy is treated as the pathology of large organizations.

3. Richard E. Neustadt, *Presidential Power, The Politics of Leadership* (New York, John Wiley & Sons, Inc., 1960), p. 181.

4. Paul H. Appleby, *Policy and Administration* (University of Alabama Press, 1949). See particularly Chapter IV, "Structure, Hierarchy, and Coordination."

5. Dean Acheson, "The President and the Secretary of State" in *The Secretary of State* (Don K. Price, ed.). Report of the 18th American Assembly held at Arden House, October 1960 (Englewood Cliffs, N.J., Prentice-Hall, Inc., 1960).

6. Bureau of the Budget, Executive Office of the President, Circular No. A-85, June 20, 1967, on "Consultation with heads of state and local governments in development of federal rules, regulations, standards, procedures, and guidelines," attaching "the President's Memorandum to Heads of Certain Agencies" of November 11, 1966.

7. James L. Sundquist (with the collaboration of David W. Davis), *Making Federalism Work* (Washington, The Brookings Institution, 1969), Chapters 2 and 3.

8. Robert S. McNamara, *The Essence of Security: Reflections in Office* (New York, Harper & Row, 1968).

9. *Government Contracting for Research and Development* (Bell Report) —Senate Committee on Government Operations, Senate Documents Vol. 2, Misc. II., 87th Congress, 2nd session (Jan 10–Oct 13, 1962), (Washington, U. S. Government Printing Office, 1962).

10. Herbert Emmerich, ed. "Administrative Problems of Multipurpose Diplomacy," Symposium in *Public Administration Review*, Vol. XXIX, No. 6 (November–December 1969).

11. Martin Landau, "Redundancy, Rationality, and the Problem of Duplication and Overlap," in *Public Administration Review*, "Symposium on Federal Executive Reorganization," Vol. XXIX, No. 4 (July–August 1969), p. 346.

12. James W. Fesler, "Executive Management and the Federal Field Service," in *Report of the President's Committee on Administrative Management* (Washington, U. S. Government Printing Office, 1937). See also his "Approaches to the Understanding of Decentralization," *Journal of Politics* (August 1965).

13. Sundquist, et al. See Note 7, p. 110.

14. *Modernizing the Federal Government*, Senate Report to Establish a Commission on the Organization and Management of the Executive Branch, U. S. Senate Committee on Government Operations 1968, p. 580.

15. White House Press Releases of March 12, 1970.

16. "Presidential Commissions, Boards, and Advisory Groups Established Since 1965," prepared by Gayle T. Harris, Government and General Research Division, Legislative Reference Service, the Library of Congress as Exhibit 13, *Modernizing the Federal Government* (Establish a Commission on the Organization and Management of the Executive Branch), *Hearings,*

Subcommittee on Executive Reorganization, of the U.S. Senate Committee on Government Operations, 90th Congress, 2nd session (Washington, U.S. Government Printing Office, 1968) p. 102. This exhibit lists the following:

1967	Commissions	27
1966	Commissions	44
1965	Commissions	30

17. For a witty and informed analysis of presidential staffing problems, see William D. Carey, "Presidential Staffing in the Sixties and Seventies," *Public Administration Review*, Vol. XXIX, No. 5 (Sept.–Oct. 1969), pp. 450–458.

18. Robert Wood, "When Government Works," *The Public Interest*, No. 18 (Winter 1970), pp. 39–51.

19. Stephen K. Bailey, "Managing the Federal Government," in *Agenda for the Nation* (Washington, The Brookings Institution, 1968) p. 301.

INDEX

Price Fixing Committee, 42
Primaries, 144
Prime minister's office, 28
Prince, The, 26
Priorities, 24
Private enterprise, 126, 179
    Hoover Commission II and,
        103–104, 109, 112, 117, 123
Privatization, 179
Procedural standardization, 191
Production Credit Associations, 64
Program formulation, 3
Program implementation, 3
Property and Management Service,
    223
Prussia, 26
Public affairs careers, 35–36
Public assistance, 74, 219
Public corporation, British, 28. *See
    also* Government corporation
Public finance, 26
Public Health Service, 211, 226, 227
Public housing, 156, 220
Public lands, 130
Public power, 109
    Hoover Commission II on, 115
Public roads, 193
Public Roads Administration, 96
Public Service Education Bill, 141
Public works, 211
Public Works Administration, 78
Public Works and Economic
        Development Act (1965), 239

Quasi-judicial agencies, 240–241
    Hoover Commission II on, 117
Quasi-judicial boards, Brownlow
        Committee on, 54
Quasi-judicial commissions, 12–13
Quasi-judicial functions, 44

Radcliffe-Maude, Lord, 28
Railroad unions, 68
Ramspeck, Robert, 120
Rand Corporation, 16
Rayburn, Sam, 205, 210
Reapportionment, 152

Recentralization, data processing
        and, 195–196
Reconstruction, 23, 31
Reconstruction Finance Corporation,
        14, 112, 160, 254
Reeves, Floyd W., 61
Reform movements, 7, 8
Regional agencies, 237–240
Regional Agricultural Credit
        Corporations, 65
Regional boards, 140
Regional commissions, 239–240
Regional councils, British, 28
Regional development, 192
Regionalism, 192–197
Regional office, 194, 195, 196
Regulatory agencies
    Brownlow Committee on, 117
    Hoover Commission I on, 117
    Hoover Commission II on, 117
Regulatory commissions, 136
    executive control of, 55
    Hoover Commission I on, 13, 164
    See also Independent commission
Regulatory functions, 44
Removal power, 12–13, 30, 42, 92,
        136, 164, 210
Renegotiation Board, 241
Reorganization
    across-the-board view, 189–191
    aims of, 11, 154–162
    bottom view, 185–188
    Brownlow Committee view of,
        52–53
    concurrent resolution veto and,
        166
    Congress and, 29, 129–135, 166
    congressional amendment of plans
        for, 169
    congressional committees and,
        130, 131, 167
    as congressional prerogative,
        165–166
    congressional roadblocks to,
        161–162
    consultation and, 185–186
    as continuing process, 7–25, 60,
        88, 162, 163, 181